Games and Natural Language Processing (Games & NLP 2020)

Marseille, France
11 – 16 May 2020

Editor:

Stephanie M. Lukin

ISBN: 978-1-7138-1260-9

LREC 2020 WORKSHOP
Language Resources and Evaluation Conference
11–16 May 2020

**Games and Natural Language Processing
(Games & NLP 2020)**

PROCEEDINGS

Edited by: Stephanie M. Lukin

Proceedings of the LREC 2020 Workshop
Games and Natural Language Processing
(Games & NLP 2020)

Edited by: Stephanie M. Lukin

For more information:
European Language Resources Association (ELRA)
9 rue des Cordelières
75013, Paris
France
http://www.elra.info
Email: lrec@elda.org

Introduction

Welcome to the Games and Natural Language Processing Workshop!

This workshop examines the use of games and gamification for Natural Language Processing (NLP) tasks, as well as how NLP research can advance player engagement and communication within games. The Games and NLP workshop aims to promote and explore the possibilities for research and practical applications of games and gamification that have a core NLP aspect, either to generate resources and perform language tasks or as a game mechanic itself. This workshop investigates computational and theoretical aspects of natural language research that would be beneficial for designing and building novel game experiences, or for processing texts to conduct formal game studies. NLP would benefit from games in obtaining language resources (e.g., construction of a thesaurus or a parser through a crowdsourcing game), or in learning the linguistic characteristics of game users as compared to those of other domains.

The workshop received 16 submissions, 12 of which were accepted into the proceedings.

Workshop website: `https://sites.google.com/view/gamnlp2020/`

Stephanie M. Lukin, Chris Madge, Jon Chamberlain, Karën Fort, Udo Kruschwitz, James Ryan
May 2020

Organising Committee

- Stephanie M. Lukin, co-chair (U.S. Army Research Laboratory)
- Chris Madge, co-chair (Queen Mary University of London)
- Jon Chamberlain (University of Essex, UK)
- Karën Fort (Sorbonne Université, France)
- Udo Kruschwitz (University of Regensburg, Germany)
- James Ryan (BBN Technologies, US)

Programme Committee

- Richard Bartle (University of Essex, UK)
- Valerio Basile (University of Turin, Italy)
- Johan Bos (University of Groningen, Netherlands)
- Chris Cieri (Linguistic Data Consortium, University of Pennsylvania, US)
- Seth Cooper (Northeastern University, US)
- James Fiumara (Linguistic Data Consortium, University of Pennsylvania, US)
- Paulo F. Gomes (Samsung Research America, US)
- Andrew Gordon (University of Southern California, Institute of Creative Technology)
- Bruno Guillaume (Inria Nancy Grand Est, France)
- Brent Harrison (University of Kentucky, US)
- Mathieu Lafourcade (LIRMM, France)
- Verena Lyding (EURAC, Italy)
- Josh Miller (Northeastern University, US)
- Alice Millour (Sorbonne Université, France)
- Lionel Nicolas (EURAC, Italy)
- Massimo Poesio (Queen Mary University, UK)
- Melissa Roemmele (SDL, US)

Table of Contents

Conference Program

Proceedings of the LREC 2020 Workshop Games and Natural Language Processing, pages 1–9
Language Resources and Evaluation Conference (LREC 2020), Marseille, 11–16 May 2020

Creating a Sentiment Lexicon with Game-Specific Words
for Analyzing NPC Dialogue in The Elder Scrolls V: Skyrim

Thérèse Bergsma, Judith van Stegeren, Mariët Theune
Human Media Interaction, University of Twente
Enschede, The Netherlands
tslbergsma@gmail.com, j.e.vanstegeren@utwente.nl, m.theune@utwente.nl

Abstract

A weak point of rule-based sentiment analysis systems is that the underlying sentiment lexicons are often not adapted to the domain of the text we want to analyze. We created a game-specific sentiment lexicon for video game *Skyrim* based on the E-ANEW word list and a dataset of *Skyrim*'s in-game documents. We calculated sentiment ratings for NPC dialogue using both our lexicon and E-ANEW and compared the resulting sentiment ratings to those of human raters. Both lexicons perform comparably well on our evaluation dialogues, but the game-specific extension performs slightly better on the dominance dimension for dialogue segments and the arousal dimension for full dialogues. To our knowledge, this is the first time that a sentiment analysis lexicon has been adapted to the video game domain.

Keywords: sentiment analysis, sentiment lexicon, ANEW, video games, dialogue, lore, *Skyrim*, E-ANEW

1. Introduction

Sentiment analysis is a subfield of NLP that tries to assign sentiment ratings to texts. A drawback of rule-based sentiment analysis methods is that sentiment lexicons, the lists that link specific words to sentiment values, are often not adapted to the specific domain of the text. In this research we investigate whether we can adapt an existing sentiment analysis lexicon to a sentiment lexicon for the video games domain.

Sentiment analysis for video games can be used as a stepping stone to achieve affective language recognition for game texts (such as NPC dialogue). If we can automatically distinguish positive and negative polarity in game texts, we might be able to extend this to multi-dimensional emotion recognition. This can help us to automatically assess opinion, emotion and personality of individual characters in video games. Additionally, these metrics could be a first step towards quantitative analysis for games as a whole, based on their texts. Holistic text-based metrics could be used to compare multiple games in the same genre, or find similarities between games across multiple domains. Finally, we expect that improved NLP methods for game texts can also inform natural language generation for games.

In this research we use an extended version of the Affective Norms for English Words (ANEW) list as the basis for the sentiment analysis lexicons. The Affective Norms for English Words (ANEW) list was published by Bradley and Lang (1999). It contains 1034 English words with a normative emotional rating. Bradley and Lang (1999) followed for their normative emotional rating the work of Osgood et al. (1957), who found that variance in emotional assessments can be captured in three major dimensions: valence (or polarity), arousal and dominance. These dimensions are often named the PAD dimensions in literature. See Figure 1 for an overview.

The 1034 ANEW words received their ratings from introductory psychology class students who participated as part of a course requirement. Each student rated words for all three dimensions. Warriner et al. (2013) added more words

dimension	low	high
valence (or: polarity)	unpleasant	pleasant
arousal	calm	excited
dominance	controlled	in control

Figure 1: PAD dimensions overview

to the original ANEW word list and gathered ratings for each word through Amazon Mechanical Turk (MTurk),[1] which resulted in an extended ANEW (E-ANEW) word list of 13,915 rated words. Almost all[2] previously ANEW rated words by Bradley and Lang (1999) were also included and received a new ANEW rating from the participants of MTurk. Here participants rated words for just one dimension, so a participant focused on only providing ratings for either valence, arousal or dominance. Each word received between 14 and 109 ratings for a dimension.

One possible use for ANEW rated words is predicting sentence sentiment by looking at the sentiment of the words that are in the sentence (Gökçay et al., 2012). However, ANEW consists only of words that are included in an English dictionary. Consequently, sentiment analysis for texts that contain many technical words, made-up words or abbreviations might not perform as well for texts that contain only common English words.

One category of texts that might contain made-up words is texts from video games. Especially role-playing games (RPGs), for example those with a fantasy or science fiction setting, often use invented words to enrich the story and to help with world building. One example of such an RPG is *The Elder Scrolls V: Skyrim* (Bethesda Game Studios, 2011), an action role-playing game (action RPG) and the fifth installment in *The Elder Scrolls* (TES) game series. *Skyrim* is widely popular. It sold 30 million copies in the

---

[1]`www.mturk.com`

[2]Only 1029 of the 1034 original words were included, because five were lost due to programmatic error

first five years of its release in 2011, and on average, players spend 150 hours in *Skyrim* (Suellentrop, 2016). The game has an open-world setting: players have the freedom to travel to any place in the game at any time, and quests can be completed in any order or even ignored completely. The world in *Skyrim* is populated by 1087 non-playable characters (NPCs). Together they have over 60,000 lines of dialogue (Senior, 2011). In *Skyrim*, all NPCs have their own daily routines: they go to bed at certain times, do chores and run errands, and talk to other NPCs. NPCs also function as quest-givers in the game. They might ask the player to do something for them, such as retrieving a family heirloom from a cave filled with necromancers, or accompanying them during their travels on a dangerous road.

Although NPCs speak English, some of the words they use cannot be found in an English dictionary. Many words are made-up and are part of *The Elder Scrolls'* lore that the developers created to enrich the game world for the players. This research focuses on sentiment analysis of dialogue of NPCs. We want to find out whether existing (such as ANEW or E-ANEW), or extended (such as lexicons adapted to a game, a game series or genre) English sentiment analysis lexicons are suitable to compute sentiment ratings for NPC dialogue in a fantasy setting. Specifically, we consider a lexicon to be suitable if it produces sentiment ratings that are comparable to those given by human raters. We compare human sentiment ratings of *Skyrim* dialogue with ratings computed using the E-ANEW lexicon and a *Skyrim*-specific extension of E-ANEW.

2. Related work

2.1. Domain-specific sentiment lexicons

Studying and comparing the performance of a genre specific lexicon is especially popular for social media text. Nielsen (2011) examined the performance of sentiment analysis for Twitter by using the ANEW list and comparing this with sentiment analysis that uses a new word list that was specifically constructed for the language that is often seen on micro-blogs, such as Internet slang acronyms (e.g. *LOL* and *WTF*) and obscene words.

Similarly, Hutto and Gilbert (2014) created VADER (Valence Aware Dictionary for sEntiment Reasoning), a rule-based model for sentiment analysis on social media texts. In their lexicon they included emoticons (e.g. *:-)*), slang with sentimental value (e.g. *nah* and *meh*) and acronyms. This resulted in a lexicon with 7,500 words. Each entry was rated by ten human raters. Aside from using a self-made lexicon, VADER also takes into account how syntax and punctuation can influence the perceived sentiment of a text.

2.2. Computing sentiment score from word ratings

In our research we computed sentiment scores by identifying words and their PAD values, summing these values for each PAD dimension and dividing them by the number of words with a PAD value in the sentence. Taking the mean to compute a sentiment score has previously been done by (Guerini et al., 2012) to measure the message impact of Google AdWords and (Staiano and Guerini, 2014) to perform sentiment analysis on crowd-annotated news.

Nielsen (2011) also tried variations on the computation by not normalizing words, by normalizing the sum by looking only at words with a non-zero valence value (a technique that diminishes returns of values with a neutral meaning (Guerini et al., 2012)), by only taking into account the words with the most extreme valence values, and by changing the valence values to +1, 0 and -1.

2.3. NLP on game texts

Most research on games and NLP deals with generating textual content for games; there is only limited work on analyzing game texts. Louis and Sutton (2018) created language models of character and action descriptions in a role-playing game (RPG) with the goal of inferring the latent ties between actions and characters. Urbanek et al. (2019) crowdsourced a collection of player interactions in a fantasy text adventure, and used it to train generative and retrieval models to predict action, emote, and dialogue sequences. Kerr and Szafron (2009) present a machine learning approach for classifying the level of sophistication of dialogue lines (trained on movie dialogues), which they tested on a manually annotated collection of dialogue lines from the game *Neverwinter Nights*.

Existing work on sentiment analysis in a game context is generally aimed at the analysis of texts produced by players of video games rather than NPCs. Fraser et al. (2018) perform sentiment analysis on utterances of users talking to a character based on an NPC from *The Elder Scrolls V: Skyrim*. Others apply sentiment analysis to game-related tweets (Sarratt et al., 2014), game reviews (Borgholt et al., 2015; Panagiotopoulos et al., 2019), and chat messages on a video game streaming platform (Barbieri et al., 2017). Whether these texts are about games or used inside games, they are likely to include game-specific words, and thus all these applications could potentially benefit from using a game-specific sentiment lexicon. We are not aware of any previous work on using a game-specific sentiment lexicon for sentiment analysis.

3. Data

For this research we used the following language resources:

1. lore from *The Elder Scrolls*: a dataset of in-game books, letters and notes from games in *The Elder Scrolls* series, scraped from a fan-website

2. a plaintext file with *Skyrim* dialogue lines

3. the extended ANEW word list from Warriner et al. (2013) with 13,915 rated words

4. an English lexicon

3.1. *The Elder Scrolls'* lore

The first dataset contains the text of all in-game documents from games in *The Elder Scrolls*. The collection consists of 4,890 books, letters and notes. The texts were scraped from *The Imperial Library* website,[3] a website that collects in-game documents from *The Elder Scrolls*.

---

[3] https://www.imperial-library.info/books/all/by-category

A is for Atronach.
B is for Bungler's Bane.
C is for Comberry.

Figure 2: Example book *ABCs for Barbarians* from the Imperial Library dataset

Property	Value
Conversation	FormID: 000AF489
Quest ID	DialogueSolitude
Quest branch	DialogueSolitudeFalkBranch3
Quest topic	DialogueSolitudeFalkBranch3Topic
Subtype	CUST
Id	0
Text	Of course he does. What sort of a question is that?
Notes	Annoyed

Figure 3: An example entry from the Thuum.org dialogue dataset

3.2. *Skyrim* dialogue file

The second resource is a text file with in-game dialogue from *Skyrim*. The dataset was acquired from Thuum.org,[4] a fan website that is dedicated to documenting *Skyrim*'s dragon language. Thuum provides a text file[5] which contains more than 34,000 dialogue entries from the base game.

Each entry consists of a conversation identifier, a quest identifier, a quest branch identifier, the topic of the quest, a dialogue subtype,[6] an identifier for the entry, 1-3 lines of dialogue, and optional direction notes for voice actors.

3.3. Extended ANEW word list

The extended ANEW word list (Warriner et al., 2013) contains 13,915 words and their ratings.[7] Ratings range from 1 (unpleasant, calm, controlled) to 9 (pleasant, excited, in control), with 5 signifying a neutral rating.

Each entry contains 65 values, listing the mean valence, arousal and dominance ratings given by participants, standard deviation (SD), the number of ratings each word received during the crowd-sourcing experiment, as well as those values for different demographic groups of participants: all participants, females, males, higher educated, lower educated, old people and young people.

Only a few of the 65 values from the E-ANEW dataset are necessary for this research: the word itself, the mean rating and standard deviation from all participants for valence, arousal and dominance.

---

[4] https://www.thuum.org/
[5] https://www.thuum.org/library/Dialogue.TXT
[6] https://en.uesp.net/wiki/Tes5Mod:Mod_File_Format/DIAL
[7] http://crr.ugent.be/archives/1003

3.4. English words lexicon

We used a public lexicon of 466,549 English words. It was retrieved from a GitHub repository[8] and is based on the dataset from Project Gutenberg,[9] which contains mostly public domain books with more than 57,000 items, and the Moby Project,[10] which consists of more than 177,000 words and their pronunciation.

4. Game-specific sentiment lexicon

In order to investigate whether sentiment analysis for NPC dialogue improves when we use a game-specific sentiment analysis lexicon (E-ANEW-TES), we want to compare human sentiment ratings for NPC dialogue with sentiment ratings calculated using E-ANEW, and a *Skyrim*-specific extension of E-ANEW. In this section we explain how we created the latter.

4.1. Creating a game-specific word list

We tokenized and stemmed the text of the dataset with TES lore, filtered out unique words and ordered these by frequency. All words that occurred in the English lexicon were removed. We manually removed English words that were not part of our English lexicon, such as the word *false*. This left us with 13,831 words considered to be unique to *The Elder Scrolls*, most of which are nouns and names.

We created a custom stemmer, i.e. a mapping from word variations to their stems, for *Skyrim*-specific words with a naive unsupervised approach: we checked whether words in our word list (i.e. stems) also occurred with additional letters appended (i.e. variations). This way we could detect both regular plural nouns, such as *nirnroot* (singular) → *nirnroots* (plural) and related adjectives, such as *khajiit* (singular) → *khajiiti* (adjective). Filtering out word variations led to a more representative frequency list of words. Finally, we removed all words that occurred less than 10 times. The final list contained 965 word stems and an additional 119 word variations.

For an example of word list entries, see Figure 4.

4.2. Calculating sentiment ratings with word2vec

The next step lies in providing each word in our game-specific word list with a value for valence, arousal and dominance, so that we can use them for calculating a sentiment rating for a line of NPC dialogue. From here on, we call the *Skyrim* lexicon with PAD values *E-ANEW-TES*, where TES stands for *The Elder Scrolls*.

We use the ratings of the E-ANEW words to extrapolate a sentiment rating for game-specific words. Specifically, we average the ratings of the three most similar E-ANEW words to calculate the PAD values for a game-specific word. We use word2vec (Mikolov et al., 2013) to find the most similar E-ANEW words for each game-specific word.

Word2vec turns words into vectors that represent the context of those words. We can use those vectors to find similar words in a dataset: words that are used in similar contexts

---

[8] https://github.com/dwyl/english-words
[9] https://www.gutenberg.org/
[10] http://www.gutenberg.org/ebooks/3202

Word	Frequency	Meaning
tamriel	936	Tamriel is one of several continents located on Nirn (the world of *The Elder Scrolls*). All *The Elder Scrolls* games to date have focused on the continent of Tamriel.
khajit	661	Khajiit are cat-like people who come from Elsweyr region in Tamriel.
vivec	613	Lord Vivec the Warrior-Poet is one of the three immortal god-kings of Morrowind, alongside Sotha Sil and Almalexia. His residence is in the eponymous city.
daedra	613	Daedra is the term for the entities who inhabit the realms of Oblivion in *The Elder Scrolls*. They are viewed as gods or demons by the inhabitants of Tamriel.
morrowind	574	Morrowind is a province in the northeastern corner of Tamriel. It is the homeland of the Dark Elves (or Dunmer).
barenziah	569	Barenziah was a long-lived Dunmer (Dark Elf) woman who was a part of the royal family of Mournhold. She experienced many important events throughout her life, and had a number of notable descendants.

Figure 4: The six most frequently occurring words from *The Elder Scrolls'* lore dataset, English words removed.

have similar vectors. In this project, we used Gensim's implementation of word2vec for Python.

We applied word2vec on the lore dataset to obtain word vectors for each of the game-specific words. We use a context window size of eight (i.e. for each word, the algorithm takes the eight words before and after that word into account) to find words that are more semantically close than only topically related (Jurafsky and Martin, 2008).

We calculate the PAD values for a game-specific word by averaging the PAD values of the three E-ANEW words that have the highest probability of occurring in the context of the game-specific word. If we use more than three words to calculate the PAD values, averaging the values means we might end up with mostly neutral PAD values for game-specific words. On the other hand, using three words for calculation mitigates the possibility of word2vec mistakes, and prevents that one ANEW word determines the PAD values too much.

4.3. Validating the word2vec model

Fifteen words from the E-ANEW list that also occur in the *Skyrim* lore (e.g. *sword*, *inn*, *werewolf* in contrast to *phone*, *satellite*, *streetcar*) were randomly chosen as validation set to determine whether the model provides good E-ANEW-TES ratings with the TES lore as training data. We filtered out English words that have a specific meaning in the context of *Skyrim*, such as *shout* ('dragon shouts' are a form of magic in Skyrim), *cat* (*Skyrim* contains humanoid cats) and *empire* (the Empire is a political entity and denotes a faction name in *The Elder Scrolls*).

We calculated the PAD values for each word in our validation set, so we could gauge whether the PAD values are within acceptable limits. A PAD value for E-ANEW-TES is considered satisfactory if the value stays within the boundaries of the standard deviation (SD) of the E-ANEW rating of that same word. For example, the E-ANEW valence rating for sword is 5.27 and the SD is 1.58, meaning that an E-ANEW-TES rating for sword will only be considered satisfactory if it is somewhere between 3.69 and 6.85, which it is with an E-ANEW-TES rating of 4.43. We retrained the word2vec model until the results provided all fifteen words with a satisfactory rating. Another fifteen random words were selected and tested which also stayed within the SD of

Parameter	Value	Description
size	125	Size of the dense vector to represent each word
window	8	Maximum distance between the target word and its neighbouring word
min_count	9	Minimum frequency count of words in the corpus
workers	10	Number of threads
epochs	50	Number of iterations over the corpus

Figure 5: Gensim word2vec parameters that we used to obtain the word vectors for words in the TES Lore dataset.

the original E-ANEW ratings. See Figure 5 for an overview of the word2vec parameters that we used.

4.4. Example

As an example, we show how the E-ANEW-TES rating is calculated for the game-specific word *Septim*. In *The Elder Scrolls*, Septim is the name of the ruling dynasty of the Empire until the end of the Oblivion Crisis. If we apply word2vec on the TES lore dataset with the aforementioned parameters, and query the resulting vector space for the words closest to *septim*, we get the words in Figure 6.

To calculate the PAD values for *septim*, we need the three words with the highest probability that also have an E-ANEW rating. These are the words *throne*, *empire* and *emperor*, which is particularly apt given the meaning of the word. We average the PAD-values of the related E-ANEW words, as shown in Figure 7.

We repeated this procedure for each of the 965 words of our game-specific word list. The words with their respective PAD values, together with the words from E-ANEW, make up our game-specific sentiment lexicon: E-ANEW-TES.

5. Sentiment analysis on game text

5.1. Calculating game text ratings

To obtain a sentiment rating for a game text, e.g. a piece of NPC dialogue, we follow the calculation method of Nielsen

Word	Probability
reman	0.39224135875701904
katariah	0.3528633713722229
cassynder	0.34252333641052246
throne	0.328492671251297
empire	0.3217410445213318
divines	0.32171204686164856

Figure 6: This table shows the words that, according to our word2vec model, have the highest probability of occurring in the context of the word *septim* in *The Elder Scrolls'* lore. The first three words are names of NPCs related to the Septim dynasty. *Divines* is a reference to the Nine Divines, another name for the pantheon of the Empire, of which Tiber Septim is a member.

Word	Valence	Arousal	Dominance
throne	5.45	5.22	6.19
empire	5.36	4.59	5.95
emperor	4.68	4.25	5.32
septim	5.163	4.686	5.82

Figure 7: To calculate the valence, arousal and dominance values for the word *septim*, we average the mean PAD value of the three related E-ANEW words *throne*, *empire* and *emperor*.

(2011): we search the game text for words from our sentiment lexicon and for each sentiment dimension (valence, arousal and dominance) separately, we average the values of these words to obtain a sentiment rating for the game text as a whole.

See Figure 8 for an example of a dialogue snippet for which we want to obtain a sentiment rating, and a table that shows how the sentiment rating is calculated for valence.

5.2. Selecting evaluation dialogue

To be able to compare the performance of E-ANEW and E-ANEW-TES, we need to apply both sentiment lexicons to dialogue snippets that contain game-specific words. We also need to keep in mind that we want humans to rate the dialogue snippets as well, so we can compare the sentiment lexicon performance to a gold standard of human ratings.

There were various approaches we could take for selecting evaluation dialogue. We could source dialogue snippets from *Skyrim*'s main questline, which contains roughly 35,000 words of dialogue. However, the main questline contains only one *Skyrim*-specific word for every 33 words of text. This is especially problematic for when we want to compare E-ANEW and E-ANEW-TES performance with human ratings: this would mean that our human raters have to rate many dialogue snippets before we have collected enough information to properly evaluate the performance. We could pick a different quest, but this has another clear drawback: a quest tends to repeat the same *Skyrim*-specific words instead of touching upon a broad variety. To illustrate:

"In the **year** 3E 41, **Emperor** Pelagius Septim **was murdered** in the **Temple** of the **One** in the **Imperial City**. **Cut** down by a **Dark Brotherhood assassin**."

E-ANEW		E-ANEW-TES	
Word	Valence	Word	Valence
year	5.15	year	5.15
emperor	4.68	emperor	4.68
be	6.18	be	6.18
murder	1.48	murder	1.48
temple	5.3	temple	5.3
one	6.09	one	6.09
imperial	4.50	imperial	4.50
city	6.12	city	6.12
		3E	4.50
		septim	5.16
Mean valence	5.01	Mean valence	4.97

Figure 8: A dialogue entry from the *Skyrim* dialogue file that contains the word *Septim*. Each bold word has an E-ANEW rating and the underlined word has an E-ANEW-TES rating. The table underneath shows how the sentiment rating for valence is calculated for each lexicon.

even *Skyrim*'s main quest consists of more than 1000 *Skyrim*-specific words, but only 76 of those are unique. If only a small part of a quest is selected, then the variation decreases even further.

Another approach would be to single out the sentences with a higher *Skyrim*-specific word occurrence. However, providing human raters with one sentence in isolation could make it more difficult for them to understand the context in which the sentence is said, which might negatively influence the quality of human ratings.

We decided to evaluate the sentiment lexicons on multiple independent dialogues, i.e. dialogues that do not belong to the same quest or the same NPCs. The dialogues were grouped by their identification number, see Section 3.2., and filtered on length. All dialogues should consist of four dialogue segments (entries from the *Skyrim* dialogue file that consist of 1-3 sentences each). Additionally, evaluation dialogues should contain at least three unique game-specific words. We selected five dialogues from the remaining subset for our evaluation. For an example dialogue, see Figure 10. All evaluation dialogues can be found in Figure 9. In the rest of this paper, we will refer to each segment or complete dialogue with the corresponding id from that table.

In addition to rating each dialogue as a whole, we also rated each dialogue segment separately.

6. Evaluation

To evaluate the performance of both the E-ANEW and E-ANEW-TES sentiment lexicons, we compare their sentiment ratings for the evaluation dialogues with those of human raters.

Dialogue	Segment	Text
d1	s1	Before the **Oblivion Crisis**, many **elves called** <u>Winterhold</u> their **home**. More **visited** the **College** from <u>Morrowind</u> every **year**.
	s2	After, **growing distrust** of **magic made life difficult** for many. Some **left** rather than **endure** the **growing hatred** from the **local** <u>Nords</u>.
	s3	**Others returned home** after the **Red Year**, when <u>Vvardenfell</u> **erupted** and **caused** much **destruction**.
	s4	<u>Winterhold</u> itself **died** in the **years** between then and now. What's **left** out there **is a husk**. Only the **College** really **remains**.
d2	s5	They**'re** the **rulers** of the <u>Aldmeri</u> **Dominion** – what **used** to **be** the **Imperial provinces** of Summerset **Isle** and <u>Valenwood</u>.
	s6	The <u>Thalmor</u> **take the arrogance** of **high elves** to the **extreme** – they **believe** they **are** the **rightful rulers** of all of <u>Tamriel</u>.
	s7	For a **century** or more, the <u>Thalmor</u> **had been picking** away at the **Empire**. <u>Valenwood</u> **was** the **first**, then the **province** of <u>Elsweyr</u>.
	s8	But even the **Blades didn't see** the **Great War coming**. We **underestimated** the <u>Thalmor</u>, and they **destroyed** us.
d3	s9	Yes, I **was hired** to **protect** the **others** as we **walk** the **roads** of <u>Skyrim</u>.
	s10	It **is a thankless task** and I **would** rather **be back home** in <u>Elsweyr</u>, but I **have little choice**.
	s11	Ahkari **freed** me from a **prison** in <u>Cyrodiil</u>, and now I **must repay** my **debt** to him.
	s12	A **word** of **advice**, my **friend** – **do** not **mix gambling** and **drink**. **Taken** together, they **will empty** your **pockets** of every <u>septim</u>.
d4	s13	No **doubt General** Tullius and his **friends** in the **Empire will tell** you that I **owe** them my **loyalty**, and perhaps I **do**.
	s14	<u>Ulfric Stormcloak</u> **would say** that I **owe** my **allegiance** to the Nord **people** as they **fight** for Skyrim's **independence**. Perhaps this **is** also true.
	s15	The **day might come** when I **am forced** to **draw** my **sword** for **one side** or the **other**.
	s16	But that **day has** not **come** yet.
d5	s17	**Back** in 42 I **was stationed** in <u>Hammerfell</u>, on **leave** in **Sentinel**, **trying** to **track** down some **refugee relatives** who **had fled persecution** in <u>Alinor</u>.
	s18	Suddenly an **explosion** of **magic** in the **refugee quarter**. <u>Thalmor</u> mages **were attacking the** <u>Altmer</u> dissidents who **were resisting** with **magic** of their own.
	s19	I **ran** to the **scene** with **other** Legionaries who **were stationed** there, but the **entire quarter was** a smoking **ruin** by the **time** we **arrived**.
	s20	Everyone **was dead**. **Wholesale slaughter**. The **Dominion**, not **content** with **killing** dissidents at **home**, **came** to <u>Hammerfell</u> to **finish** the **job**.

Figure 9: Overview of the dialogues and dialogue segments used for evaluation. Words that are **bold** are part of the E-ANEW word list and words that are <u>underlined</u> have an E-ANEW-TES rating.

6.1. Collecting human ratings

Since Warriner et al. (2013) collected at least 14 ratings per word for the E-ANEW lexicon, we aimed for at least 14 participants. In order to collect representative ratings for snippets with game-specific words, we searched specifically for participants that were familiar with *Skyrim*.

We collected sentiment ratings from a group of 15 participants via a digital questionnaire. Participants were asked to rate all dialogue segments and all complete dialogues on all three PAD dimensions.

To fulfil the familiarity requirement, the instructions began with a list of twenty *Skyrim*-specific terms occurring in the evaluation dialogues. This list contained both terms that are part of the 965 *Skyrim*-specific words used for this research (e.g. *Hammerfell*, *Ulfric*) and words that are unique for *The Elder Scrolls* series but that are not part of that list (e.g.

the Blades, *Summerset Isle*). Participants were encouraged to search the Internet for more information if they did not know a particular term. If a participant was familiar with the meaning of a term, they could check the box in front of it. Checking off all game-specific terms was a prerequisite for continuing with the rating.

We provided participants with a short description of the context of each dialogue. For an example, see Figure 10.

All participants rated all five dialogues. For each dialogue they gave fifteen ratings; they rated each dialogue segment separately, of which there are four, and the dialogue as a whole on valence, arousal and dominance. Each participant provided 75 ratings in total.

A summary of the ratings from our participants is presented in Figure 11.

The player will meet with Delphine, who is a member of the Blades, to talk about an infiltration into a Thalmor party. The player can ask Delphine who exactly the Thalmor are and she will answer:

Dialogue text

They're the rulers of the Aldmeri Dominion – what used to be the Imperial provinces of Summerset Isle and Valenwood. The Thalmor take the arrogance of high elves to the extreme – they believe they are the rightful rulers of all of Tamriel. For a century or more, the Thalmor had been picking away at the Empire. Valenwood was the first, then the province of Elsweyr. But even the Blades didn't see the Great War coming. We underestimated the Thalmor, and they destroyed us.

Figure 10: A dialogue from our evaluation set, together with the context that was presented to participants in our experiment. *Aldmeri*, *Valenwood*, *Thalmor*, *Tamriel* and *Elsweyr* are *Skyrim*-specific words with an E-ANEW-TES rating.

6.2. Comparing lexicon ratings with human ratings

To compare the performance of the two lexicons, we consider both the number of satisfactory ratings and the correlation between human sentiment ratings and the ratings computed with the lexicons. A calculated E-ANEW or E-ANEW-TES rating is considered *satisfactory* if it stays within the boundaries of the standard deviation (SD) of the human rating for the same dialogue or dialogue segment. For an example, see Section 4.3.

Figure 12 shows the number of satisfactory ratings for both lexicons. For E-ANEW, 11, 17 and 20 dialogue segments have a satisfactory rating (out of 20 total) and 4, 5 and 5 complete dialogues have a satisfactory rating (out of 5 total) for respectively valence, arousal and dominance. For E-ANEW-TES the results are comparable. For segments, the results are the same. For the complete dialogues, there is one less dialogue with a satisfactory rating for valence.

We calculated the correlation between the human ratings and the sentiment ratings computed with each lexicon. Since it is not possible with only 15 participants to determine whether the human ratings are normally distributed, we calculated the correlation with a metric for parametric variables (Pearson correlation) and one for non-parametric variables (Spearman correlation). However, in both cases the results are comparable, with a slightly better performance by our game-specific lexicon E-ANEW-TES.

The correlation scores between the human ratings and E-ANEW and the human ratings and E-ANEW-TES are presented in Figure 13. For each correlation, we also report the significance as a 2-tailed p-value. The p-value was calculated using SciPy's built-in significance test[11] for the

---

[11]For more information, see the documentation of SciPy 1.4.1. https://docs.scipy.org/doc/scipy/reference/generated/scipy.stats.pearsonr.html

Pearson correlation and the Spearman correlation.

7. Discussion

If we look at the results in Figure 12 and Figure 13, we cannot conclusively state that our game-specific lexicon performs significantly better than E-ANEW.

If we look only at satisfactory ratings, E-ANEW-TES performs slightly worse than E-ANEW, since it has one less dialogue segments with a *satisfactory* rating for valence.

When we look at Pearson correlation scores between human ratings and the two lexicons, E-ANEW performs better for the valence dimension, and E-ANEW-TES performs better on arousal and dominance, independent of the length (e.g. segments or complete dialogues) of the evaluation text.

If we consider the Spearman correlation, E-ANEW-TES performs slightly better than E-ANEW. It performs better than E-ANEW on dominance for segments and on arousal for whole dialogues. E-ANEW performs better on valence for segments. For all other sentiment dimensions and text types, both lexicons perform equally well. However, except for arousal, most correlation scores are not significant. This is probably due to the small amount of participants in our evaluation experiment.

When we calculate a sentiment rating for a dialogue segment or a complete dialogue, we take only a few game-specific words into account. On average, this was one word per dialogue segment (with a maximum of three) and five words per complete dialogue (with a maximum of eight words). This low density of recognized game-specific words makes it hard for E-ANEW-TES to perform significantly better than E-ANEW. amount However, analyzing texts with a large number of recognized words (both E-ANEW words and game-specific words) can also become problematic. Since we average the values of all recognized words, recognizing more words in a text will inevitably lead to the ratings that approach a neutral rating of 5. Similarly, longer texts might also contain more words from our lexicon, which also invariably leads to more neutral ratings and decreased performance.

We selected our evaluation dialogues with the evaluation process in mind: dialogues were selected for containing at least four game-specific words, with at least three of those words unique to the dialogue. However, most dialogues from the game will not satisfy these constraints. This means that when choosing a *Skyrim* dialogue at random, the performance might be worse than in the ideal situation used for this research.

8. Improvements

There are multiple possibilities for improving both our game-specific lexicon E-ANEW-TES and sentiment analysis for games in general.

A possible improvement is creating a game-specific lexicon that also includes n-grams, i.e. game-specific terms that consist of multiple words. For example, the bigrams *Oblivion Crisis* and *Red Year* from [d2] would receive four E-ANEW ratings, since *oblivion*, *crisis*, *red* and *year* all occur in its lexicon. However, the bigrams have their own particular meaning in *The Elder Scrolls*. Additionally, words that are names in *The Elder Scrolls* but also appear in our English

	dialogue segments			complete dialogues		
	valence	arousal	dominance	valence	arousal	dominance
highest rating	6	7.133	5.533	5.667	6.133	5.667
lowest rating	2.667	3.533	3.467	3.267	4	3.533
mean rating	4.257	4.783	4.390	4.187	5.08	4.387
mean SD	1.414	1.920	2.301	1.392	1.826	2.020

Figure 11: Human ratings for dialogue segments and complete dialogues obtained from 15 participants. Sentiment ratings range from 1 (unpleasant, calm, controlled) to 9 (pleasant, excited, in control).

		Number of satisfactory ratings	
		E-ANEW	E-ANEW-TES
segments	val	11	11
	ar	17	17
	dom	20	20
dialogues	val	4	3
	ar	4	4
	dom	5	5

Figure 12: Number of segments and dialogues with a *satisfactory* sentiment rating, as calculated using the E-ANEW and E-ANEW-TES lexicons. The results of the two lexicons are comparable.

word list (e.g. *Empire* and *nord*) often have a different meaning in *Skyrim*. This is not reflected in the current E-ANEW-TES word list. Additionally, future work should focus on larger-scale evaluation with more participants, more evaluation dialogues and texts of different lengths. It would also be interesting to apply the same method on in-game text from other games. Finally, instead of simply averaging the sentiment ratings of the lexicon words, we could apply more sophisticated methods for calculating the sentiment rating for a text.

9. Conclusion

The inclusion of game-specific or genre-specific words in a sentiment lexicon seems a suitable approach for improving sentiment analysis for games. However, text for which we want to calculate a sentiment rating should have a high density of game-specific words before using a game-specific lexicon makes a noticeable difference.

E-ANEW-TES, the E-ANEW extension that also includes game-specific words performed better on complete *Skyrim* dialogues than E-ANEW. However, the performance difference between E-ANEW-TES and E-ANEW is very small. In most cases, the performance of E-ANEW-TES was the same as that of E-ANEW.

The code, datasets and results of this research are available on Github: `https://github.com/jd7h/sentiment-lexicon-skyrim`.

10. Acknowledgments

This research is partially supported by the Netherlands Organisation for Scientific Research (NWO) via the DATA2GAME project (project number 055.16.114).

11. References

Barbieri, F., Espinosa-Anke, L., Ballesteros, M., Soler-Company, J., and Saggion, H. (2017). Towards the understanding of gaming audiences by modeling Twitch emotes. In *Proceedings of the 3rd Workshop on Noisy User-generated Text*, pages 11–20. Association for Computational Linguistics.

Bethesda Game Studios. (2011). *The Elder Scrolls V: Skyrim*. Game [PC]. Bethesda Softworks, Rockville, Maryland, US.

Borgholt, L., Simonsen, P., and Hovy, D. (2015). The rating game: Sentiment rating reproducibility from text. In *Proceedings of the 2015 Conference on Empirical Methods in Natural Language Processing*, pages 2527–2532. Association for Computational Linguistics.

Bradley, M. M. and Lang, P. J. (1999). Affective norms for English words (ANEW): Instruction manual and affective ratings. Technical Report C-1, Center for Research in Psychophysiology, University of Florida.

Fraser, J., Papaioannou, I., and Lemon, O. (2018). Spoken conversational ai in video games: Emotional dialogue management increases user engagement. In *Proceedings of the 18th International Conference on Intelligent Virtual Agents*, IVA '18, page 179–184. Association for Computing Machinery.

Gökçay, D., İşbilir, E., and Yildirim, G. (2012). Predicting the sentiment in sentences based on words: An exploratory study on ANEW and ANET. In *2012 IEEE 3rd International Conference on Cognitive Infocommunications (CogInfoCom)*, pages 715–718. IEEE.

Guerini, M., Strapparava, C., and Stock, O. (2012). Ecological evaluation of persuasive messages using Google AdWords. In *Proceedings of the 50th Annual Meeting of the Association for Computational Linguistics*, pages 988–996. Association for Computational Linguistics.

Hutto, C. J. and Gilbert, E. (2014). VADER: A parsimonious rule-based model for sentiment analysis of social media text. In *Eighth international AAAI Conference on Weblogs and Social Media*, pages 216–225.

Jurafsky, D. and Martin, J. (2008). *Speech and Langauge Processing*. Pearson Education (US).

Kerr, C. and Szafron, D. (2009). Supporting dialogue generation for story-based games. In *Proceedings of the Fifth AAAI Conference on Artificial Intelligence and Interactive Digital Entertainment*, AIIDE'09, page 154–160. AAAI Press.

Louis, A. and Sutton, C. (2018). Deep Dungeons and Drag-

		E-ANEW		E-ANEW-TES	
		Pearson correlation	p-value	Pearson correlation	p-value
Segments	Valence	**0.3662**	0.1123	0.3399	0.1426
	Arousal	0.3373	0.1459	**0.3581**	0.1210
	Dominance	0.5291	0.0164	**0.5853**	0.0067
Dialogues	Valence	**0.7520**	0.1426	0.6902	0.1971
	Arousal	0.5474	0.3396	**0.6435**	0.2414
	Dominance	0.7276	0.1635	**0.7632**	0.1333

		E-ANEW		E-ANEW-TES	
		Spearman correlation	p-value	Spearman correlation	p-value
Segments	Valence	**0.3786**	0.0997	0.3583	0.1209
	Arousal	0.3336	0.1506	0.3336	0.1506
	Dominance	0.5019	0.0241	**0.5584**	0.0105
Dialogues	Valence	0.8000	0.1041	0.8000	0.1041
	Arousal	0.4000	0.5046	**0.7000**	0.1881
	Dominance	0.9000	0.0374	0.9000	0.0374

Figure 13: Pearson correlation and Spearman correlation between the human ratings and E-ANEW and human ratings and E-ANEW-TES. Entries are bold if one of the lexicons performed better than the other. The p-value is a 2-tailed p-value that indicates the probability that two uncorrelated datasets produce the same correlation. Most of the correlations are not significant ($p \leq 0.05$). This is probably due to the small number of data points.

ons: Learning character-action interactions from role-playing game transcripts. In *Proceedings of the 2018 Conference of the North American Chapter of the Association for Computational Linguistics: Human Language Technologies, Volume 2 (Short Papers)*, pages 708–713. Association for Computational Linguistics.

Mikolov, T., Sutskever, I., Chen, K., Corrado, G. S., and Dean, J. (2013). Distributed representations of words and phrases and their compositionality. In C. J. C. Burges, et al., editors, *Advances in Neural Information Processing Systems 26*, pages 3111–3119. Curran Associates, Inc.

Nielsen, F. Å. (2011). A new ANEW: evaluation of a word list for sentiment analysis in microblogs. In *Proceedings of the ESWC2011 Workshop on 'Making Sense of Microposts': Big things come in small packages*, pages 93–98. CEUR-WS.org.

Osgood, C. E., Suci, G. J., and Tannenbaum, P. H. (1957). *The measurement of meaning*. University of Illinois press.

Panagiotopoulos, G., Giannakopoulos, G., and Liapis, A. (2019). A study on game review summarization. In *Proceedings of the Workshop MultiLing 2019: Summarization Across Languages, Genres and Sources*, pages 35–43. INCOMA Ltd.

Sarratt, T., Morgens, S.-M., and Jhala, A. (2014). Domain-specific sentiment classification for games-related tweets. In *AAAI Conference on Artificial Intelligence and Interactive Digital Entertainment*, pages 32–34.

Senior, T. (2011). Skyrim has 60,000 lines of dialogue, new dragon shouts revealed, horses confirmed. https://www.pcgamer.com/skyrim-has-60000-lines-of-dialogue-new-dragon-shouts-revealed-horses-confirmed/. Last accessed on 2019-11-15.

Staiano, J. and Guerini, M. (2014). Depeche Mood: a lexicon for emotion analysis from crowd annotated news. In *Proceedings of the 52nd Annual Meeting of the Association for Computational Linguistics*, pages 427–433. Association for Computational Linguistics.

Suellentrop, C. (2016). Skyrim creator on why we will have to wait for another elder scrolls. https://www.rollingstone.com/culture/culture-features/skyrim-creator-on-why-well-have-to-wait-for-another-elder-scrolls-128377/. Last accessed on 2019-11-15.

Urbanek, J., Fan, A., Karamcheti, S., Jain, S., Humeau, S., Dinan, E., Rocktäschel, T., Kiela, D., Szlam, A., and Weston, J. (2019). Learning to speak and act in a fantasy text adventure game. In *Proceedings of the 2019 Conference on Empirical Methods in Natural Language Processing and the 9th International Joint Conference on Natural Language Processing (EMNLP-IJCNLP)*, pages 673–683. Association for Computational Linguistics.

Warriner, A. B., Kuperman, V., and Brysbaert, M. (2013). Norms of valence, arousal, and dominance for 13,915 English lemmas. *Behavior research methods*, 45(4):1191–1207.

Proceedings of the LREC 2020 Workshop Games and Natural Language Processing, pages 10–16
Language Resources and Evaluation Conference (LREC 2020), Marseille, 11–16 May 2020
© European Language Resources Association (ELRA), licensed under CC-BY-NC

ClueMeIn: Obtaining More Specific Image Labels Through a Game

Christopher G. Harris
School of Mathematical Sciences
University of Northern Colorado
Greeley, CO 80639 USA
christopher.harris@unco.edu

Abstract
The ESP Game (also known as the Google Image Labeler) demonstrated how the crowd could perform a task that is straightforward for humans but challenging for computers – providing labels for images. The game facilitated the task of basic image labeling; however, the labels generated were non-specific and limited the ability to distinguish similar images from one another, limiting its ability in search tasks, annotating images for the visually impaired, and training computer vision machine algorithms. In this paper, we describe ClueMeIn, an entertaining web-based game with a purpose that generates more detailed image labels than the ESP Game. We conduct experiments to generate specific image labels, show how the results can lead to improvements in the accuracy of image searches over image labels generated by the ESP Game when using the same public dataset.

Keywords: ESP Game, Image Labeler, Games With a Purpose, GWAP, Computer Vision

1. Introduction

There are numerous benefits to image recognition and labeling (i.e., tagging), such as providing better accuracy in image searches to greater accessibility for visually impaired users. Despite impressive advances in computer vision, many challenges remain in image recognition; it remains an intractable problem. Unlike machines, humans are capable of image recognition and labeling but require incentives. Games With A Purpose (GWAP) are a class of games that developed to bridge the gap between human and machine abilities. One goal of GWAPs is to aid in annotation or labeling of items for training machine learning algorithms.

In 2004, the ESP Game was created to assist in these tasks of image recognition and labeling (Von Ahn and Dabbish, 2004). By integrating image recognition and labeling tasks into an entertaining game, it provides an incentive to human players by aligning game performance with task achievement.

The ESP Game randomly matches two players with no other means of communication. The two players are shown the same image, and they both enter words that can be used to describe the image. The objective is for the two players to enter the same word or phrase, which earns them points and becomes a label, or tag, to describe the image. Labels successfully assigned to that image become "taboo" words, which do not earn points in future games. There is a time limit to increase player engagement: players have 150 seconds to label 15 images.

One clear limitation of the ESP Game is that the tags given to the images are generic and rarely provide enough information to discriminate between *similar* images (see Figure 1). In this paper, we introduce a game, ClueMeIn, to address this problem. We designed ClueMeIn to generate more specific image labels, to improve image search accuracy, to train machine learning algorithms, and to increase accessibility for the visually impaired. In the next section, we discuss the limitations of the ESP Game as

an image labeler; in Section 3, we describe other games that have also been designed to label images. In Section 4, we discuss the design and creation of ClueMeIn. We describe experiments in Section 5, followed by analysis in Section 6. Last, we conclude and mention future work in Section 7.

2. Limitations of the ESP Game

The ESP Game was adapted in 2008 as the Google Image Labeler. Starting with a collection of 350k images, the game later used randomly selected images from the web to create its image dataset.

One limitation of the ESP Game is that players are given incentives to type the most obvious labels, which maximizes agreement with other players (and consequently points). Due to its reliance on matching, the ESP Game rewards players providing generic terms and punishes players for the use of more informative (but rare) terms. The reward mechanism ensures players are more likely to achieve a match if they enter generic terms as opposed to specific ones. This has been demonstrated through a game-theoretic approach by Jain and Parkes (2009). Moreover, the generic nature of the ESP Game labels defeats the advantages that human computation provides.

Figure 1: A game to distinguish between similar images, such as these boats, can create more meaningful labels.

The use of more generic terms by players also encourages redundancies in the labels; Weber, Robertson, and Vojnovic (2009) indicated that 81% of images labeled with the "guy" were also labeled with "man." Thus, the more general the generated terms, the less informative they are in describing the image.

A second limitation of the ESP Game is that generic labels such as "car" provide little benefit to image collections, except at a superficial level; a search on "car" on any popular image search engine, such as those provided in Bing or Google, will return more than 100M images. Many labels have a strong association with one another and can be predicted through simple word association, like "sky" and "clouds." Also, there is a strong tendency to rely on colors as labels – an aspect of computer vision that machines can already detect with high accuracy. Therefore, the ESP Game favors general labels for an image over specific ones, as this is the best strategy to match other players and to generate the most points. However, this is less useful for generating labels for search tasks.

A third limitation is that labels can be ascertained using language models or other means, limiting the human-added value. For example, Weber, Robertson, and Vognovic developed a program to play the ESP Game without the need to evaluate the actual image. Their program disregards the visual content of the images and predicts likely tags by analyzing the taboo words and then applies a probabilistic language model. It manages to agree with the human partner on a label for 69% of images, growing to 81% of images with at least one assigned taboo term. Thus, human players provide little additional information to the existing tags even when taboo words are used. ClueMeIn overcomes these limitations by providing more informative labels than the ESP Game is able to do; our focus is on having participants identify a single image from a set of similar images by specifying increasingly precise labels.

3.   Related Work

Since its initial development, the ESP Game has inspired other image labeling games. *Peekaboom*, by the same creators as the ESP Game, looks for pixel boundaries of objects in images (Von Ahn, Liu, and Bloom, 2006). Human annotators enhance image metadata to create better learning algorithms. While the outputs are different from the ESP Game, the methods of collecting data are similar.

Karido uses a collaborative framework to tell works of art apart (Steinmayr et al., 2011). In Karido, nine similar images are randomly selected from a given database of artwork with the objective of increasing tag diversity. Players take turns either playing the Guesser or describer of the image selected by the system to be described. To discourage random guessing, the score of both players is reduced as a penalty if a wrong image is selected. This penalty exceeds the bonus for selecting the correct image.

Phetch is not designed to collect image labels but to collect entire sentences that described an image (Von Ahn et al., 2007). Three to five players play each round of Phetch, one of which is randomly selected as the describer while the remaining players become seekers. Initially, a picture is shown to the describer, who enters descriptive sentences to guide the seekers. The seekers use a search engine within the game to locate the described image. If a seeker selects the correct image, that seeker and the describer are awarded a score bonus. Once the correct image has been found, the winning seeker becomes the describer in the subsequent round. To discourage random guessing, points are deducted whenever a seeker makes an incorrect guess.

One issue with the ESP Game is the lack of tag diversity. Ho et al. created *KissKissBan* (2009), which introduces a third player and a competitive element in KissKissBan. The first two players (called a couple) try to achieve the same goal as in the ESP Game. The third player in KissKissBan, called the blocker, is competing with the other two players. Before each round begins, the blocker can see the image and has seven seconds to enter as many words as possible, which the couple is not allowed to use. Unlike the taboo words in the ESP Game, the couple cannot see this list of words. If one of the players in the couple enter a blocked word, five seconds are deducted from their allotted time. If the timer runs out before the couple achieves a match, their scores are decreased and the blocker's score is increased; if the couple has a successful match, their score increases while the blocker's decreases.

PhotoSlap by Ho et al. (2007) is a web-based variation of Snap, a popular card game. PhotoSlap engages users in an interactive game that capitalizes on the human ability to quickly decipher whether the same person shows up in two consecutive images presented by the computer. The game mechanism encourages rational play; in other words, from a game-theoretic view, the optimal player strategy is not to collude, but balance cooperation with competition.

Picture This, by Bennett et al. (2009) is designed not to label images directly, but rather to improve query results using existing tags. Other image labeling tools exist in non-gamified formats as well. *LabelMe* (Russell et al. 2007), a web-based tool for annotating images and sharing those annotations within a community of users, provides an easy-to-use interface for manual labeling of object information, including position, shape, and object label. Likewise, *ImageTagger* (Fiedler, Bestmann, and Hendrich, 2018) is a collaborative labeling tool that allows also includes an automated photo annotation option.

4.   ClueMeIn: Designing for Informative Labels

ClueMeIn falls into the class of inversion-problem games, as defined by Von Ahn and Dabbish (2004) In these games, one player transforms a given input (the selected goal image) into an intermediary output (i.e., the textual description). The second player tries to transform the intermediary output back into the original input (i.e., by selecting the correct image). Inversion-problem games are designed for player success to be associated with the degree to which the intermediary output becomes a representation of the original input.

4.1 Dataset

For our dataset, we use the IAPR TC-12 image retrieval benchmark, a collection of 20k images created for the CLEF cross-language image retrieval track (ImageCLEF) (Grubinger, 2006) In our initial experiment, we manually selected 473 similar images on several themes (e.g., boats, waterfalls, birds, churches). We assigned these images to 40 image pools based on a single theme (e.g., sailboats, waterfalls, clouds). Image pool sizes ranged between 5 and 18 with a mean size of 11.83. ClueMeIn randomly assigned images for a single image pool in groups of 3 to 9 for each game session. As with the ESP Game, clues provided by players for an image in earlier games became "taboo" words for that image in subsequent games. To test image similarity, we focused on images taken at different angles and of very similar items, such as those seen in Fig. 2.

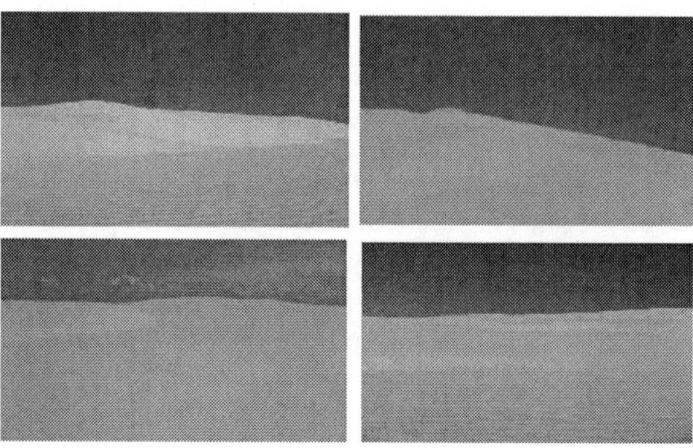

Figure 2: Some images are challenging to come up with unique labels, such as with these four images.

4.2 Game Design

Unlike the ESP Game, which examines a single image, our game, ClueMeIn, presents the pair of players with between three and nine *similar* images. These similar images can be selected using those with identical labels from the ESP Game or other sources. ClueMeIn is designed to develop labels that distinguish similar images from one another. It, therefore, focuses more on providing informative labels without the penalties associated with generic labels.

Players take turns playing two roles- one player serves as the *Guesser* while another serves as the *Cluegiver*. Players are each presented with the same set of images in a randomized order. The game identifies the one image for the Cluegiver to describe to the Guesser (see Fig. 3). Because the order is randomized, providing clues based on the relative position of each image will not help describe a specific image, nor will providing comparative words (most *term+er*, least *term+er*, *term+est*, etc.) as these are not permitted. As in Karido, label inputs are restricted to a maximum of three words and all punctuation is removed. Because there is less of a focus on matching and more of a focus on using the human-provided clues to discriminate

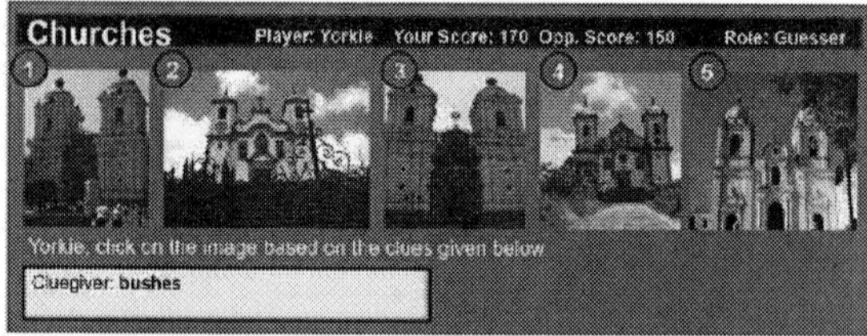

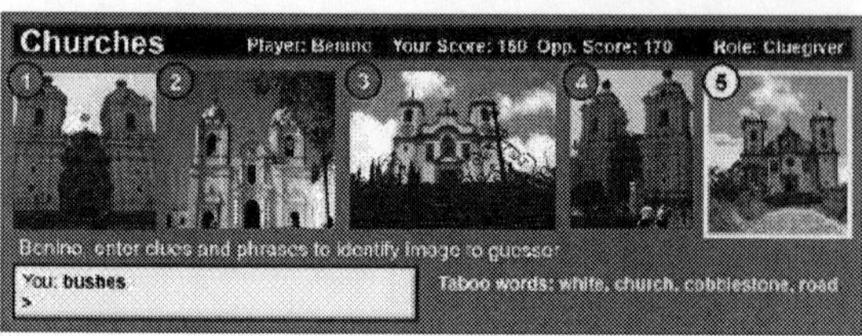

Figure 3: Screenshots from the game indicating the view of Guesser (top) and Cluegiver (bottom). Players take turns in each role and have different incentives to facilitate meaningful clues.

between images, the information contained in the labels themselves is better at describing that image.

In ClueMeIn, each of the two players serves as Guesser and Cluegiver five times on different sets of images either from the same image pool or different image pools. Each player alternates between the two roles, Guesser and Cluegiver, in an attempt to maximize the number of points. ClueMeIn assigns points based on different behaviors.

- *Cluegivers* are given points based on how unique their clues (words or phrases) are – we examine the label frequency, and once a clue has been mentioned three times (across multiple games), it is added to the list of "taboo" words. By dividing the number of labels supplied for that image overall by the number of instances the label has appeared previously, we arrive at a raw score. We apply some normalization and smoothing to arrive at an overall score for that label, rewarding more unique labels more than commonly-used ones. As each image is evaluated more frequently, the label quality increases since the more commonly-used clues are awarded fewer points or become taboo words after they are given for the third time for that image. Taboo and comparative clues are not conveyed to the Guessers; however, an error message is returned to the Cluegiver, indicating the word is off-limits.

- *Guessers* are given points based on how few guesses they use to identify the correct image. They can only make a single guess after a clue has been provided by the Cluegiver. We count the number of guesses, minus the chance they would guess randomly as the raw score. We apply some normalization and some smoothing to arrive at an overall score for a correct selection. Therefore, if five images are presented, Guessers are given more points for guessing the first image correctly than guessing the second time correctly out of the remaining four.

- To prevent the Cluegiver from supplying intentionally useless labels or the Guesser from making intentionally poor guesses, a portion of points are assigned equally to both players per session based on their mutual performance. Although this reward is the opposite of the penalty assigned for random guessing in Karido, it has a similar effect. The number of points given to each is 25% of the combined number of points the two players achieve in that round (see Fig. 4 for an example). Players were provided this information in advance to persuade them not to be adversarial.

4.3 Game Interface

The game interface was designed in Flash to be played through a web browser. Image categories, each pulled from a separate image pool, were randomly selected, as were the images from each pool. Each participant could only evaluate a given group of images once. All players had the option to create and log into an account or remain anonymous (but were tracked by a userID only). ClueMeIn provides a leaderboard for players who logged in to see their overall rank (given as a percentile) for the day and the overall campaign (see Fig. 5).

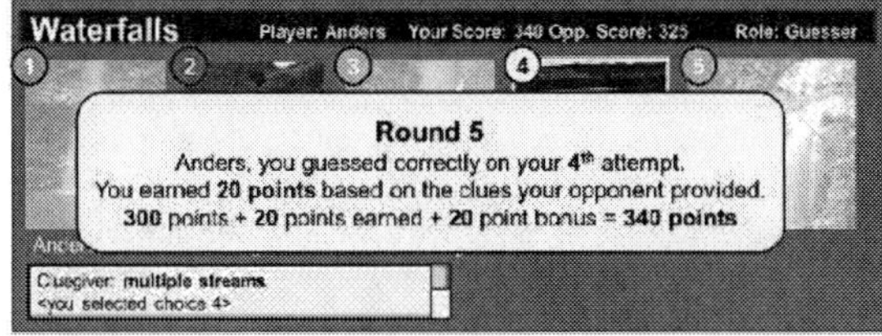

Figure 4: Screenshot of the information given to the players at the end of each round. The bonus given is 25% of the number of points earned by both Guessers and Cluegivers.

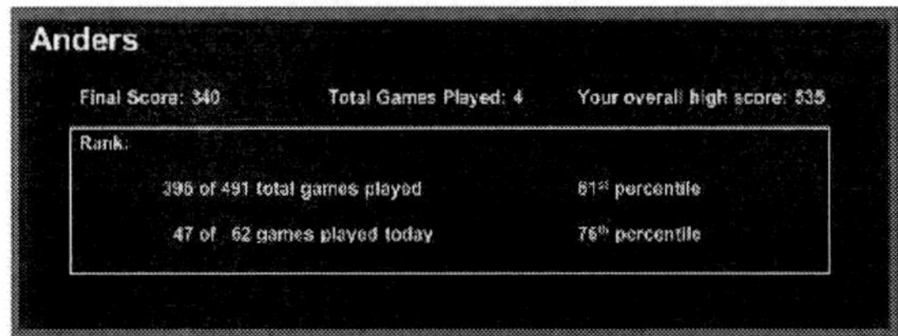

Figure 5: A screenshot of the information given to each player who logs in (players can also play anonymously).

4.4 Other Game Design Considerations

We also ran some small usability experiments to determine the best method for achieving informative labels. We examined the use of a countdown timer, but the competitive nature of our game often made the two players more adversarial – some players intentionally slowed each other down to achieve a higher score. A survey of player satisfaction suggested we get rid of the timer (which we did). We plan to explore other options to enhance the speed of the games.

Deciding how cooperative versus competitive to make the game was another consideration. There is some emerging research (e.g., Siu, Zook, and Riedl, 2014; Siu and Riedl, 2016) that examines the role of competition vs. cooperation in games. Von Ahn and Dabbish (2008) argue that games like the ESP Game work better because it is cooperative, while most entertainment-related games work best when the environment is competitive. Emmerich, K., & Masuch (2013) found that the desirable game characteristics of immersion and flow were greater in competitive gaming formats, while empathy was greater in cooperative gaming formats. We experimented with cooperation by taking the average of the scores obtained by the Guesser and Cluegiver and giving the same score to each. While this seems equitable, it made the game less enjoyable based on our player satisfaction survey. We found that providing the scoring approach for each player described earlier made it competitive without producing adverse effects, such as misleading clues or bad guesses.

5. Experiments

We conducted a series of experiments over six weeks to evaluate the design of our game. These experiments build on the preliminary studies found in Harris (2018). For label generation, we recruited and randomly distributed 40 participants, comprised of students all proficient in the English language from a four-year university, into two groups with a 60-40 split.

5.1 Gathering Labels

We then replicated the ESP Game format using the 473 images in our dataset. Our objective was to determine the labels the ESP Game could generate; this became our *baseline*. We had 16 participants (average age = 23.2, males = 13) play 373 five-round games of the ESP Game, generating a total of 2098 labels, or 4.44 labels per image. Of these 2098 labels, 997 (47.5%) were "taboo" at the end of the six-week gaming period (i.e., they had been given as clues three or more times).

Next, we had 24 participants (average age = 22.4, males = 18) play a total of 886 games of ClueMeIn with the same 473 images, averaging 36.9 games per participant. We gathered a total of 4514 unique labels across the 473 images, averaging 9.54 labels per image. Of these 4514, taboo labels totaled 2437 (54%) at the end of the campaign.

5.2 Determining Label Quality

We evaluated the quality of the generated labels from the ESP Game and ClueMeIn; high-quality labels should be specific enough to identify an image from a pool of images.

To accomplish this, we provided the generated labels obtained for all images to 10 participants (who did not participate in the labeling tasks). Four were asked to use the 2098 labels generated by the ESP Game and the other six using the 4514 labels from ClueMeIn.

Each participant was asked to identify which image (from the 473 total images) was best represented by the provided label. When the labels were created, participants were only able to see the subset of images from that pool that appeared in that round of the game; however, good quality labels should identify the correct image (even those that were unseen as choices in the game) when a particular label was created. Although we divided up the labels among the participants, 20% of the image labels were evaluated by more than one participant to examine inter-rater reliability (IRR), a measure of consistency among observational ratings provided by multiple coders. We obtained a Fleiss' κ of 0.610 and 0.672 for the ESP Game and ClueMeIn evaluators, respectively, indicating substantial agreement (Landis and Koch, 1977). Participants performed the label matching task independently (i.e., not as a group).

Each of the 10 participants evaluated multiple searches. Some of the searches were provided with search results in three formats:

- *ordered* lists (ordered in decreasing order by term frequency, but no frequency was provided)
- *unordered* lists (a list of search terms listed in random order without the knowing the number of times players generated each term
- *ordered weighted* lists (ordered in decreasing order by term frequency, where the frequency count was provided)

The number of searches participants received with each type of list, whether they received the ClueMeIn generated list of terms vs. the ESP Game list of terms, as well as the assignment of list type to each search was each independently and randomly determined.

When participants were provided with an unordered list, the average accuracy (calculated as the number of correctly assigned labels/total number of labels) was 68.0% for those generated by the ESP Game and 88.7% for those generated by ClueMeIn, a substantial difference. This shows that even when information about the frequency of terms is not given, the quality of labels generated using ClueMeIn is superior to those generated for the same images using the ESP Game.

When an ordered weighted list was provided, the average accuracy increased to 78.1% for those generated by the ESP Game and 96.6% for those generated by ClueMeIn, also a large difference. Since both the ESP Game and ClueMeIn results were provided with the same type of list. Again, these results showing a consistent jump in accuracy indicate that it was not the dataset used, but the game format, that made a difference in label quality.

The improvement of results between the three list types as the information becomes more meaningful (first ordered, then both ordered and weighted) is attributable to a form of bias called *search result bias*. A violation of search neutrality, this bias occurs when people scan a list of terms from top to bottom and perceive the ones towards the top are more important than those further down the list (Kulshrestha et.al., 2019). This has known to have an impact on various aspects of daily life, from searching through a phone directory to find a business to the order candidate names are listed on election ballots. However, we examine these because most labels have an implied order, and the use of these ordered, weighted list of labels provides a more realistic scenario than the unordered list.

We note that while participants selected from all 473 images, the pools were distinct enough that possible labels were, in practice, restricted to a single pool of images (e.g., sailboats). Although the average image pool size to select a given a label from was small (11.83), we believe the method in which labels generated for an image show promise to enhance the accuracy of image searches overall.

6. Analysis

Better quality labels help us generate more meaningful annotations for images, more descriptive image tags for the visually impaired, and richer information for training machine learning algorithms. The better accuracy achieved by human evaluators indicates the design of the ClueMeIn game by which labels are generated for an image show promise to enhance the accuracy of image searches overall relative to that used in the ESP Game. We also note the number of labels (4514 vs. 2098) and the diversity (the number of non-taboo tags: 2077 vs. 1101) was more than double using ClueMeIn; this is also a measure which implies the richer language used in creating labels through ClueMeIn.

One may observe that more games were played of ClueMeIn than the ESP Game; however, both game campaigns ended when the rate of new label generation fell below 0.5 (defined as the average number of new non-taboo labels generated for an image per round of the game). This also indicates the ability of ClueMeIn to generate more diverse labels. With a larger pool of images, we believe the diversity of labels would increase with ClueMeIn (due to the need to create specific labels to distinguish between similar images), but not necessarily with the ESP Game (which examines a single image at a time).

We used the 2015 version of the Linguistic Inquiry and Word Count (LIWC) to evaluate aspects of the language used in each label. Our analysis using LIWC is limited because our labels are limited to three words and contained a few of the features normally common in free-form text. Some comparisons on key linguistic features between the ESP Game and ClueMeIn labels were possible and are given (in a normalized form) in Table 1.

Metric	ESP Game	ClueMeIn
Words>6 letters	0.768	0.845
Dictionary words	0.923	0.881
Use of Numbers	0.217	0.294
Use of Quantifiers	0.265	0.338
Cognitive Terms	0.373	0.460
Perceptual Terms	0.318	0.377

Table 1: Comparison of LIWC metrics between labels obtained from the ESP Game and ClueMeIn

From this, we can see that the language used in the ClueMeIn labels use longer words (>6 letters), more numbers and quantifiers, use words that are more cognitive and more perceptual but use fewer dictionary words than labels generated on the same dataset using the ESP Game.

These are linguistic characteristics often associated with more specific, meaningful terms (e.g., Chuang et.al. 2012, Pitt and Samuel, 2006).

We designed ClueMeIn to be entertaining – that is, participants enjoy playing the game and don't perceive it as a task. To examine this, we asked our 40 participants to evaluate the game they were assigned to play on enjoyment (how much fun it was to play relative to other games) and engagement (how sticky the game was) on a five-point scale, 1 = lowest, 5 = highest. Participants, on average, found the ClueMeIn game more enjoyable (3.58 vs. 3.06) and more engaging (3.71 vs. 3.38) than the ESP Game, indicating a greater potential for participants to enjoy the game and play for longer periods. See Fig. 6 for a box-and-whisker plot of the results for each.

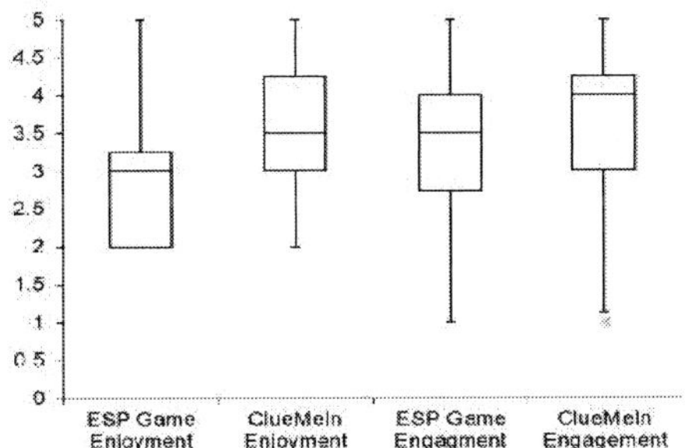

Figure 6. A box and whisker plot comparing enjoyment and engagement for the ESP Game and ClueMeIn.

7. Conclusion and Future Work

We have implemented an entertaining web-based game, ClueMeIn, to provide more specific image labels and improve the accuracy of image searches. The design of ClueMeIn addresses some of the weaknesses of the popular ESP Game (Google Image Labeler). While the ESP Game was designed to provide broad labels, advancements in computer vision have propelled past what the ESP Game was intended to accomplish. ClueMeIn can build upon the initial tags generated by the ESP Game to create image pools (i.e., "house") which in turn can provide a game

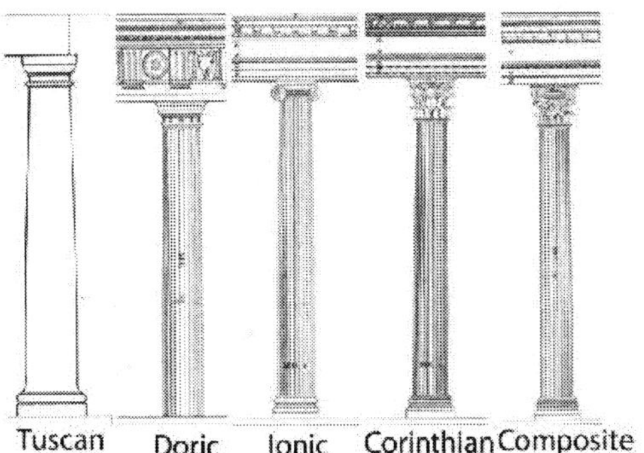

Figure 7. Five classical orders of columns. ClueMeIn can help illustrate the differences in these orders, enhancing word embeddings and leading to more descriptive labels. Image from Mitrović (1999).

environment to compare similar images of houses with one another, forcing the adoption of more specific labels, (i.e., "Greek Revival architecture"). This increase in granularity can be repeated (all houses with a "Greek Revival architecture" label can then be compared using ClueMeIn once again to get even more specific labels). It can also advance word embeddings that tied to images; people not familiar with architecture may understand columns (see Fig 7), but more specific labels will help build word embeddings that capture the similarities and differences.

As the clues get more specific and the list of "taboo" words grows, the clues that separate images become less and less important to the images. This feature is especially true when identifying the image from a larger pool of similar images. In Fig. 8, we see that the words used to separate these two images, 'grass' and "rocks," will be winning clues in our game but are not very descriptive of the image overall.

Figure 8. Sometimes seemingly irrelevant facts can separate two similar images. "Rocks" was a label given to the image on left, but "grass" was a label given to the image on the right. We resolve this by assigning weights to these labels based on Cluegiver frequency

Some challenges remain. One challenge is how the game should properly weigh the labels. Image labels identified in earlier sessions become "taboo" words in later sessions for other players, but these labels contain more obvious identifiers and need to be weighed higher in the label metadata. We are currently exploring how to properly model and apply term weights to these image labels.

We will continue to apply the game to an expanding pool of similarly themed images. Once the pool of images is sufficiently large (e.g., "cars"), we plan to examine the game's labeling effects on large-scale image searches. Initial results are promising.

We also plan to explore how we can make the game more enjoyable and immersive for players. We are exploring the addition of game elements to improve the flow of the game. We are also looking at other game mechanisms such as scoring, collaborative vs. competitive elements, and how to reward players who devote a significant amount of time (and provide significant value) recognizing and labeling images in ClueMeIn.

One further use for ClueMeIn is that it has the possibility of helping language learners understand and apply terms in a second language to images they already know and understand, help build a better list of synonyms and possibly help build a stronger, more robust set of word embeddings that can be tied to a specific image.

8. Bibliographical References

Bennett, P. N., Chickering, D. M., & Mityagin, A. (2009). Picture this: preferences for image search. *In Proceedings of the ACM SIGKDD Workshop on Human Computation* (pp. 25-26).

Chuang, J., Manning, C. D., & Heer, J. (2012). "Without the clutter of unimportant words" Descriptive keyphrases for text visualization. *ACM Transactions on Computer-Human Interaction (TOCHI),* 19(3), 1-29.

Emmerich, K., & Masuch, M. (2013). Helping friends or fighting foes: The influence of collaboration and competition on player experience. *In FDG* (pp. 150-157).

Fiedler, N., Bestmann, M., & Hendrich, N. (2018). Imagetagger: An open-source online platform for collaborative image labeling. *In Robot World Cup* (pp. 162-169). Springer, Cham.

Grubinger, M., Clough, P., Müller, H., & Deselaers, T. (2006). The iapr tc-12 benchmark: A new evaluation resource for visual information systems. *In International workshop ontoImage* (Vol. 2).

Harris, C. (2018). ClueMeIn: Enhancing the ESP Game to Obtain More Specific Image Labels. *In Proceedings of the 2018 Annual Symposium on Computer-Human Interaction in Play Companion Extended Abstracts* (pp. 447-452).

Ho, C. J., Chang, T. H., & Hsu, J. Y. J. (2007). Photoslap: A multi-player online game for semantic annotation. *In Proceedings of the National Conference on Artificial Intelligence (Vol. 22, No. 2, p. 1359).* Menlo Park, CA; AAAI Press; MIT Press.

Ho, C. J., Chang, T. H., Lee, J. C., Hsu, J. Y. J., & Chen, K. T. (2009). KissKissBan: a competitive human computation game for image annotation. *In Proceedings of the acm sigkdd workshop on human computation* (pp. 11-14).

Jain, S., & Parkes, D. C. (2013). A game-theoretic analysis of the ESP Game. *ACM Transactions on Economics and Computation (TEAC),* 1(1), 1-35.

Kulshrestha, J., Eslami, M., Messias, J., Zafar, M. B., Ghosh, S., Gummadi, K. P., & Karahalios, K. (2019). Search bias quantification: investigating political bias in social media and web search. *Information Retrieval Journal*, 22(1-2), 188-227.

Landis, J. R., & Koch, G. G. (1977). The measurement of observer agreement for categorical data. *Biometrics*, 159-174.

Mitrović, B. (1999). Palladio's Theory of the Classical Orders in the First Book of I Quattro Libri Dell'Architettura 1. *Architectural History*, 42, 110-140.

Pitt, M. A., & Samuel, A. G. (2006). Word length and lexical activation: Longer is better. *Journal of Experimental Psychology: Human Perception and Performance*, 32(5), 1120.

Robertson, S., Vojnovic, M., & Weber, I. (2009). Rethinking the ESP game. *In CHI'09 Extended Abstracts on Human Factors in Computing Systems* (pp. 3937-3942).

Russell, B. C., Torralba, A., Murphy, K. P., & Freeman, W. T. (2008). LabelMe: a database and web-based tool for image annotation. *International journal of computer vision*, 77(1-3), 157-173.

Siu, K., Zook, A., & Riedl, M. O. (2014). Collaboration versus competition: Design and evaluation of mechanics for games with a purpose. *In FDG*.

Siu, K., & Riedl, M. O. (2016). Reward systems in human computation games. *In Proceedings of the 2016 Annual Symposium on Computer-Human Interaction in Play* (pp. 266-275).

Steinmayr, B., Wieser, C., Kneißl, F., & Bry, F. (2011). Karido: A GWAP for telling artworks apart. *In 2011 16th International Conference on Computer Games (CGAMES)* (pp. 193-200). IEEE

Von Ahn, L. and Dabbish, L. (2004). Labeling images with a computer game. *SIGCHI conference on Human factors in computing systems (CHI '04).* 319-326. ACM.

Von Ahn, L., & Dabbish, L. (2008). Designing games with a purpose. Communications of the ACM, 51(8), 58-67.

Von Ahn, L., Ginosar, S., Kedia, M., & Blum, M. (2007). Improving image search with phetch. *In 2007 IEEE International Conference on Acoustics, Speech and Signal Processing-ICASSP'07 (Vol. 4, pp. IV-1209).* IEEE.

Von Ahn, L., Liu, R., & Blum, M. (2006). Peekaboom: a game for locating objects in images. *In Proceedings of the SIGCHI conference on Human Factors in computing systems* (pp. 55-64).

Proceedings of the LREC 2020 Workshop Games and Natural Language Processing, pages 17–25
Language Resources and Evaluation Conference (LREC 2020), Marseille, 11–16 May 2020
© European Language Resources Association (ELRA), licensed under CC-BY-NC

Cipher: A Prototype Game-with-a-Purpose for Detecting Errors in Text

Liang Xu & Jon Chamberlain

University of Essex, Wivenhoe Park, Colchester, Essex, UK
{lx18921,jchamb}@essex.ac.uk

Abstract

Errors commonly exist in machine-generated documents and publication materials; however, some correction algorithms do not perform well for complex errors and it is costly to employ humans to do the task. To solve the problem, a prototype computer game called Cipher was developed that encourages people to identify errors in text. Gamification is achieved by introducing the idea of steganography as the entertaining game element. People play the game for entertainment while they make valuable annotations to locate text errors. The prototype was tested by 35 players in a evaluation experiment, creating 4,764 annotations. After filtering the data, the system detected manually introduced text errors and also genuine errors in the texts that were not noticed when they were introduced into the game.

Keywords: Game with a purpose, error detection, gwap, distributed knowledge acquisition, text correction

1. Introduction

Text error detection techniques have been widely used in a variety of applications, e.g., spell checkers and Optical Character Recognition (OCR) readers. Studies have explored methods to improve the accuracy of word correction, with several techniques commonly used for solving the problem. Dictionary-matching, common error list analysis and targeted error detection approaches have been employed to address general and simple errors like misspelling and non-word mistakes in articles (Kukich, 1992). For more complex errors, e.g., grammar errors and errors which rely on context, there are computational models for detection and correction of errors, such as the Statistics Language Model (SLM) (Kukich, 1992). It is still challenging to detect complex errors and the above methods might not detect them all. To solve the problem there are applications which use human effort that is to say, people who have high proficiency in the language are employed to do the proofreading task. They are paid to find all the errors in the text, especially those errors that computers cannot detect. The disadvantage of this approach is the cost of annotators.

Computers outperform humans in many tasks; however, they are still not powerful enough to beat humans in fields such as creative work, emotion detection, context-based analysis and so on. Therefore, we use human processing abilities to solve the problems that machines are not good at (Quinn and Bederson, 2011; Chamberlain et al., 2013). In our project, a computer game was designed to motivate people to find text errors, which is based on the idea of a Game With A Purpose (GWAP) (Von Ahn, 2006). GWAPs are able to reduce the cost of human effort to solve computational problems through gamification. In this research steganography is used as part of the game design to improve enjoyment and help to achieve the data collection goal. The purpose of the prototype was to evaluate human performance in text error detection through an entertaining game. In the game, every decision of error detection from a player is an annotation, whether it is correct or not.

This research aims to answer two questions: 1) How good are humans at identifying errors in text? and 2) Is it possible to build a game to motivate people to detect errors in text? First, this paper summarises related work in the field of text error detection and correction, as well as notable games used for language annotation. Section 3 presents the methodology and design of the prototype game called *Cipher*, developed to detect errors in text. Game implementation is explained in Section 4. Section 5 presents the results from a lab-based evaluation of players using the game, followed by discussion of the applications of the game and its limitations.

2. Related Work

2.1. Error detection and correction

Text error detection and correction techniques have three common problems. The first problem is non-word error detection. Any word or string that cannot be found in the dictionary might be a non-word error. The most common instances are spelling mistakes, for example, "anatomy" is misspelled as "anonomy". The second problem is isolated-word error correction that is to correct the detected non-word errors in text. The third problem is context-based word correction. The errors which rely on the context are difficult to detect, because they are correctly spelled words which are not correctly used in the context, for example, "off" when it should be "of". Both words are spelled correctly but the former will not fit the specific context. The research (Kukich, 1992) is a gist of some of the techniques used in the detection of text errors in research as summarized by Kukich:

2.1.1. Non-word detection techniques

Dictionary lookup is the most common and direct spelling error detection approach. Every target word is compared to the word in the dictionary, one by one, to check if they match. A correct word will find a counterpart in the dictionary while a wrong word will not. To achieve this, a hash table is used to compare the hash address of the target word with the address of the word in the dictionary (Knuth, 1973). However, the size of the dictionary for comparison might influence the dictionary access speed and efficiency. A solution is that the category of the dictionary chosen to match the target word is related to its application or domain, which narrows down the range of search vocabulary (Mishra and Kaur, 2013).

N-gram analysis can also be used. The value of *n* is often 1, 2, or 3, which represents the n-letter subsequence of the target word. This approach is a comparative analysis of each n-gram with the corresponding word in a preprocessed n-gram table which is metamorphosed from a dictionary or a specific corpus. The related applications perform well in detecting errors in machine-produced text, for example, electronic-documents generated by OCR devices, but they are not good at detecting hand-written errors (Riseman and Hanson, 1974).

2.1.2. Isolated-word correction techniques

The process of word correction is more difficult than error detection. In most situations, text errors require not only to be found but also correctly modified. Thus, there are some techniques for non-word error correction (Kukich, 1992; Mishra and Kaur, 2013):

The **Minimum Edit Distance Algorithm** was first introduced to explain the minimum steps to modify a word from its wrong form to its correct form (Wagner, 1974). The ways of modification include insertion, deletion, and replacement. There are several useful algorithms based on this idea that compute the minimum edit distance between a text error and its correspondent correct counterpart .

The **Similarity Key Algorithm** assigns a key to those words that look alike (e.g. far, for, form, from, fool). Therefore, all similar words have the same key and those corresponding words are the values of the key. When a spelling mistake is detected, according to the key of this error, all the similar words which have the same key will be attached as correcting candidates. The advantage of the method is that there is no need to compare the error to every word in the lexicon or corpus one by one, which saves processing time and promotes the efficiency of correction process (Odell and Russell, 1918).

A **Rule Based Algorithm** is a process of collecting the features of common spelling mistakes compared to their correct forms and turning the features into different rules. For example, the word "gracefull" is an error because the last letter of its correct form "graceful" has been repeated, which is a feature of the error. According to the rules which can be applied, text errors can be detected and corrected (Yannakoudakis and Fawthrop, 1983).

When it comes to probability for text recognition and error correction, there are two different probabilities which can be applied: **transition probability** and **confusion probability**. Transition probabilities are the probabilities of a letter followed by another letter correctly. Confusion probabilities are the probabilities of a wrong letter appearing after a correct letter. Algorithms based on the two probabilities are useful in text recognition preprocessing and word correction (Bledsoe and Browning, 1959).

Neural Networks (NNs) play an important role in spelling error correction. The correction ability of NNs becomes more accurate with large scale spelling error data for training. Some spelling correction applications record users' spelling mistakes as the training data to train the Neural Networks, then those frequent spelling errors associated with the user's misspelling habits can be easily corrected and even predicted (Rumelhart et al., 1986).

2.1.3. Context-based correction techniques

For this type of error (the hardly detectable errors), the performance for real-word error correction achieved by existing empirical studies is not as promising as the performance for isolated-word error correction. Real-word errors could be syntactic errors or semantic errors, thus, it is more difficult to detect or correct this type of error. It has been suggested that around 40% of all text errors are context-based errors (Mitton, 1987).

2.1.4. Summary

The core of these techniques is based on algorithms. Furthermore, different types of errors have different detection and correction techniques. The model built for this project uses human effort through a game and deals with all kinds of errors in text. For context-based errors particularly, this model is expected to find those errors that computer algorithms cannot find because humans are better than machines at understanding context and finding hard to detect errors.

2.2. Games with a Purpose

Computers are able to replace humans in many fields; however, there are still some tasks that human perform at better than computers. The idea of a Game With A Purpose (GWAP), proposed by Luis von Ahn, was to design an entertaining game that motivates people to solve a computational problem (Von Ahn, 2006). The problem is typically one which computers cannot solve it yet. The GWAP idea benefits from three conditions (Von Ahn and Dabbish, 2008): Firstly, the ubiquity of the Internet to provide a connected workforce is an important factor. There are more people who use the Internet every day and almost everything in daily life is involved with it. Secondly, some computational problems are challenging for computer algorithms but not complicated for human beings, such as syntax annotation, labelling objects within an image, common-sense collection and so on. Lastly, computer games are popular and an increasing number of individuals spend considerable time playing them. The approach has been increasingly applied to many fields such as text analysis, image recognition, Internet search reinforcement, security monitoring, information filtering, etc (Lafourcade et al., 2015).

2.2.1. The ESP Game & Peekaboom

The *ESP Game* is a web-based game focusing on labelling images (Von Ahn and Dabbish, 2008). In the game, two players are given the same image and both players use a word to describe the picture. If the outputs of the two players are identical, they win the game. In total, more than 200,000 people played the game and it collected 50 million image labels. *Peekaboom* is another example in which the goal of the game is to not only label the image contents generally but also locate specific image objects within each image, based on the data from the ESP game (Von Ahn et al., 2006). According to the usage statistics, *Peekaboom* collected 1,122,998 pieces of data with 14,153 players in one month. The *ESP Game* and *Peekaboom* were used to improve Internet search performance, especially for searching pictures which contain noisy information (Von Ahn and Dabbish, 2008). Additionally, *CAPTCHA*, an automated cryptographic program introduced by Luis von Ahn, is a successful example of the recognition competition between humans and computers, although it is not a GWAP (Von Ahn et al., 2003). The test result differentiates humans from computers.

2.2.2. Phrase Detectives

GWAPs are also used in language annotation. *Phrase Detectives* is an online game with the purpose for identifying semantic connections in vocabulary under a certain context (Chamberlain et al., 2008). More specifically, the goal of the game is to encourage people to detect anaphoric coreference (the word or phrase used to replace the former mentioned object in the text). For example, in the sentence: "Tom and Mike are friends and they study in the same university", the players need to annotate "they" as reference to the earlier mentioned entity "Tom and Mike". *Phrase Detectives* used players to annotate the text, as well as validate the decisions of other players in order to optimise the data collection process (Chamberlain et al., 2018).

2.2.3. Digitalkoot

OCR devices are able to achieve recognition accuracy of a character as high as 99% for documents with high scan quality; however, word recognition accuracy decreases with word length to around 95% for a five-letter word (Kukich, 1992). *Digitalkoot* is designed to minimise the effort to detect and correct OCR errors in old Finnish newspapers. *Digitalkoot* is divided into 2 parts: verifying OCR outcomes and using human OCR (humans reading the text). In the first part, several words generated by OCR devices are shown to players. They need to decide whether those words are correctly recognised compared to the original text within the images. The second part is to encourage players to type each word with a given word image to build a bridge to make the game character cross successfully. In 51 days, 4,768 players played the game. They spent 2,740 hours on the game and finished 2.5 million tasks. Compared with 85% recognition accuracy by using OCR devices, the game players achieved 99% accuracy for recognising the text (Chrons and Sundell, 2011).

2.2.4. Designing GWAPs

GWAPs can be an effective method to collect data. GWAPs are less expensive in the long term than other approaches for using human power to solve problems, such as Amazon Mechanical Turk. To design a GWAP, there are some suggestions according to the reviewed games (Von Ahn and Dabbish, 2008; Chamberlain et al., 2013). First of all, the key to developing such games is enjoyability. It is important that people enjoy playing the game and we obtain the data as a side effect. Furthermore, GWAPs attempt to solve computational problems which are divided into smaller tasks. Designing a successful GWAP relies on how to introduce those tasks without influencing the game-design mechanics (Chrons and Sundell, 2011). Engaging game elements can be added to increase player enjoyment such as time limit, score rewarding, rankings, level setting and so on. Moreover, it is essential to apply some evaluation metrics to GWAPs and make sure the obtained results are correct. The performance of GWAPs can be evaluated by metrics, such as Cost per Acquisition, Monthly Active Users, and Average Lifetime Play (Chamberlain et al., 2017).

2.2.5. Summary

In the context of the *ESP Game* and *Peekaboom*, the object recognition competition between humans is to help computers improve the ability of image labelling. The model built for this project tries to solve the error detection problem with the help of humans. The idea of making annotations of text errors is inspired by *Phrase Detectives* which makes annotations of anaphoric coreference. The evaluation metrics that apply to *Phrase Detectives* are also used in the project, which help in optimising the data collection process. When compared to *Digitalkoot*, the game which detects OCR errors, our project has the potential for detecting context-based errors.

3. Methodology

How good are humans at identifying errors in text? This is the over-arching question for the project. In order to answer the question, artificial errors are generated in texts which players must detect and the average correction accuracy achieved by players used as a benchmark. The assumption is that humans can detect most errors in a given text and based on this assumption, the second research question is: *is it possible to build a game to encourage people to detect errors in text?* Errors commonly exist in printed materials and electronic documents, but humans can detect them and thus we build a game to identify errors in text with the help of game participants who are entertained to play the game while we collect useful data. We combine the two research questions and explore if a game can improve the performance at the correction task. When we analyse the data, we are also identifying errors we did not know. With more people playing the game, more errors can be identified and the error detecting performance improved overall.

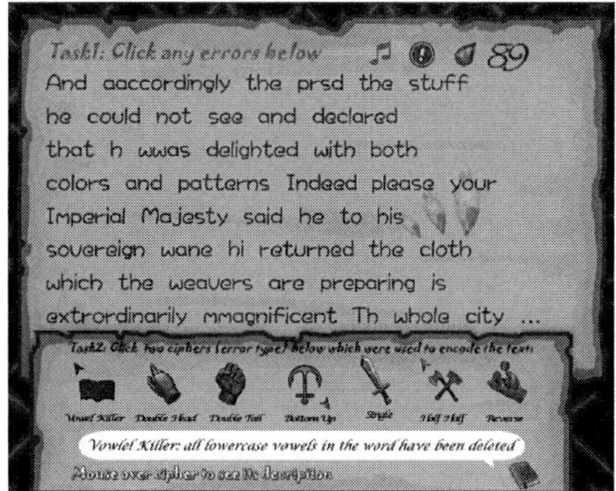

Figure 1: A screenshot from the gameplay of *Cipher*

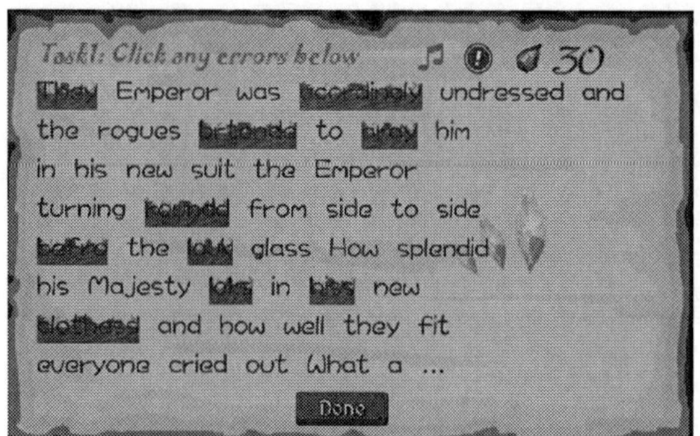

Figure 2: An example of cipher and common errors in a round of the game.

3.1. Cipher: A game to detect errors in text

Cipher is a single-player game that focuses on a text-based problem. Inspired by *Phrase Detectives*, the game is a text analysis game and collects data from players about annotation of words or phrases (Figure 1). *Cipher* encourages people to detect errors in text and was experimentally tested following a previously published strategy (Pearl and Steyvers, 2010) by inviting people to play the game offline to simulate an online GWAP. The participants include university students and friends of the authors, mostly in the 18-21 age range with English as a second language. The idea of steganography is used as an interesting game element for gamification. This turns the error detection task to cipher seeking. Ciphers create simple errors with certain features which would be found easily while more complex errors are also introduced as distractors for motivation, which would challenge players. The methodology for data collection and analysis combines qualitative and quantitative approaches. We focus not only data quantity, but also data quality, filtering the data according to players' performance and the number of players. It is also important to get players' opinions on the game as one of the essential evaluation metrics. By the experimental strategy, players are asked to play *Cipher* for at least 30 minutes. Their data are processed by filtering out data generated by those players whose correction accuracy and annotation accuracy are less than a threshold value.

There are also errors assumed to be the real errors in the text, we term as **unknown errors**, that must be distinguished from a mistake made by the player. The number of players who detect the same unknown error is also used as a filter to process the data.

3.2. Artificial error distractors

Automatically generated error data has been used to improve the performance of error detection and correction in previous studies. Artificial error data are easy to produce and can be applied to train and evaluate error detection systems, evaluate the robustness of Natural Language Processing techniques and be negative evidence in the form of automatically distorted sentences in unsupervised learning (Foster and Andersen, 2009). This approach was used in *Cipher* where, in each round, 10 artificial errors consist of 6 cipher-generated errors (3 similar errors generated by each cipher) and 4 common errors. Common errors are chosen from 3 common error corpora (Aspell, Birkbeck, and Wikipedia)[1] and then are introduced by replacing the correct counterparts in the game text. They can be non-word errors or real-word errors. Figure 2 is an example of errors in the text in the game. In the picture, "acordingly", "aray", "loks", "roundd", "hiss", and "clothess" are cipher errors. "They", "brtende", "befro", and "louk" are common errors. The cumulative correction accuracy (detected errors / round*10) of a player demonstrates how good the player is at error detection. Moreover, a total of 15 errors (5 in each article) were manually added into 3 articles from which the short text in each round is chosen from. They are used to evaluate the game's ability in error detection as a system on the assumption there were no genuine unknown errors in the articles.

3.3. Cipher mechanism

The idea of introducing cipher-generated errors is to turn the error checking task to cipher deducing, which is to make the serious game task entertaining for gamification purpose. To define ciphers, we make certain rules to alter the correct words in the text. In fact, these rules are the actual "ciphers". In each round, a piece of short text was encoded by two ciphers. Each cipher generates 3 similar errors, i.e., they have the same error feature (Figure 2). Ciphers that were used in the game were:

- **Vowel killer** All lowercase vowels in the word have been deleted (e.g., "th" from *the*, "hr" from *her*, "bk" from *book*);

- **Double head** The first letter has been repeated (e.g., "tthe" from *the*, "yyou" from *you*, "dday" from *day*);

- **Double tail** The last lowercase letter in the word has been repeated (e.g., "roundd" from *round*, "hiss" from *his*, and "clothess" from *clothes*);

- **Bottom up** The first letter in the word has been swapped with the last (e.g., "eids" from *side*, "mottob" from *bottom*, "tuis" from *suit*);

- **Single** One of two consecutive identical letters in the word has been deleted (e.g., "acordingly" from *accordingly*, "aray" from *array*, "loks" from *looks*);

- **Half half** The first half part of the word has been swapped with the rest (e.g., "itsu" from *suit*, "ndidsple" from *splendid*, "typem" from *empty*);

- **Reverse** The word has been reversed (e.g., "drow" from *word*, "hctam" from *match*, "thgil" from *light*).

As cipher-generated errors are rule-based and do not often occur in the real world, we also introduce errors from the common error corpora to simulate common typographical errors. There are 4 common errors (random error features)

---

[1]https://www.kaggle.com/bittlingmayer/spelling, accessed 13/2/2020

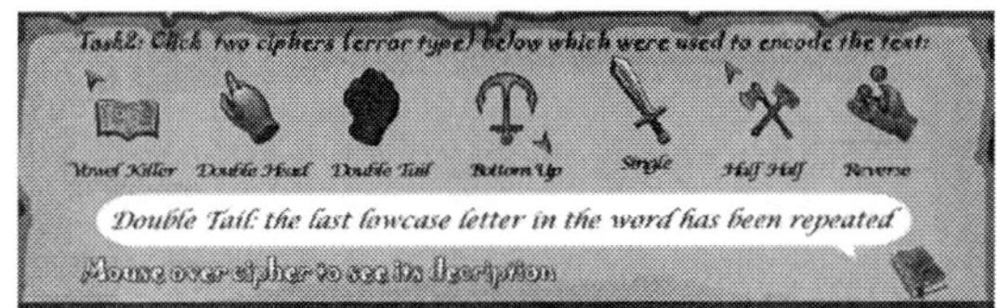

Figure 3: Cipher panel.

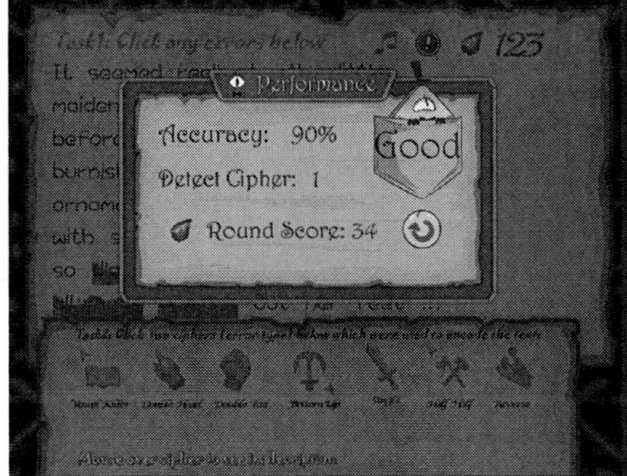

Figure 4: Player's performance panel.

besides 6 cipher errors making 10 **known errors** that have been introduced by the game per round.

Players have two tasks: At first, they need to find all the errors in the text and click them; Then they need to identify the ciphers according to the errors they have found and the descriptions of ciphers (Figure 3). The aim of the game is to find all the errors and then deduce the ciphers with according error features. Players' performance (correction accuracy, ciphers detected, and scores) was given at the end of the game after players confirmed and selected the ciphers according to the errors they found (Figure 4).

About text in the game, short text was randomly chosen from 3 articles in each round. In each article, there were 5 errors which have been manually added to determine the performance of the system. The 10 known errors in each game round were randomly generated by algorithms after the piece of text has been chosen and were intended to make the game fun and for appropriate rewards to be given to the players for correctly detecting an error. Although all texts were previewed by the authors before being used in the game, there may be some genuine errors in the text which was assessed in posthoc analysis.

4. Implementation

Cipher was developed in Unity game engine. Game graphics resources mostly come from Unity Asset Store[2] and the logo was a picture of the fictional character *Bill Cipher* from *Cleanpng*.[3] The implementation was divided into 4

---

[2]https://assetstore.unity.com/, accessed 13/2/2020.

[3]https://www.cleanpng.com/, accessed 13/2/2020.

parts: login & registration panel, text display panel, cipher panel and performance panel.

Login & registration panel When a player registered an account, a piece of player information data is created in the database. The players are required to login to the game so that their game information data can be updated in the database while they are playing the game.

Text display panel A short piece of text was randomly chosen from one of 3 xml documents. 10 errors are introduced into the text including 6 cipher errors and 4 common errors. More precisely, 4 correct words are replaced by 4 common mistaken words from common error corpus. There are 2 ciphers each round which encode the text by adding 6 errors randomly (3 errors with the same feature generated by each cipher algorithm). Finally, the modified text is shown to the players. Every word in the text is clickable.

Cipher panel A player needs to find all the errors in the given text by clicking them. When the player clicks an error, a piece of annotation data is created in the database. After the player finds all the errors and presses the "done" button, the cipher panel which contains 7 different ciphers is shown to the player. If the player finds the 2 ciphers , he will win the game and be rewarded with the score. The description of the cipher pops up when the mouse hovers over each cipher.

Performance panel The player is rewarded with 3 points for correctly identifying an error and 7 points for finding a cipher. After the player chooses 2 ciphers (whether correct or not), the result panel will pop out, which displays correction accuracy (correctly detected errors / 10), the number of ciphers found, and scores obtained in the round. Scores are accumulated each round. The player's information is updated in the database.

4.1. Data storage

Data collection is divided into three parts, stored in a table in MySql database. When a player detects and clicks an error, it is considered as an annotation. This annotation information includes the word Id, the name of the article where the word comes from, the correct form (plus wrong form as comparison if it is a game-introduced error) of the word, a Boolean flag representing if it is a known error ('Y' is Yes and 'N' is No), and the username of the player who clicked the word. This piece of annotation information is recorded in the table "annotation". The table "player" in the database has all the players' usernames and passwords. The table "playerinfo" stores the game information of the players including the scores the player has obtained, the number of rounds the player played, time the player spent in the game, the number of annotations the player made, the number of known errors the player detected, average correction accuracy (number of found errors / number of rounds*10), and annotation accuracy (number of found errors / number of annotations).

5. Results

The purpose of the game is to collect useful data while people are playing the game. The prototype game was tested by asking experimental participants to play the game. Participants were all unpaid volunteers and the experimental

Table 1: Unknown errors detected (CP=1, AA=0.2, and CA=0.2).

Word id	Story	Word	# clicked players
w473	Little match girl	Rischt	14
w482	Little match girl	burnt	4
w396	Emperor's new clothes	unft	3
w1942	Emperor's new clothes	exmating	2
w910	Little match girl	grandthern	2
w405	Swineherd	ill-humored	2
w570	Swineherd	cub	2
w115	Emperor's new clothes	wardrob	1
w823	Emperor's new clothes	atternd	1
w151	Swineherd	thad	1
w381	Swineherd	hummon	1
w708	Swineherd	mology	1
w1675	Swineherd	tecking	1

play time for each participant was at least 30 minutes. In 2 weeks, there were 35 participants who played the game and 25 of them played for more than 30 minutes. In total, players spent around 24 hours and 50 minutes playing the game. The game generated 4,764 pieces of annotation data, i.e., a click from the player who believes they have found an error, whether it is correct or not.

3 parameters were used as filters for the results: correction accuracy (number of found known errors by a player / number of rounds*10); annotation accuracy (number of found known errors by a player / total number of annotations from the player); and the number of clicked players (the number of players who made annotations on the same unknown word error). The difference between correction accuracy and annotation accuracy is that the former represents how accurate a player is at error correction while the latter shows how effective the player is at error correction.

While players were detecting errors, the game also recorded unknown errors. An unknown error can be either a genuine error in the text (or an error manually introduced into the text) or a mistake made by the player. The former is the target error (true positive) and the latter is considered as noise (false positive). Based on the collected data, we measure the variables: the number of true positives, the number of false positives, and thus recall and precision, were analysed by tuning 3 parameters: clicked player (CP), annotation accuracy (AA) and correction accuracy (CA). Initially,

the values of all parameters were very low (CP=2, AA=0.2, and CA=0.2), which could be considered as no filter applied, because there was no player whose correction accuracy or annotation was below 20%. Then we changed each parameter gradually and observed the measure variables. Lastly, the relationships between parameters and measured variables were plotted to see which parameters were important for improving correction performance of the system.

Of the 35 experimental participants, 28 of them achieved correction accuracy of more than 70% and 29 of them achieved annotation accuracy of more than 70%. There were 20 players whose correction accuracy was more than 80% and 15 players whose annotation accuracy was more than 80%.

Based on the collected data, the number of true positives, the number of false positives, recall, and precision were analysed with tuning 3 parameters: clicked player (CP), annotation accuracy (AA) and correction accuracy (CA). With parameters (CP, AA and CA) tuning, the relationship between the filters and the measure variables (number of target error and noise, recall and precision) were plotted in Figure 5 - 10. When the number of clicks from players is used as a filter we observe that noise is effectively reduced with filter at 4 player clicks, similar to the findings in the validation analysis in *Phrase Detectives* (Chamberlain et al., 2018), see Figure 5. We also observe an increase in precision when more player clicks are used but a lower recall due to the low number of players in the game experiment, see Figure 6. A similar effect is observed with the reduction of noise by using annotation and correction accuracy as a filter, i.e., by increasing the requirement for player ability, the number of incorrect judgements is reduced, see Figures 7 and 9. Likewise, we observe recall significantly drop when annotation and correction accuracy is used as a filter due to player exclusion and the low number of players in the experiment, see Figures 8 and 10.

Table 1 shows the unknown error detected results when the values of all parameters were very low, which can be considered as no filter applied. In this case, the values for CP, AA, and CA are 1, 0.2, and 0.2 respectively. 13 unknown errors were detected by players. 10 of them are manually added errors: "unft" (unfit), "grandthern" (grandmother), "exmating" (examining), "cub" (cap), "wardrob" (wardrobe), "atternd" (pattern), "thad" (that), "hummon" (humor), "mology" (melody) and "tecking" (taking). In total, there were 15 (5 in each story) manually introduced errors (66.6% detection rate). All 5 added errors in the story *Swineherd* were detected. Three unknown errors not introduced into the texts but were detected by players include:

"Rischt", or "R-r-ratch" in a different version of the story *Little match girl*, represents the sound of striking a match;

"burnt" is past tense in American English;

"ill-humored" is commonly used in American English.

In addition, old English words such as "hitherto", "Fie" and "swineherd" were also detected, which are rarely used nowadays (noted by player 3, 4 and 13 respectively).

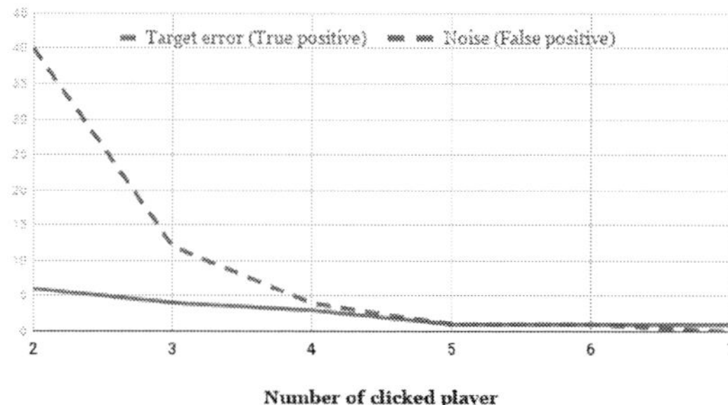

Figure 5: The number of target error and noise change when the number of clicked player is the filter.

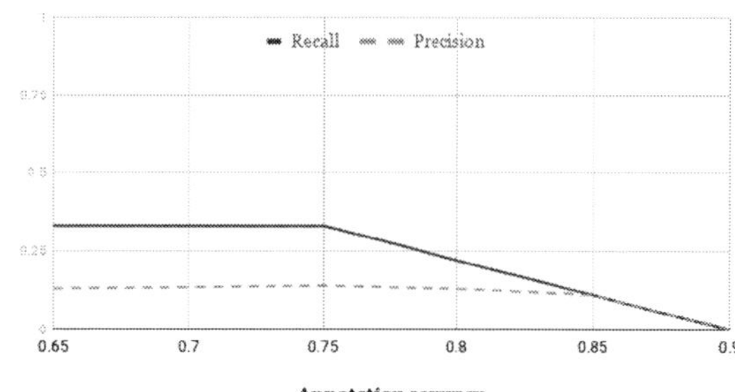

Figure 8: Recall and precision values with tuning parameter annotation accuracy.

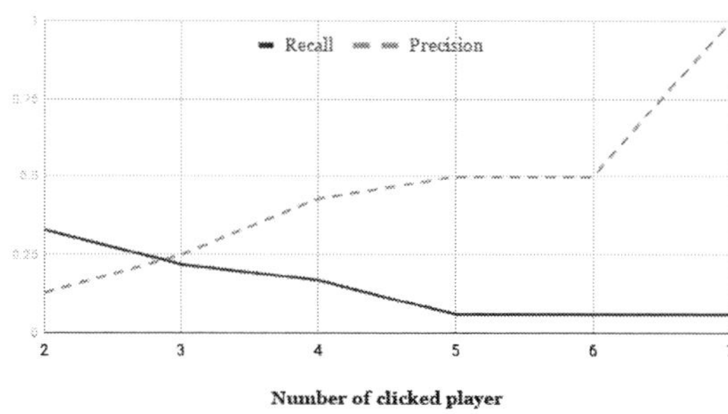

Figure 6: Recall and precision change when the number of clicked player is the filter.

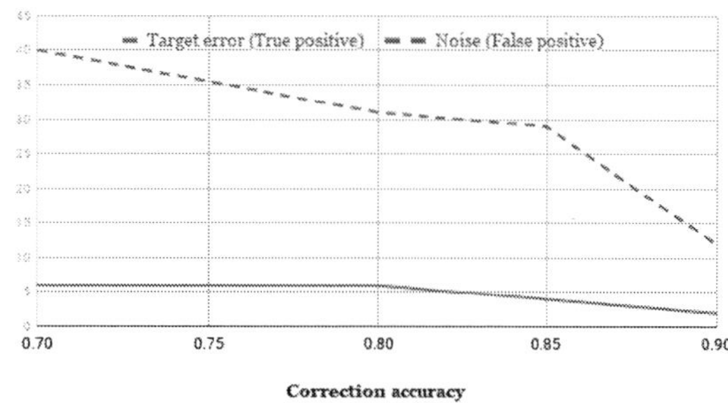

Figure 9: Number of target error and noise change when correction accuracy is the filter.

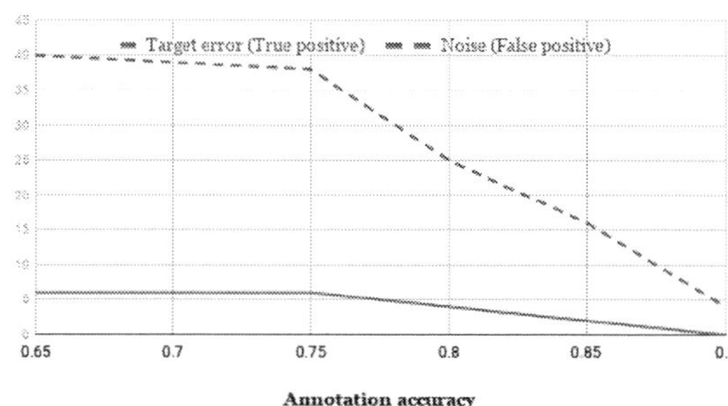

Figure 7: The number of target error and noise change when annotation accuracy is the filter.

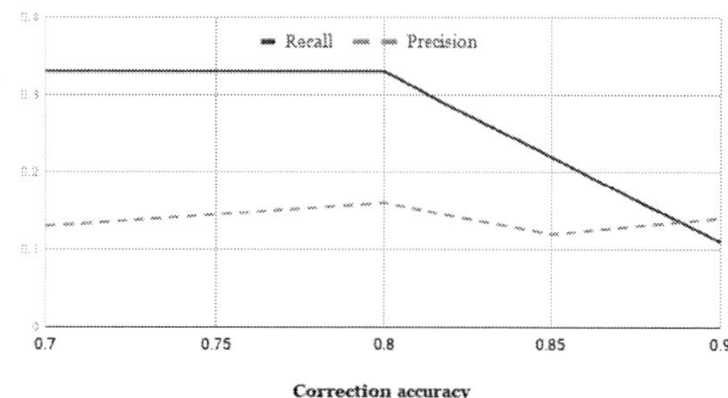

Figure 10: Recall and precision values with tuning parameter correction accuracy.

6. Discussion

Correction accuracy represents how accurate each player is in word correction. By calculating correction accuracy of each player, we can answer the first research question. 29 of 35 players' correction accuracy is higher than 70% and 20 players achieved more than 80%. 3 players reached more than 90% correction accuracy. These values suggested high performance of humans in error detection.

Initially we set the values of the 3 parameters, clicked player (CP), annotation accuracy (AA), and correction accuracy (CA) 2, 0.2 and 0.2 respectively in case there was too much noise (false positives). From the results, "unft", "grandthern" and "exmating" (manually added errors) were detected by players. Furthermore, there were some errors which we did not introduce into the documents. "Rischt" is the noise of striking a match in the context and its correct form is "R-r-ratch" in a version of the original text. The latter makes more sense in the context. We found that some players got confused between "burnt" and "burned" and "humored" and "humoured". In fact, "burnt" and "humor" are preferred in American English, therefore, some players considered them as errors. Players also detected that the types of English for some words used in the documents were not standard English because they annotated some old English words such as "Fie" (meaning "for shame" in other versions of the text), "hitherto" and "swineherd", which are uncommon. Figure 11 indicates the frequencies of the 3 old English words mentioned over time.

We did not know these errors until we looked at the data from the game. When players were finding errors in the text, they did find genuine errors and detected some problems we did not previously know.

We wanted to know if the game was engaging for players to encourage them to help us solve the problem. For the experiments, participants needed to play for over 30 minutes; however, many players played for more than 1 hour because they enjoyed the game. Verbatim comments from participants during the experiments include:

> "This game is a bit addictive. I really would like to play the game if it is released online."

> "It is an interesting game. Moreover, this game has some educational meaning. I think it will be really helpful for school students to play this type of game."

> "The game UI combined with the ear worm of the background music makes the text-based game a bit fun."

When evaluating the effectiveness of the system in detecting errors, we used 3 parameters (CP, AA, and CA) to try to improve the performance. From the graphs (Figure 5 – 10), we found precision overall would ascend but would fall to 0 if the parameter reached a certain value. As the parameter value goes up, the system keeps better players while eliminating bad players. There were fewer answers gradually, but the obtained results were more likely to be true positives. However, when the parameter value was too high, all players were excluded, which causes the decline of precision. When it comes to recall, it was always declining with each parameter increasing. The result explained that noise was generated while players were finding true positives. If we would like to get more true positives, we would get more noise as well. In conclusion, the performance of the system in word correction depends on how we tune the parameters.

There are some limitations with the project. The game was running offline on a small scale. The number of people who tested the game was sufficient for a prototype test but more would be needed for large-scale data collection. Enough participants played the game and created useful data which allowed us to explore the documents and find out new information. Furthermore, this is an English language game

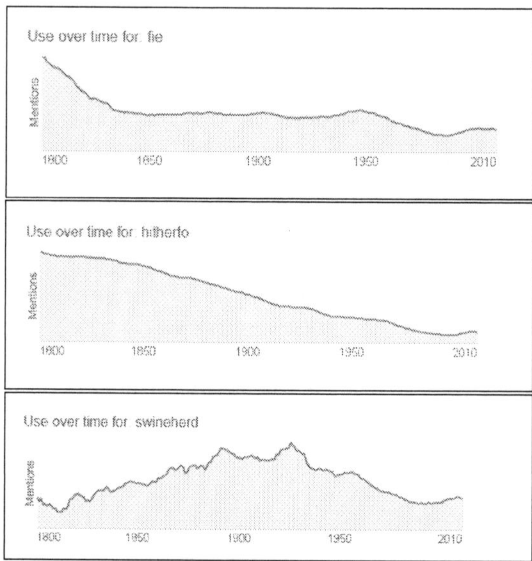

Figure 11: "fie", "hitherto" and "swineherd" used over time from Google dictionary.

but most participants were English learners rather than native speakers. This is partly because English learners are more interested in this language game for the motivation of practicing their English skills while playing the game and partly because of the limited number of participants. Therefore, there was more noise (false positives) detected, which influences the detection results. However, we defined filters to improve the outcomes. Even though most of the participants were non-native speakers, they still achieved high performance in error detection and found genuine errors and problems which we did not know.

7. Conclusion

It is common that some errors are found in publication materials and electronic documents. Existing commercial spelling-checking applications struggle to detect complicated text errors and it is expensive to employ humans to find errors. In this paper, we described a GWAP methodology for error detection. We found that people are able to easily identify errors in text and they were encouraged to do the tasks by playing an enjoyable game. Several genuine errors were detected, indicating the GWAP approach is useful to identify novel errors in text already checked by a proofreader. Parameters such as clicked players (number of players who detected the error), correction accuracy (detected errors / rounds*10), and annotation accuracy (detected errors / the total number of annotations) can be used to measure game performance. In addition, we found that the game has the potential for helping language learners. Participants reported that they enjoyed the game and found the unusual language interesting. A GWAP approach to error detection and correction would be useful as a support tool for OCR software, or as part of a wider pipeline looking to build fully corrected and annotated documents for large, collaboratively-produced language resources.

8. Bibliographical References

Bledsoe, W. W. and Browning, I. (1959). Pattern recognition and reading by machine. In *Papers presented at the December 1-3, 1959, eastern joint IRE-AIEE-ACM computer conference*, pages 225–232.

Chamberlain, J., Poesio, M., and Kruschwitz, U. (2008). Phrase detectives: A web-based collaborative annotation game. In *Proceedings of the International Conference on Semantic Systems (I-Semantics' 08)*, pages 42–49.

Chamberlain, J., Kruschwitz, U., and Poesio, M. (2013). Methods for engaging and evaluating users of human computation systems. In *Handbook of Human Computation*. Springer.

Chamberlain, J., Bartle, R., Kruschwitz, U., Madge, C., Poesio, M., et al. (2017). Metrics of games-with-a-purpose for nlp applications.

Chamberlain, J., Kruschwitz, U., and Poesio, M. (2018). Optimising crowdsourcing efficiency: Amplifying human computation with validation. *it - Information Technology*, 60:41–49.

Chrons, O. and Sundell, S. (2011). Digitalkoot: Making old archives accessible using crowdsourcing. In *Workshops at the Twenty-Fifth AAAI Conference on Artificial Intelligence*.

Foster, J. and Andersen, O. (2009). Generrate: generating errors for use in grammatical error detection. In *Proceedings of the fourth workshop on innovative use of nlp for building educational applications*, pages 82–90.

Knuth, D. E. (1973). The art of computer programming, vol. 3, addison-wesley. *Reading, MASS*.

Kukich, K. (1992). Techniques for automatically correcting words in text. *Acm Computing Surveys (CSUR)*, 24(4):377–439.

Lafourcade, M., Joubert, A., and Le Brun, N. (2015). *Games with a Purpose (GWAPS)*. John Wiley & Sons.

Mishra, R. and Kaur, N. (2013). A survey of spelling error detection and correction techniques. *International Journal of Computer Trends and Technology*, 4(3):372–374.

Mitton, R. (1987). Spelling checkers, spelling correctors and the misspellings of poor spellers. *Information processing & management*, 23(5):495–505.

Odell, M. K. and Russell, R. (1918). Patent numbers 1261167 (1918) and 1435663 (1922). *Washington, DC: US Patent Office*.

Pearl, L. and Steyvers, M. (2010). Identifying emotions, intentions, and attitudes in text using a game with a purpose. In *Proceedings of the naacl hlt 2010 workshop on computational approaches to analysis and generation of emotion in text*, pages 71–79. Association for Computational Linguistics.

Quinn, A. J. and Bederson, B. B. (2011). Human computation: A survey and taxonomy of a growing field. In *Proceedings of the 2011 SIGCHI Conference on Human Factors in Computing Systems (CHI'11)*, pages 1403–1412.

Riseman, E. M. and Hanson, A. R. (1974). A contextual postprocessing system for error correction using binary n-grams. *IEEE Transactions on Computers*, (5):480–493.

Rumelhart, D., Hinton, G., and Williams, R. (1986). Learning internal representations by error propagation in parallel distributed processing", de rumelhart, jl mcclelland eds.

Von Ahn, L. and Dabbish, L. (2008). Designing games with a purpose. *Communications of the ACM*, 51(8):58–67.

Von Ahn, L., Blum, M., Hopper, N. J., and Langford, J. (2003). Captcha: Using hard ai problems for security. In *International Conference on the Theory and Applications of Cryptographic Techniques*, pages 294–311. Springer.

Von Ahn, L., Liu, R., and Blum, M. (2006). Peekaboom: a game for locating objects in images. In *Proceedings of the SIGCHI conference on Human Factors in computing systems*, pages 55–64. ACM.

Von Ahn, L. (2006). Games with a purpose. *Computer*, 39(6):92–94.

Wagner, R. A. (1974). Order-n correction for regular languages. *Communications of the ACM*, 17(5):265–268.

Yannakoudakis, E. J. and Fawthrop, D. (1983). The rules of spelling errors. *Information Processing & Management*, 19(2):87–99.

Proceedings of the LREC 2020 Workshop Games and Natural Language Processing, pages 26–33
Language Resources and Evaluation Conference (LREC 2020), Marseille, 11–16 May 2020
© European Language Resources Association (ELRA), licensed under CC-BY-NC

Game Design Evaluation of GWAPs for Collecting Word Associations

Mathieu Lafourcade (1), Nathalie Le Brun (2)

(1) LIRMM, Université de Montpellier
161 rue Ada - 34095 Montpellier Cedex 5 - France
mathieu.lafourcade@lirmm.fr
(2) Imagin@t, France - imaginat@imaginat.name

Abstract

GWAP design might have a tremendous effect on its popularity of course but also on the quality of the data collected. In this paper, a comparison is undertaken between two GWAPs for building term association lists, namely JeuxDeMots and Quicky Goose. After comparing both game designs, the Cohen kappa of associative lists in various configurations is computed in order to assess likeness and differences of the data they provide.
Keywords: lexical network, associative dictionary, game design, comparing association lists

1. Introduction

The aim of the JeuxDeMots[1] project is to design Games With a purpose (GWAPs) to build a large lexical knowledge base (KB). Among the types of relations between terms that structure this network, free association is the one used to infer more precise semantic relations. It should be noted that there has long been a strong interest in associative dictionaries and/or thesauri (like the famous Roget's Thesaurus). What we want to evaluate here is the influence of game design on the quality of the data collected, especially the words that players provide when asked to indicate ideas associated with a target term.

After presenting the lexical network, we compare the main lexical data acquisition game to a new game, Quicky Goose[2] (QG), which proceeds from radically different choices in terms of game design. For a given term, we evaluate the similarity and divergence of the sets of associated terms obtained with each of the game modes, and we try to define the aspects of game design that play a key role.

2. Context: building a large lexical network

In JeuxDeMots (JDM), the main game of the project, players earn and collect words by providing lexical and semantic associations to terms proposed by the system. JDM is a two player GWAP (Game With A Purpose, (Ahn, 2006)) which is both cooperative (a player cannot play "against" another one as at the end of a game all rewards are equally attributed to both players) and competitive (players fight to achieve the best ranking).

Playing games, in order to fill the lexical network, is a kind of indirect crowdsourcing, where people (players) do not negotiate their contribution beforehand. In some cases, direct crowdsourcing (with negotiation between contributors) is desirable. Indeed, some lexical relations might be too complicated to be playable without some linguistic knowledge. That is the case for a telic role, which is the goal/purpose of an object (or action). For instance, a butcher knife has a telic role of cutting meat. It is to be differentiated from the instrument of a predicate, which indicates what can be done with the object. A butcher knife could be used to stab someone, but this is not its telic role.

2.1. RezoJDM

As mentioned above, the structure of the lexical network (RezoJDM) we are building involves nodes and relations between nodes. Such a structure was initially introduced in the end of 1960s by Collins and Quillian (1969), developed by Sowa and Zachman (1992) and by Fellbaum (1998), used in the small worlds by Gaume et al. (2007), and more recently clarified by Polguère (2014). Every node of the network is composed of a label (which is a term or an expression, or potentially any kind of string), a type (regular term, symbolic information, part of speech, etc.) and a weight, and includes all possible meanings.

The JDM lexical network has a predefined list of around 120 relation types, and around 40 of them are playable in the JDM game. Players cannot define new relation types by themselves. Other games of the JDM project, having a different design, are dedicated to other relations (different from the 40 playable relations of the main game). The JDM relation types fall into several categories:

Lexical relations - synonymy, antonyms, expression, lexical family. These types of relations relate to vocabulary and lexicalization.

Ontological relations - generic (hyperonymy), specific (hyponymy), part of (meronymy), whole of (holonymy), mater/substance, instances (named entities), typical location, characteristics and relevant properties, etc. Such relations concern knowledge about world objects.

Associative relations - free associations, associated feelings, meanings, similar objects, more and less intense (Magn and anti-Magn). These relations are rather about subjective and global knowledge; some of them can be considered as phrasal associations.

Predicative relations - typical agent, typical patient, typical instrument, location where the action takes place, typical manner, typical cause, typical consequence etc. These relations link a verb (or action noun) as starting node to the values of its arguments (in a very broad sense) as ending nodes.

Some relation types are typical of some noun classes or specific domains. For example, for a noun referring to an

---

[1] http://www.jeuxdemots.org/jdm-accueil.php
[2] http://www.jeuxdemots.org/quicky.php

intellectual work (book, novel, movie, piece of art, etc.), the relation "author" is defined. In case of a medical entity, "targets" and "symptoms" relations are defined.

Word senses (or usages) of a given polysemous term T are represented as standard nodes $T>glose_1$, $T>glose_2$, ..., $T>glose_n$ which are linked by refine(ment) relations (of type `r_semantic_raf`) to the term T. Glosses are terms that help the reader to identify the proper meaning of the term T. For example, consider the French term *frégate* (Eng. frigate):

- frégate refine frégate>navire
- frégate>navire refine frégate>navire>ancient
- frégate>navire refine frégate>navire>modern
- frégate refine frégate>oiseau

A frigate can be either a ship or a bird (both English and French show the same ambiguity for this word), and when it is a ship it can be either an ancient ship (with sails) or a modern one (with missiles and such).

As it can be seen from the above example, word refinements are organized as a decision tree, which is more advantageous for lexical disambiguation than a simple list of different meanings.

A particular meaning of a polysemous term is considered a standard term, it can be "played" like any other term. The general polysemous term includes (in principle) the union set of all possible relations for each of the different meanings. In practice, we proceed the other way around, trying to distribute relations from the general term to the proper senses.

Negative Relations - A given relation is weighted, and its weight can be negative or positive. A negative weight is only the result of some contributing process (not possible through the games) where volunteers add information to the lexical network. The interest of negative relations is that they can be at the origin of inhibition processes allowing a semantic analysis system to reject (rather than select) certain meanings during a lexical disambiguation task.

- frégate>navire refine coque
- frégate>oiseau refine<0 coque

If we consider the sentence (in English): *The frigate had her hull breached.* Obviously, the negative relation immediately forbid in this sentence the frigate from being a bird. Thus, negative relations are of primary interest to represent contrastive phenomena among the various meanings of a given term. This later aspect is critical in any approach of lexical embedding. Lexical embedding of words deeply relies on associated information.

2.2. Related Work and Research Questions

Other GWAPs are available to collect word associations. In (Vickrey et al., 2008) three online games are mentioned (Categorilla and Categodzilla and Free Association) that were designed to collect semantic associations in the form of structured data. Users are asked to supply words to fulfill specific categories, for example, "Types of bird", "A thing that cries" etc. The game "Free Association" is based on the popular game Taboo and just asks players to provide words in relation to a target word (stimulus or seed, in the psycholinguistics jargon). There is a taboo list of forbidden words which comes from SemCor and Google unigram data.

The game Verbosity (Ahn et al., 2006) also aims to collect linguistic data and semantic facts. The principle of the game is to propose riddles (a term that a user must make another user guess through the proposal of semantic relations.) In Grác and Nevěřilová (2010), a game similar to Verbosity is presented, but with a strong time constraint of 3 minutes.

In Parasca et al. (2016), an interesting analysis shows how a game can produce data that go beyond automatic extraction based on the distributional hypothesis. The presented game, Word Sheriff, handles word associations as well as more precise semantic relations.

All in all, there are quite no recent GWAPs in NLP to collect word associations. In this context, there are no studies on the effect of game design on data collection. For instance one might ask what effect does the time constraint have on the quality and quantity of data collected? What would be the bias if players could control the proposed target terms ? How to ensure a satisfactory sampling of terms to be proposed without introducing bias?

3. Comparing: two GWAPs for Free Word Associations

We compare the JeuxDeMots and Quicky Goose GWAPs, in order to assess the influence of their respective design on the collection of word associations. Both games concern French language, although they can be adapted to any language.

3.1. JeuxDeMots - A Sophisticated Environment

JeuxDeMots (JDM) was launched late Summer 2007 and since then, more than 1.470.000 games have been played. It should be noted that other games are part of the overall project and contribute to building the lexical network. The user environment is quite sophisticated in order to induce an engagement in players so that they play longer and more often. Although it can be played occasionally, the game is designed to encourage long-term investment, as the goal is to capture, steal, protect and hoard words (which is loosely based on the Pokemon game).

The relevant game design elements of the main game of the JeuxDeMots project are as follows:

- The term to be played with (the target term) is randomly selected;
- the relation (game instruction) is given at the beginning of the game;
- The answers given are compared with those of another player, on the same term with the same instruction. Answers common to both players are added to the lexical network, or strengthen the relation if it already exists.
- Points are computed according to the number of associations common to both players, and the point amount is notified to the user at the end of the game;

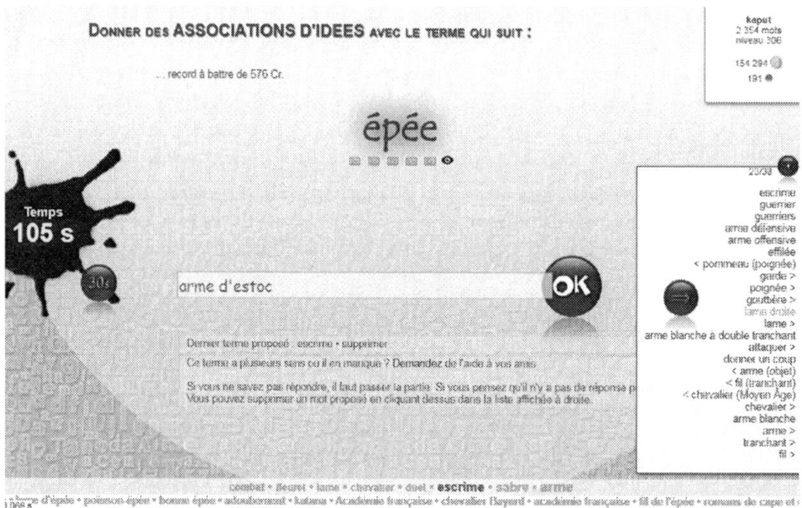

Figure 1: in-going play of JDM. The target word is *épée*. The player has already proposed a number of terms (list on the right).

- a game lasts one minute by default; a timer indicates the remaining time.

Beside elements related to player ranking, JeuxDeMots features *credits*, a virtual money allowing players to have some game control. People can invest directly or indirectly their credits to do the following:

- automatic re-launch of the game (same term and same instruction) which will be confronted with that of another player. This is only allowed below a certain gain threshold.

- buying *competences*, which unlocks the use of more relations

- buy more time while playing;

- investing tokens into his/her last game, so that it will be proposed to more people;

- giving a gift to other players, to encourage them to play with a specific term and relation.

All game features are designed to increase the player's engagement while fostering data quality. The time constraint is an important element in making the game exciting and challenging, although not all players appreciate this constraint: some of them tend to buy a lot of time at the beginning of the game, to reduce stress. And since buying time consumes money, these players are driven to play more, in order to get more virtual money.

3.2. Quicky Goose - A Fast and Simple Direct Approach

Quicky Goose was launched late December 2019, with some word to mouth advertisement on Facebook. Since then, more than 180.000 games have been played, from more than 1000 IP addresses. Registration is not required to play, but someone who is already registered on JDM can play Quicky Goose with his/her account.

The interesting game design elements of Quicky Goose (QG) project are the following:

Figure 2: End of JDM game with display of results. Common words are used for computing points.

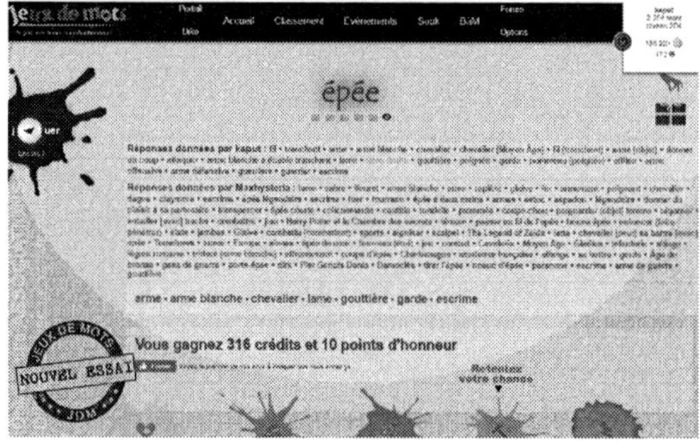

Figure 3: End of JDM game with display of results, with alternative results after retry

- The term to be played with (the target term) is randomly selected ;

- The player has the possibility to change relation (instruction) for the current term during the game; but only a subset of all possible relations is available; but a relation that has already been played and then neglected in favor of a new one cannot be chosen again during the current game;

- Answers are compared to the state of the lexical network;

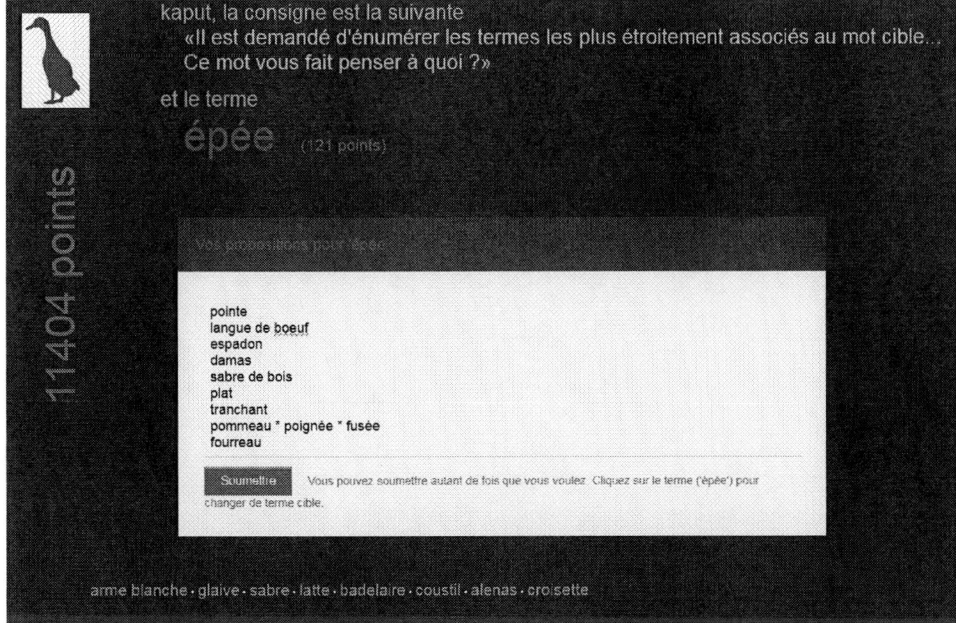

Figure 4: The main screen of the GWAP Quicky Goose. From top to bottom we can see: the instruction, the target term along with current points, the form for entering proposals, and a sum up of already proposed terms. On the left is displayed the *grand total* of points (cumulative points) earned by the player since its first game of QG.

- points are computed on the basis of the presence of each proposed term in the network, either already validated or awaiting validation, or its absence (new proposal); points are added as proposals are made, in real time;
- There is no time limit.

If a term proposed by a player is not already linked to the target term in the network, it is stored in a temporary place. If a certain number of different players (empirically set to 5) propose the same association, then it is added to the lexical network. If they are not registered, players are identified by their IP address. Thus, the same proposal cannot be given several times by the same player. The creation weight is set to 5 and each subsequent association increases it by 1. As such, the weight strictly translates the number of times two terms have been associated. In JDM by contrast, a new association enters the lexical network if at least two players have made this association and met by chance during a game (player A is playing on the recorded game of player B who already made this association). As the other player is not known during the game, collusion is not possible.

Displaying points earned for each proposed word during the course of the game (and not at the end) makes the game highly addictive for some people. Players tend to beat their own record (proposing more terms, earning more points). Although QG is considered a purely casual game, the average playing time tends to exceed that observed on JDM, because as people are not subject to the time constraint, they continue to make proposals until they have no more ideas.

Selection of target words - QG uses the JDM lexical network (which is in open access) to select a target word to propose to the player. By default, QG selects common words (this is a possible attribute of network terms in Rezo-

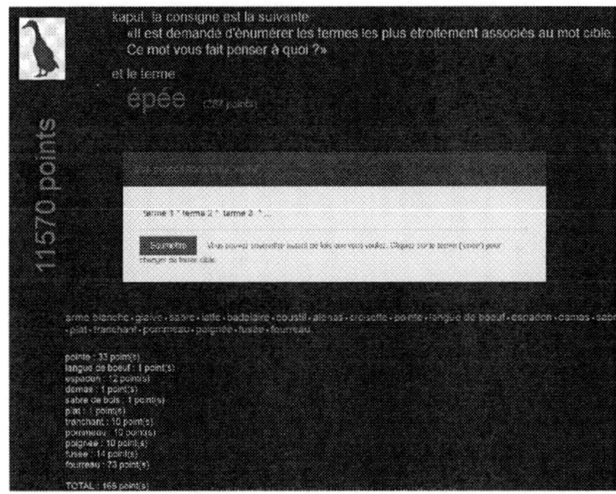

Figure 5: The proposed terms are displayed below with points earned for each one. Once a term is proposed, is cannot be proposed again.

JDM) but can alternatively propose target terms according to a theme, freely chosen by the player: then only words linked to the theme in RezoJDM are proposed. It should be stressed that a purely random word selection from a pre-defined list is not suitable, and would tend to make player either bored or desperate because very unusual or improbable target terms are then proposed to him/her. So it is preferable, when possible, to use a preexisting knowledge base.

Having plenty of time - with QG, players have all the time they want to propose word associations. For difficult relations, such as "telic role", this aspect of the game is welcome since the player can think about his/her answers, their quality, relevance and diversity increases.

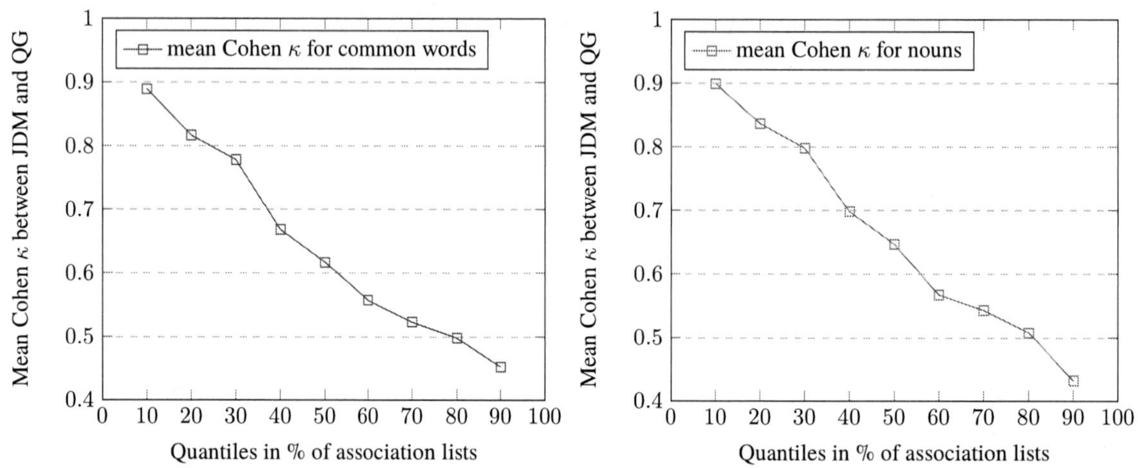

Figure 6: (left) mean Cohen κ between associative list of JDM and QG for 2800 common words (Nouns, Verbs, and Adjectives) for free associations; (right) mean Cohen κ between associative list of JDM and QG for 3200 Nouns for free associations ;

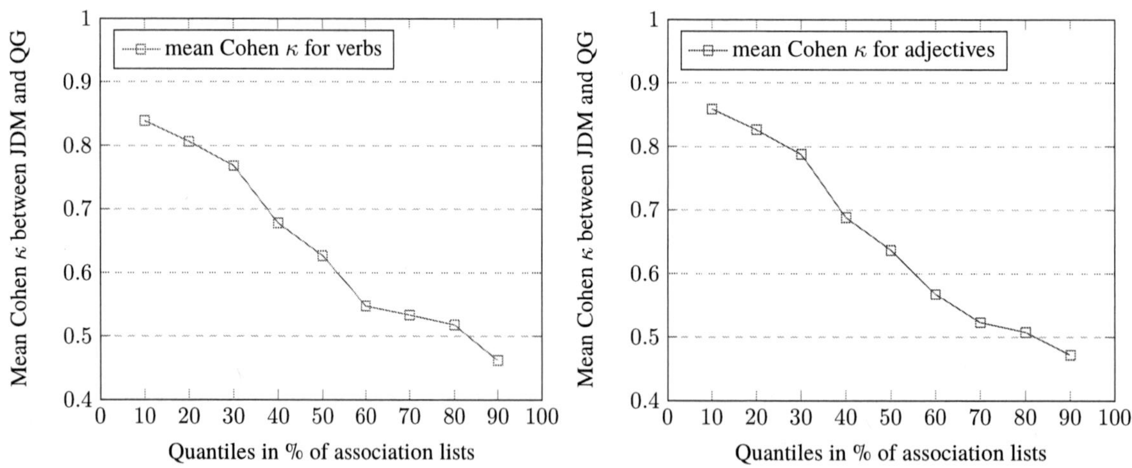

Figure 7: (left) mean Cohen κ between associative list of JDM and QG for 890 verbs for free associations ; (right) mean Cohen κ between associative list of JDM and QG for 1450 adjectives for free associations.

4. Evaluating: Agreement Between Associative Lists and Effects of Game Designs

We evaluated the associations made by the players, both in JDM and in QG. What are the similarities and differences between the two game modes in terms of the data collected? What is the value of data collected using one of the two game modes, that are not collected using the other ? Which game features induce these differences?

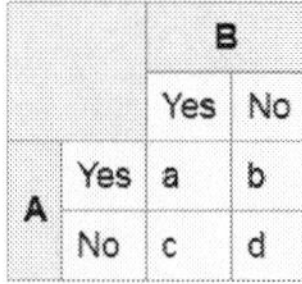

Figure 8: Situations for the Cohen κ (from Wikipedia). In our evaluation the d situation is not possible and thus is always equal to 0. At least one list contains the tested term.

4.1. Quantitative assessment

The methodology for evaluating agreement is as follows: for a given target word T, we took both association lists produced with JDM and with QG respectively. We can compute an agreement (Cohen κ) for quantiles of the list. We adopted an approach with 10 quantiles. The first quantile corresponds to the first (most activated) 10% terms of the association list. The second quantile, are terms ranked between 10% up to 20% (not included), and so on. Choosing the number of quantiles was a difficult question. In many studies quartiles are used (four quantiles of 25%), but in our case it was to be a bit coarse. One of the motives for a finer quantification (using 10 quantiles of 10% rather than quartiles) is that the data behave according a power law and not an average distribution, and as such the variations of the distribution are much stronger at the beginning (first quantiles).

The value of the agreement of the Cohen κ is a global measure of the answers to questions like "is the word A present in the n% quantile of associations for relation t for term B ?" For example, "is *mouse* present in the 10% quantile of associations for relation `r_associated` (free associations) for *cat* ?" Formally we ask each association list (from JDM and QG) and their answer is either "yes" or "no". Note that case with both answering "no" is not possible as we compare both lists, hence a given term is necessarily at least in one of the lists.

The domain of the agreement is every time the union of terms of both lists, and not all the possible terms existing in JDM. If we had proceeded this way, the agreement would always have been meaninglessly close to 1, because there is an overwhelming number of terms no whatsoever related to each other. In our evaluation the d case in figure 8 is always equal to 0.

This assessment evaluates only the rank of the associated words, not their actual weight. The weight is only significant when comparing terms within the same list. Hence relying on weights to compare two lists produced through different means would be meaningless. Also, knowing the exact rank of a term in one list in order to compare it to its rank in the other list is not really meaningful. What is required for evaluation is just whether the two terms are in the same part of the distribution curve.

In figure 6 it appears that the agreement between JDM and QG association lists is very high in the first quantiles. That is to say, that the strongest associations are very similar (if not identical). As intuitively expected, the Cohen kappa decreases as the rank of the associations increases (their strength is decreasing). We can see that the global highest agreement concerns nouns, adjectives, and finally verbs. Indeed, finding association to verbs is felt to be not quite so easy, as people often focus on synonyms and potential patients (eat an apple). But more often than not, the number of possible answers is high, hence a lower agreement than for nouns. For adjectives, beside synonyms and antonyms, the more recurrent associations are the typical targets (red apple, red car, red skirt, etc.) even though the "complete" association list is both very large and illusory to achieve.

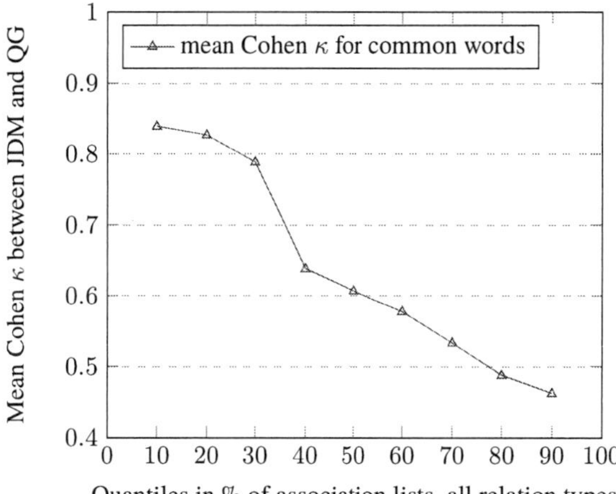

Figure 9: Mean Cohen κ between associative list of JDM and QG for 2800 common words (Nouns, Verbs, and Adjectives) for any relation type, except for free associations.

The agreements for other relations than associated ideas (figure 9) are not fundamentally different than the ones for associated ideas. What we can notice the Cohen κ agreement is very strong up to the first 30%, then drops sharply to around 0.63. The main reason is that in general for precise semantic relations there are fewer obvious possible answers than for free associations. Hence the agreement between JDM and QG is lower because due to the time constraint people usually don't have time to propose a high number of relevant answers. Some players "confessed" that since they have unlimited time in QG, they consult online encyclopedias and dictionaries or even hard books. Given the purpose of the project (building a lexical semantic resource) we can only approve of such behavior. Some might mock such players as "information extractors from external existing resources" to be opposed to players that are "information extractors from internal existing resources" (namely their brain).

4.2. Qualitative assessment

For the qualitative assessment, we tried to evaluate two aspects: a) number of false or dubious terms in associations, b) the quality of terms in disagreement in association lists (i.e those belonging to only one of the two lists).

Errors - We looked for terms that are not common to both lists and semi-automatically evaluated whether they should be considered errors. For over 7000 associations lists (over 3500 for JDM and 3500 for QG) corresponding to about 500.000 terms, we found around 1% terms (around 5000 "rogue" terms) than were not in both lists. We first made a random manual evaluation of around 500 terms (10%) and did not find any wrong, and only 13 that might be considered as far fetched. For example, *chat* (cat) and *Alice* are associated (probably because of their link with the *Cheshire Cat*) has been considered as far fetched.

In a more systematic way and by exploiting the RezoJDM, we tried to (automatically) assess if a rogue term A could be indirectly linked to the target term B through an intermediate term C. For example, *pavé* is linked to *main* in the QG association list but not in JDM (not in rezoJDM, hence). But in rezoJDM, we can have *pavé* (A) linked to *lancer* (C) linked to *main* (C). Thus, we consider the association between *pavé* and *main* to be correct (which is the case). With this method, only 25 rogue associations were found not linkable through an intermediate nodes. By manually checking those associations, 17 were considered as correct and 8 as far fetched. None were considered as clearly false.

Undoubtedly, there are (of will be) errors in associations, nevertheless they seem to be quite uncommon and hard to spot automatically, and even human judgment might be difficult in some cases. The JDM filtering (2 players encountering) and the QG filtering (5 independent contributions) appears to behave as expected reducing the amount of errors entering the KB (rezoJDM). During the development of these games, theses respective number (2 and 5) of different users for confirming an association have been determined empirically, trying to have a good balance between recall and precision.

Terms in disagreement - It is difficult to compare two lists that were constructed on different time scales (13 years for JDM, and 2 months for QG). However, it is possible to normalize the heaviest list (with the highest strongest score) to the weakest by linearly reducing weights to the weakest. The reduction is linear as all weights are divided by the maximum weight.

After normalization, comparison shows that QG association lists are richer than those of JDM, but tend to be much "flatter" (smaller relative difference between term weights). In contrast, JDM association lists have higher weight variations (more contrast), even if globally term ranks are the same for the first quantiles.

Again, in QG people tend to be very creative, proposing quite often terms that do not yet exist in rezoJDM, but in most cases are very relevant.

4.3. Impact of the Game Design Choices

We did a very small survey by asking the identified players about the features of QG and/or the features of JDM. Their

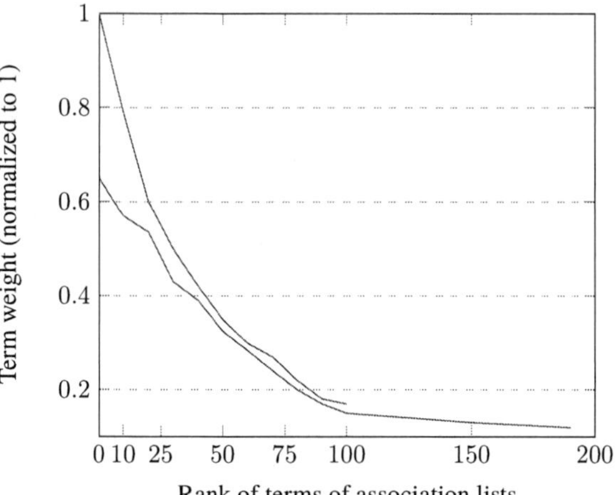

Figure 10: Illustration of typical association lists (JDM purple, QG blue), weights are normalized to 1. The QG plot is flatter but longer than the JDM plot.

answers are consistent with our evaluation of association lists.

The time constraint in JeuxDeMots has a very strong impact on the data collected. It makes the game exciting for many people, but some people find it stressful. Without a time constraint, players produce more associations, so that lead to a quite longer tail of associations. However, the collected data are a bit less spontaneous. It does however not have much impact on the strongest associations.

The immediate display of points gained during the game (like in QG) encourages longer play time and proposing more associations. In JDM, getting the result only at the end of the game makes it like a kind of bet, leads to either excitement or disappointment. In the overall, players produce more associations when the points are distilled during the process. True players play JDM, and most don't care to contribute but instead are obsessed with ranking, and other rewards. People minded to contribute plays QG, even if they think they are players.

Being able to change the instruction during the game seems to be appreciated by players (whether they already played JDM or not). The (little) constraint of not allowing to propose again an already proposed term, even with another instruction is controversial. Some people think this is an unnecessary restriction, others see that as a game challenge. After playing a little, some players keep some associations for the most appropriate instruction. The set and order of instructions is defined along with the nature of the term (noun, verb, adjective, adverb, ...) and with some experience the player does anticipate the "most appropriate place" where the candidate association belongs. This aspect makes the game challenging and just a direct "put all of them here" kind of activity. Furthermore, for data quality sake, this feature induces players to properly distributed associated terms among semantic relations.

The number of players (after scaling) of QG is much higher than JDM (> 1000 in two months for QC, and > 10000 in 13 years for JDM), even if the novelty effect is taken into account. The simplicity of QG tend to favor the number of players, but the turnover is higher than in JeuxDeMots (6 days versus 24 days). The distribution of players according to their number of games done, follows in both case a power law (few people playing a lot, and most people playing occasionally).

5. Conclusion

In this paper we have presented a comparison between two GWAPs for building term association lists, namely JeuxDeMots and Quicky Goose. After comparing game design in both games, we computed the Cohen kappa of associative lists in various configurations in order to assess major differences in obtained data.

It appears that game with a time constraint is more exciting for many but tend to produced less flourishing associative lists than games without this time constraint. This tendency is only noticeable for the long tail of associative lists, that is for less activated associated terms. Some people just prefer having as much time as they want, and collecting points and rewards this way.

We do not know yet the percentage of people who are playing both games, or whether the gamer population is strictly separated. Anyway, it seems quite clear that proposing several games with different designs in the context of the same project is a good (if not cheap) strategy for building a valuable linguistic resource.

6. Acknowledgments

This project has been funded through a PRC (CNRS) with University of Novosibirsk about Associative Dictionaries. A big thank-you to the JeuxDeMots team that made some aspects of the connectivity between Quicky Goose and JeuxDeMots technically possible.

7. Bibliographical References

Ahn, L. V., Kedia, M., and Blum, M. (2006). Verbosity: a game for collecting common-sense facts. In In Proceedings of ACM CHI 2006 Conference on Human Factors in Computing Systems, volume 1 of Games, pages 75–78. ACM Press.

Ahn, L. v. (2006). Games with a purpose. *Computer*, 39(6):92–94, June.

Collins, A. M. and Quillian, M. R. (1969). Retrieval time from semantic memory. *Journal of Verbal Learning and Verbal Behavior*, 8(2):240 – 247.

Fellbaum, C. (1998). WordNet: An Electronic Lexical Database. Bradford Books.

Gaume, B., Duvignau, K., and Vanhove, M. (2007). Semantic associations and confluences in paradigmatic networks. In From polysemy to semantic change - towards a typology of lexical semantic associations, Toulouse, France. John Benjamins Publishing Company.

Gaume, B., Ho-Dac, L. M., Tanguy, L., Fabre, C., Pierrejean, B., Hathout, N., Farinas, J., Pinquier, J., Danet, L., Péran, P., et al. (2019). Toward a computational multidimensional lexical similarity measure for modeling word association tasks in psycholinguistics. In Proceedings of the Workshop on Cognitive Modeling and Computational Linguistics, pages 71–76.

Grác, M. and Nevěřilová, Z. (2010). Acquiring nlp data by means of games. pages 109–114, 01.

Lafourcade, M., Joubert, A., and Brun, N. (2015). Games with a Purpose (GWAPS). Focus Series in Cognitive Science and Knowledge Management. Wiley.

Lafourcade, M., Mery, B., Mirzapour, M., Moot, R., and Retoré, C. (2018). Collecting Weighted Coercions from Crowd-Sourced Lexical Data for Compositional Semantic Analysis. In isAI: International Symposium on Artificial Intelligence, volume LNCS of *New Frontiers in Artificial Intelligence*, pages 214–230, Tokyo, Japan, June.

Lafourcade, M. (2007). Making people play for Lexical Acquisition with the JeuxDeMots prototype. In SNLP'07: 7th International Symposium on Natural Language Processing, page 7, Pattaya, Chonburi, Thailand, December.

Machida, Y., Kawahara, D., Kurohashi, S., and Sassano, M. (2016). Design of word association games using dialog systems for acquisition of word association knowledge. In Proceedings of the 5th Workshop on Automated Knowledge Base Construction, pages 86–91.

Mitchell, T., Cohen, W., Hruschka, E., Talukdar, P., Yang, B., Betteridge, J., Carlson, A., Dalvi, B., Gardner, M., Kisiel, B., Krishnamurthy, J., Lao, N., Mazaitis, K., Mohamed, T., Nakashole, N., Platanios, E., Ritter, A., Samadi, M., Settles, B., Wang, R., Wijaya, D., Gupta, A., Chen, X., Saparov, A., Greaves, M., and Welling, J. (2018). Never-ending learning. *Commun. ACM*, 61(5):103–115, April.

Parasca, I.-E., Rauter, A. L., Roper, J., Rusinov, A., Bouchard, G., Riedel, S., and Stenetorp, P. (2016). Defining words with words: Beyond the distributional hypothesis. In Proceedings of the 1st Workshop on Evaluating Vector-Space Representations for NLP, pages 122–126, Berlin, Germany, August. Association for Computational Linguistics.

Polguère, A. (2014). From writing dictionaries to weaving lexical networks. *International Journal of Lexicography*, 27(4):396—418.

Singh, P., Lin, T., Mueller, E. T., Lim, G., Perkins, T., and Li Zhu, W. (2002). Open mind common sense: Knowledge acquisition from the general public. In Robert Meersman et al., editors, On the Move to Meaningful Internet Systems 2002: CoopIS, DOA, and ODBASE, pages 1223–1237, Berlin, Heidelberg. Springer Berlin Heidelberg.

Sowa, J. F. and Zachman, J. A. (1992). Extending and formalizing the framework for information systems architecture. *IBM Systems Journal*, 31(3):590–616.

Vickrey, D., Bronzan, A., Choi, W., Kumar, A., Turner-Maier, J., Wang, A., and Koller, D. (2008). Online word games for semantic data collection. In Proceedings of the Conference on Empirical Methods in Natural Language Processing, EMNLP '08, page 533–542, USA. Association for Computational Linguistics.

Proceedings of the LREC 2020 Workshop Games and Natural Language Processing, pages 34–38
Language Resources and Evaluation Conference (LREC 2020), Marseille, 11–16 May 2020
© European Language Resources Association (ELRA), licensed under CC-BY-NC

The challenge of the TV game *La Ghigliottina* to NLP

Federico Sangati[1], Antonio Pascucci[1], Johanna Monti[1]
L'Orientale University of Naples - UNIOR NLP Research Group[1]
Via Duomo 219 Naples (Italy)[1],
{fsangati,apascucci,jmonti}@unior.it

Abstract

In this paper, we describe a Telegram bot, *Mago della Ghigliottina* (*Ghigliottina Wizard*), able to solve *La Ghigliottina* game (*The Guillotine*), the final game of the Italian TV quiz show *L'Eredità*. Our system relies on linguistic resources and artificial intelligence and achieves better results than human players (and competitors of *L'Eredità* too). In addition to solving a game, *Mago della Ghigliottina* can also generate new game instances and challenge the users to match the solution.

Keywords: Telegram Bot, Linguistic Games, Artificial Intelligence

1. Introduction

In this paper, we present *Mago della Ghigliottina*, a Telegram bot able to solve *La Ghigliottina* (*The Guillotine*), the final game of the Italian TV quiz show *L'Eredità*. Given a set of five words (clues), the competitor has to guess the sixth word (solution) that is linked with each of these five clues. For example, given the five clues: *pie, bad, Adam, core, eye* the solution is *apple*, because: *apple-pie* is a kind of pie; *bad apple* is a way to refer to a trouble maker; *Adam's apple* is the prominent part of men's throat; *apple core* is the center of the apple; *apple of someone's eye* is a way to refer to someone's beloved person. The game is one of the most popular games in Italy, viewed by nearly three million spectators (approximately 20% share). Audience at home also enjoys participating in the game and tries to match the solution. Some players compete in *Ghigliottini-amo*[1], an app that enables people to challenge each other while the game is being broadcasted. *Mago della Ghigliot-tina* participated as *UNIOR4NLP* (Sangati et al., 2018) in the shared task NLP4FUN (Basile et al., 2018), which was part of the EVALITA 2018 (Caselli et al., 2018), a periodic evaluation campaign of Natural Language Processing (NLP) and speech tools for the Italian language.[2]

The paper is organized as follows: in Section 2 we present *La Ghigliottina* TV game and its rules. In Section 3 we make a brief overview about NLP systems related to games. In Section 4 we describe our approach to solve the game: how we built our artificial player and how the system attempts at finding the correct solution. In Section 5 we describe *Mago della Ghigliottina*. Conclusions and Future Work are in Section 6.

2. *La Ghigliottina* game

L'Eredità represents one of the most popular TV games in Italy and in 2020 reached its 18th season. The game involves seven competitors that challenge each other in elimination games. The player who reaches the final game (named *La Ghigliottina*) can win the jackpot. The game works as follows: given a set of five words (clues), the player has to guess a sixth word (the solution) that is linked

with the five clues. The five clues are unrelated to each other, but each is in relation with the solution. In figure 1 we show an example of the game.

Figure 1: A screenshot of *La Ghigliottina*. In this case, the solution is *cassa*: i) *cassa del cinema* (*cinema box office*), ii) *grancassa* (*bass drum*), iii) *cassa comune* (*petty cash*), iv) *battere cassa* (*beat the check*), and v) *coda alla cassa* (*checkout line*)

3. NLP and games

Games represent an interesting playground to conduct research in NLP and Artificial Intelligence (AI) (Yannakakis and Togelius, 2018). There are a number of popular TV quiz based on language games, such as *The Wheel of Fortune* and *Who Wants to be a Millionaire?*. The current work focuses on *La Ghigliottina*, which is particularly interesting for AI and NLP because it is based on how words are connected to each other. OTTHO (Semeraro et al., 2009; Basile et al., 2014) represents the first artificial player of the game and exploits resources from the web such as Wikipedia to build i) a lexicon and a knowledge repository and ii) a knowledge base modeling represented by an association matrix which stores the degree of correlation between any two words in the lexicon. Word correlations are detected by connecting lemmas to the entries in the dictionary definition, pair of words occurring in proverbs, movie or song

---

[1] https://appadvice.com/app/ghigliottiniamo/1447355292
[2] http://www.evalita.it

titles, and pair of similar words by exploiting Vector Space Models (Salton et al., 1975).

4. Our approach to solve *La Ghigliottina*

Our approach uses similar resources with respect to the OT-THO system. However, regarding word relations we don't focus on word similarity but on a restricted set of syntactic constructions (patterns).

4.1. Preliminary steps in building our artificial player

Building an automatic solver for *La Ghigliottina* game requires three preliminary steps: game analysis, definition of linguistic patterns, and extraction of linguistic resources.

Game analysis We analyzed a sample of 100 *La Ghigliottina* instances that we collected from past editions of the TV game. We found out that almost in all combination the clue is connected to the solution because they form a Multiword Expression (MWE). A MWE is a sequence of words that presents some characteristic behaviour (at the lexical, syntactic, semantic, pragmatic or statistical level) and whose interpretation crosses the boundaries between words (Sag et al., 2002). MWEs have to be considered as lexical items which convey a single meaning different from the meanings of its constituent words, such as in the idiomatic expression *kick the bucket* where the simple addition of the meanings of *kick* and *bucket* does not convey the meaning of *to die*. Our system has been built on this key observation. After the official dataset was released, we found out that the great majority of game instances confirmed our initial hypothesis.

Linguistic Patterns Clue words are typically nouns, verbs, or adjectives, while the solutions are typically nouns or adjectives (almost never verbs). We detected six possible clue-solution combination that generate MWEs:

- **A-B** (Noun-Adjective, Adjective-Noun, Verb-Noun, Noun-Noun) *permesso premio* ('permit price' → good behaviour license);

- **A-determiner-B** *dare il permesso* ('give the permit' → authorize);

- **A-conjunction-B** *stima e affetto* (esteem and affection);

- **A-preposition-B** *colpo di coda* ('flick of tail' → last ditch effort);

- **A-articulated preposition-B** *virtù dei forti*, part of the famous Italian proverb *La calma è la virtù dei forti* (patience is the virtue of the strong);

- **A+B**: compounds such as *radio + attività = radioattività* (radio + activity = radioactivity).

Linguistic Resources We collected the linguistic resources which we deemed necessary for the task. To this end we used the following freely available corpora:

- **Paisà**: 250 million tokens corpus automatically annotated (Lyding et al., 2014).

- **itWaC**: 1.5 billion words corpus automatically annotated (Baroni et al., 2009)

- **Wiki-IT-Titles**: Wikipedia-IT titles downloaded via WikiExtractor (Attardi, 2012).

- **Proverbs**: 1,955 proverbs from (Wikiquote, 2016) and 371 from an online collection (Dige, 2016).

In addition, we have constructed the following lexical resources:

- **DeMauro-Ext**: words extracted from "Il Nuovo vocabolario di base della lingua italiana"(De Mauro, 2016b), extended with morphological variations obtained by changing last vowel of the word and checking if the resulting word has frequency $\geq$ 1000 in `Paisà`.

- **DeMauro-MWEs**: MWEs extracted from the "De Mauro online dictionary" (De Mauro, 2016a) composed of 30,633 entries.

4.2. System description

In order to build our system, we started processing the selected corpora via standard tokenization (only single word tokens) and removal of punctuation marks and non-word patterns. Next, we constructed two lexical sets: C_{LEX} to cover the *clue* words, and S_{LEX} to cover the *solution* words. S_{LEX} (composed of 7,942 nouns and adjectives in `DeMauro-Ext`) is smaller than C_{LEX} (composed of 19,414 words from the full `DeMauro-Ext` and `DeMauro-MWEs`) because solution words are almost always nouns or adjectives as described in Section 4.1.

Secondly, we built a co-occurrence matrix M_c which stores the counts $c_{i,j}$ for every pair of words $w_i \in S_{LEX}$ and $w_j \in C_{LEX}$ such that w_i co-occurs with w_j in the resources according to patterns described in Section 4.1. Co-occurrence patterns were extracted from `Paisà` and `itWaC` with weight $w = 1$, from `DeMauro-MWE` with $w = 200$, from `Proverbs` with $w = 100$, and from `Wiki-IT-Titles` with $w = 50$. The weight were chosen manually taking into account the likelihood that a pattern in a given corpus represented a valid MWE. Compound patterns (A+B) were extracted from C_{LEX}: for every word w in C_{LEX} if $w = ab$, a and b are both in C_{LEX}, and a and b have at least 4 characters, the count for the pair (a, b) is incremented by 1 in the co-occurrence matrix.

Thirdly, for every pair of words w_i and w_j in M_c, we populate the association-score matrix M_{pmi} via the Pointwise Mutual Information measure:

$$M_{pmi}(w_i, w_j) = \log \frac{p(w_i, w_j)}{p(w_i) \cdot p(w_j)} \qquad (1)$$

where

$$p(w_i) = \sum_{w_j \in C_{LEX}} M_c(w_i, w_j) \qquad (2)$$

$$p(w_j) = \sum_{w_i \in S_{LEX}} M_c(w_i, w_j) \qquad (3)$$

$$p(w_i, w_j) = \frac{M_c(w_i, w_j)}{\sum_{\substack{x \in S_{LEX} \\ y \in C_{LEX}}} M_c(x, y)} \quad (4)$$

Finally, for a given game instance with the 5 clue words $G = (w_{c1}, w_{c2}, w_{c3}, w_{c4}, w_{c5})$, we choose the solution word $\widehat{w_s} \in S_{LEX}$ such that:

$$\widehat{w_s} = \max_{w_s \in S_{LEX}} \sum_{w_c \in G} M_{pmi}(w_s, w_c) \quad (5)$$

that is, we choose the word in S_{LEX} which maximizes the score obtained by summing the pmi between each clue word and the candidate word. If two words are never seen co-occurring together in a pattern in the training corpora, we assign to them the lowest pmi value in M_{pmi}.

The system has been implemented in Python and the code is open source. After the matrix has been loaded into memory the response time on an average laptop is around 1-2 seconds.

5. *Mago della Ghigliottina* bot

Mago della Ghigliottina offers two game modalities: the first one (solution mode) allows users to insert the five clues and to challenge the bot to match the solution, while the second one (generation mode) presents the user with five clue words and challenges to find the correct solution.

5.1. Solution mode

In solution mode, it is possible to write the five clues or to send a picture with the five clues. As shown in Figure 2, *Mago della Ghigliottina* uses OCR to recognize the words from the image.

Mago della Ghigliottina returns its prediction with a degree of accuracy accompanied by an emoji face that reflects the specific degree of accuracy:

- 😎 *sono quasi certo* (I'm fairly certain, as shown in the example below).

- 🙂 *credo che* (I believe that);

- 😐 *sono abbastanza convinto* (I'm quite sure);

- 😬 *non sono sicuro, ma* (I'm not sure, but);

Until now (April 2020), $9,333$ *Ghigliottina* instances (4016 unique) have been submitted to the bot by a total of 740 Telegram users and 133 Twitter users.

Mago della Ghigliottina is automatically tested every day on the TV show instances and is able to guess the solution correctly about 2/3 of the time. It must be considered that every day several users submit the same instance of *La Ghigliottina* game, so this performance has been calculated discarding duplicates. The bot definitely outperforms humans in solving the game. In comparing the performance of our AI system with that of a top player, we analyzed the games played by Andrea Saccone, who has been the biggest champion of the Ghigliottina game so far: he was champion for 13 days (3-15 March 2018), and he managed to

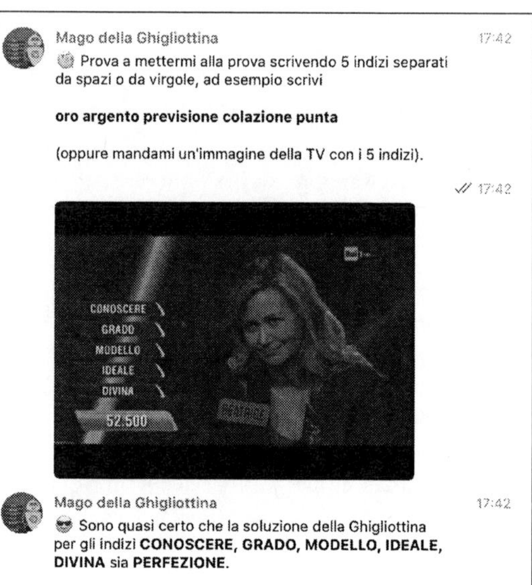

Figure 2: A screenshot from Telegram in solution mode: *Mago della Ghigliottina* accepts the picture containing the five clues and in 1-2 seconds returns its prediction with a degree of accuracy. In this case, the system correctly guesses the solution because of the following MWEs i) *conoscere alla perfezione* (to perfectly know), ii) *grado di perfezione* (degree of perfection), iii) *modello di perfezione* (model of perfection), iv) *ideale di perfezione* (ideal of perfection), and v) *perfezione divina* (divine perfection).

find the correct solution three times.[3] In comparison *Mago della Ghigliottina* was able to win the same game instances 9 times.

As mentioned in section 3, the other AI model that has been developed to solve the same task is OTTHO (Basile et al., 2014), which makes use of Vector Space Models (among other things). We observe that they achieve a precision of around 30% which is well below ours (75%).[4]

Users can send live to *Mago della Ghigliottina* the *Ghigliottina* instance. Alternatively, users can send new instances made up on the spot whenever they want, just thinking at five words related to the word they imagine as the solution. Obviously, in this case prediction performaces can drop because pairs clue-solution can never be accurate as well as those of the TV show.

5.2. Generation mode

In generation mode (Figure 3), the system can automatically create novel game instances. Using a reversed association-matrix,[5] it chooses a random word (the solu-

---

[3] The players who reach the "Ghigliottina" game (the champion) continue to participate in the subsequent episodes even if they do not guess the solution word.

[4] Unfortunately we were not able to make an exact comparison because the original data-set has not been made publicly available for copyright reasons.

[5] In generation mode, we make use of a smaller co-occurrence matrix extracted only from `DeMauro-MWEs`, in order to produce

tion) and presents a list of 5 clues with a high score. In addition, when the solution is given it provides a sentence for every clue-solution pair exemplifying the relations between the two words.

Figure 3: A screenshot from Telegram in generation mode. In this case, the solution is *scherzo* (*joke*): i) *nemmeno per scherzo* (*even as a joke*), ii) *brutto scherzo* (*bad joke*), iii) *scherzo da prete* (*sick joke*), iv) *scherzo di natura* (*trick of nature*), and v) *neppure per scherzo* (*even as a joke*)

6. Conclusions and Future Work

In this paper, we have described *Mago della Ghigliottina*, a Telegram bot that is able to solve *La Ghigliottina* game (*The Guillotine*), the final game of the Italian TV quiz show *L'Eredità*. *Mago della Ghigliottina* relies on linguistic resources and is tested every day on the TV show instances: it is able to guess on average two out of three *Ghigliottina* instances. Users can play with *Mago della Ghigliottina* also independently for the TV game by providing their own clues and asking the bot to solve the game (solution mode) or by asking the bot five new clues (generation mode). We aim to collect continuously data in order to develop a corpus with new game instances and improve our system. *Mago della Ghigliottina* is also available on Amazon Alexa[6] (simply ask *Mago della Ghigliottina* to match the solution providing it with the five clues) and Twitter[7] (users just need to write the five clues and tag @UNIOR4NLP in their tweet and the solution appears in a comment).

The methodology adopted for the bot can be successfully applied to all NLP tasks that aim at identifying co-occurrence and semantic relations between words.

As future work we intend to add a validation step by the users when they play with the bot independently from the TV game. The validation is carried out by asking users to confirm the correctness of the solution provided by the bot to their *Ghigliottina* instances. In addition, we also foresee to ask users to provide all the correct co-occurrences between their five clues and the solution they expect.

---

higher quality game instances.

[6]https://www.amazon.it/ Federico-Sangati-Mago-della-Ghigliottina/ dp/B07VHKT43F

[7]https://twitter.com/UNIOR4NLP

7. Acknowledgements

This research has been partly supported by the PON Ricerca e Innovazione 2014/20 fund. Authorship contribution is as follows: Johanna Monti is author of Sections 1, 2 and 6, Federico Sangati is author of Sections 3, 4.2 and 5, while Section 4.1 is in common between Antonio Pascucci and Johanna Monti.

8. Bibliographical References

Basile, P., de Gemmis, M., Lops, P., and Semeraro, G. (2014). Solving a complex language game by using knowledge-based word associations discovery. *IEEE Transactions on Computational Intelligence and AI in Games*, 8(1):13–26.

Basile, P., de Gemmis, M., Siciliani, L., and Semeraro, G. (2018). Overview of the evalita 2018 solving language games (nlp4fun) task. *EVALITA Evaluation of NLP and Speech Tools for Italian*, 12:75.

Caselli, T., Novielli, N., Patti, V., and Rosso, P. (2018). Sixth evaluation campaign of natural language processing and speech tools for italian: Final workshop (evalita 2018). In *EVALITA 2018*. CEUR Workshop Proceedings (CEUR-WS. org).

De Mauro, T. (2016a). Il Nuovo De Mauro (Online). https://dizionario.internazionale.it. Last accessed on the 1st October 2018.

De Mauro, T. (2016b). Il Nuovo vocabolario di base della lingua italiana (pdf version). https://www.dropbox.com/s/mkcyo53m15ktbnp/ nuovovocabolariodibase.pdf. Last accessed on the 1st October 2018.

Sag, I. A., Baldwin, T., Bond, F., Copestake, A., and Flickinger, D. (2002). Multiword expressions: A pain in the neck for nlp. In *International conference on intelligent text processing and computational linguistics*, pages 1–15. Springer.

Salton, G., Wong, A., and Yang, C.-S. (1975). A vector space model for automatic indexing. *Communications of the ACM*, 18(11):613–620.

Sangati, F., Pascucci, A., and Monti, J. (2018). Exploiting multiword expressions to solve "la ghigliottina". In *Sixth Evaluation Campaign of Natural Language Processing and Speech Tools for Italian. Final Workshop (EVALITA 2018)*, volume 2263, pages 258–263. Accademia University Press.

Semeraro, G., Lops, P., Basile, P., and De Gemmis, M. (2009). On the tip of my thought: Playing the guillotine game. In *Twenty-First International Joint Conference on Artificial Intelligence*.

Yannakakis, G. N. and Togelius, J. (2018). *Artificial intelligence and games*, volume 2. Springer.

9. Language Resource References

Attardi, G. (2012). Wikiextractor.

Baroni, M., Bernardini, S., Ferraresi, A., and Zanchetta, E. (2009). The wacky wide web: a collection of very large linguistically processed web-crawled corpora. *Language resources and evaluation*, 43(3):209–226.

Dige, A. (2016). Raccolta di proverbi e detti italiani. `http://web.tiscali.it/proverbiitaliani`. Downloaded on the 24th April 2018.

Lyding, V., Stemle, E., Borghetti, C., Brunello, M., Castagnoli, S., Dell'Orletta, F., Dittmann, H., Lenci, A., and Pirrelli, V. (2014). The paisa' corpus of italian web texts. In *9th Web as Corpus Workshop (WaC-9)@ EACL 2014*, pages 36–43. EACL (European chapter of the Association for Computational Linguistics).

Wikiquote. (2016). Proverbi italiani. `https://it.wikiquote.org/wiki/Proverbi_italiani`. Downloaded on the 24th April 2018.

Proceedings of the LREC 2020 Workshop Games and Natural Language Processing, pages 39–43
Language Resources and Evaluation Conference (LREC 2020), Marseille, 11–16 May 2020
© European Language Resources Association (ELRA), licensed under CC-BY-NC

A 3D Role-Playing Game for Abusive Language Annotation

Federico Bonetti[a,b], Sara Tonelli[b],
[a]Dept. of Psychology and Cognitive Science, University of Trento
[b]Fondazione Bruno Kessler, Trento
{fbonetti,satonelli}@fbk.eu

Abstract

Gamification has been applied to many linguistic annotation tasks, as an alternative to crowdsourcing platforms to collect annotated data in an inexpensive way. However, we think that still much has to be explored. Games with a Purpose (GWAPs) tend to lack important elements that we commonly see in commercial games, such as 2D and 3D worlds or a story. Making GWAPs more similar to full-fledged video games in order to involve users more easily and increase dissemination is a demanding yet interesting ground to explore. In this paper we present a 3D role-playing game for abusive language annotation that is currently under development.

Keywords: games with a purpose, game design, linguistic annotation, abusive language

1. Introduction

Games with a Purpose (GWAPs) have been exploited for many linguistic annotation tasks to enrich data with different information layers, ranging from word senses to anaphora. Gathering annotations from experts hired for the tasks can be expensive and time-consuming. Using gamification to collect annotations from players, instead, allows to combine the stronger motivation and the will to play again that games foster (Ryan et al., 2006) with lower average costs (Poesio et al., 2013; Vannella et al., 2014; Jurgens and Navigli, 2014). One of the main problems with GWAPs, however, is the low resemblance with commercial games, which are devised specifically for entertainment purposes (Jamieson et al., 2012). This is the case especially for existing games aimed at linguistic annotation.

Another common criticism to GWAPs is that they tend to exploit ephemeral extrinsic rewards (like collecting points, achieving high places in leaderboards, obtaining badges and so on) which might even harm motivation in the long run (Seaborn and Fels, 2015) and that do not represent the real essence of video games, as game designer Margaret Robertson claims (Robertson, 2010).

In the light of these criticisms, we show in this paper that it is possible to create a 3D video game for linguistic annotation using simple models created in Blender[1] even without domain-specific (i.e. 3D modelling) professional skills. In particular, we are presenting a role-playing game (RPG) rendered in 3D cel shading graphics (which means the style is cartoonish) with the purpose of collecting abusive language annotations. The goal is to create sentences that can be used to train a hate speech detection systems. The game is being developed with multiple target devices in mind so the ergonomics will fit both keyboard and touchscreen setups.

2. Related work

To date, there have been many attempts in the direction of gamifying a wide range of linguistic annotation tasks. These include *Phrase Detectives* for anaphora resolution (Poesio et al., 2013), *The Knowledge Towers* (Vannella et al., 2014) and *Puzzle Racer* (Jurgens and Navigli, 2014) for concept-image linking, *Infection* (Vannella et al., 2014), *OnToGalaxy* (Krause et al., 2010) and *JeuxDeMots* (Joubert et al., 2018) for semantic linking, *Argotario* (Habernal et al., 2017) for fallacious argumentation identification, *Zombilingo* (Fort et al., 2014) for dependecy syntax annotation, *Sentimentator* (Öhman and Kajava, 2018) for sentiment annotation, *Wordrobe* (Venhuizen et al., 2013) and *Ka-Boom!* (Jurgens and Navigli, 2014) for sense annotation. Researchers stress the fact that GWAPs should be designed in such a way that they integrate the task without sacrificing their 'gamefulness', otherwise the tasks may be perceived as work (Vannella et al., 2014). Some of these games try to exploit *disjoint design* (Krause et al., 2010), i.e. a technique by which the goal of the player and the goal of the task are kept separate. In particular, in *OnToGalaxy* players control a spaceship and have to shoot other spaceships with a certain label that does not satisfy the condition expressed in the instructions. We take into account that this separation, or task abstraction, could potentially harm the quality of the outcome, so tasks have to be thought very carefully. A goal that is phrased as *shoot the spaceships with a name that does not satisfy this condition* may very well drive the player's actions differently than a task that says *click on the label that satisfies the following condition*, if only because of the sense of challenge or excitement that arises. On the other hand, challenge and a gameful environment might be exactly what drives the players' actions in the right direction, to the point of improving the annotation quality over standard crowdsourcing methods (Vannella et al., 2014).

This separation is useful for hiding the task and making the whole experience feel less like work and more like play. However, hiding a task does not necessarily mean that the users must not be made aware of its presence. In fact, saying clearly that a game is useful for research purposes can be a motivator for players (Tuite, 2014).

Among the contributions we have analysed, some try to exploit this technique and we noticed that although two text-based annotation games take advantage of it – *Infec-*

---

[1]The Blender Foundation, https://www.blender.org/.

tion (Vannella et al., 2014) and *OnToGalaxy* (Krause et al., 2010) – they focus on word-level annotation tasks, while to our knowledge no existing GWAP with disjoint design performs a task at sentence level. Probably the games that push the most their looks and feel towards commercial games are *Infection* and *The Knowledge Towers*, where the player actually controls a character and is rather free to explore the virtual environment. However, as mentioned before, these games focus on word-level annotation and are in 2D, while we are experimenting with sentence-level annotation in a 3D scenery.

In Table 1 we summarise the main games developed for linguistic annotation, specifying which ones rely on disjoint design, the target of the annotation and the task. To our knowledge there is still no overlap between the sentence level annotation category and the disjoint design category.

Game	Disjoint design	Task type
Phrase Detectives (Poesio et al., 2013)	No	**Sentence level**
Zombilingo (Fort et al., 2014)	No	**Sentence level**
Sentimentator (Öhman and Kajava, 2018)	No	**Sentence level**
Argotario (Habernal et al., 2017)	No	**Sentence level**
Wordrobe (Venhuizen et al., 2013)	No	Word level
JeuxDeMots (Joubert et al., 2018)	No	Word level
OnToGalaxy (Krause et al., 2010)	**Yes**	Word level
Infection (Vannella et al., 2014)	**Yes**	Word level
Ka-Boom! (Jurgens and Navigli, 2014)	**Yes**	Word level
Puzzle Racer (Jurgens and Navigli, 2014)	**Yes**	Word level
The Knowledge Towers (Vannella et al., 2014)	**Yes**	Word level

Table 1: Feature summary.

3. Abusive Language Annotation

The goal of the game we implement is to collect data for hate speech detection (Fortuna and Nunes, 2018). Due to the increasing popularity of social media platforms such as Facebook, Twitter and Instagram, it has indeed become of crucial importance to automatically detect abusive messages online with the aim to suspend accounts, delete hate speech messages, etc. While existing hate speech detection systems have achieved good results on resource-rich languages using deep learning techniques (Basile et al., 2019), these data-intensive approaches require large amounts of high-quality annotated data for training, which are typically expensive and time-consuming to create. We therefore develop the first GWAP with the goal to annotate data to be used for hate speech detection.

We distinguish between two different linguistic tasks: the goal of the first one is to collect a set of abusive and not abusive sentences. The goal of the second task is to identify, in an abusive sentence, which expressions or words are offensive, so to have a fine-grained annotation of the sentence, isolating only the offensive strings. For both cases, the game takes in input a corpus of sentences that may contain abusive language, with the goal to annotate them. For our first experimentation, we use the Italian WhatsApp corpus of cyberbullying interactions (Sprugnoli et al., 2018), containing 10 chats for a total of 14,600 tokens. The messages had been manually annotated as offensive or not, and the semantic type of the offense was also specified (e.g. body shame, sexism, blackmail, etc.). For our game, the existing annotation has not been taken into account, but it can be used to check whether the information on offensive messages collected through the game matches the gold standard. Since users are exposed to vulgar language in this game, a disclamer is put at the beginning where they are informed about the potential harm.

The input format for the game is rather straightforward: a standard .txt/.xml file containing a conversation (made up of *name* + space + *sentence* turns if it is a .txt file). The game engine takes this file in input, splits the turns, assigns random names to the speakers and represents the chat in the game as students talking to each other.

4. Tasks

4.1. Task 1: Sentence level annotation

The protagonist of our game, a high-school student, has been given a special device by a scientist and has been appointed the mission to lower the level of bullying in the school. This level is represented by a 'security meter' in the form of a classic health bar near the player's avatar in the heads-up display. The device makes it possible to tap into other people's minds to change what they are going to say. This mechanism in particular allows to annotate sentences and constitutes Task 1. In this task players have to change what a bully says, if it contains abusive language, in order to make the expression inoffensive. This is done by clicking on the tokens that represent what the bully is thinking. The purpose of the task is twofold. The main goal is to annotate the sentence as containing abusive language or not (if it does, it is fed to task 2). The secondary goal is to obtain pairs of abusive and non-abusive sentences. The dialogue phase unfolds as follows: when the player goes near a certain group of students, it is possible to overhear their conversation. Before every message, the player is able to read the speaker's mind: a cloud is shown where tokens are freely modifiable; when the change has been made, the bullies say what the player has told them to say, then they look puzzled and run away. The task implements disjoint design in the sense that what the players do is they *make sentences inoffensive* while the underlying task mechanics consist of *marking* sentences and *providing pairs of abusive and non-abusive sentences*. The task goal is *driven* by the surface goal. Both the modified sentence and the original sentence are kept in order to have positive and negative examples. The new sentence can be similar to the original one or rewritten from scratch, since the focus is on knowing if, not how, the sentences have been modified. The game leaves players rather free to change all the tokens they want. However, it is possible that users will only change the one or two tokens required to render the sentence less offensive. This would actually help us collect pairs of sentences where the difference is minimal, so that the classifier can learn from these examples to recognise offensive messages also when they are similar to not-offensive ones.

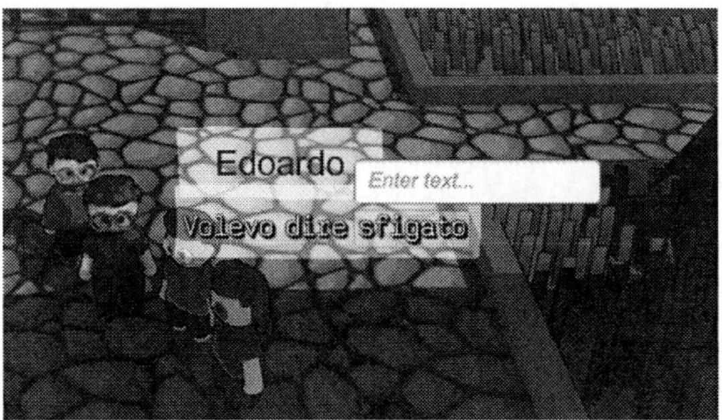

Figure 1: Game screenshot of task 1: Modifying offensive sentences.

4.2. Task 2: Word level annotation

This task consists in erasing offensive expressions off a blackboard or a wall. The snippets of texts that make up the graffiti are taken from sentences annotated in Task 1 as offensive, so this also serves as a validation phase. Players can erase tokens they think are offensive by using a sponge or a wiper. The erasing mechanics adds a layer to the interaction, since erasing by rubbing an object against a surface in correspondence of a token is different than simply clicking on a token. Again, the idea is to make the task less direct but more satisfactory. Words are considered erased when more than 2/3 of the word surface has been wiped. In order to prevent the player from erasing too many inoffensive words, we put a limit to the available game resources involved in these mechanics (such as soap) and reward low waste.

Figure 2: Game screenshot of task 2: Erasing graffiti with a sponge.

4.3. Score and quality control

To control the annotation quality, three methods are being implemented. The first one consists of randomly presenting players with gold standard annotated sentences. Players who show deviation from the gold standard are given hard feedback about their performance, with advice on how to improve it.

Another way of assessing whether players are good annotators, especially if no gold standard is available yet, is to check their response time with respect to the sentences presented. If players systematically skip sentences after a very short time, we can infer that their motivation or interest is low and rate their reliability accordingly. One way to cope with this is to either exclude the annotations or submit them to other players in the form of a specific validation task. Finally, agreement between players who annotate the same sentences will be used to add to their score. Regardless, a base score will always be given to players in both tasks, according to the amount of sentence skipping and time dedicated to the annotation. This score is partly represented in the security meter and partly used to calculate the experience points that allow the player to level up.

5. Game Design

5.1. Gameplay

The game world is intended to be, to an extent, free to roam, which means the player is allowed to explore freely, progressing with the story only when they feel ready to. During the exploration phase, it is possible to overhear conversations and intervene when hate speech is used, or erase abusive language off of walls and blackboards. These two instances of tasks reiterate themselves indefinitely, or until the player has reached a certain amount of discipline in the school that let them advance with the story.

A crucial issue is how to keep players engaged as progress is made through the story. A common datum is that games gradually increase the difficulty to keep the player challenged. This is modeled in Flow Theory applied to video games (Csikszentmihalyi, 1997; Cowley et al., 2008). However, many successful games (see *Minecraft*) do not implement difficulty as an upward curve. Rather, the player is motivated by the possibility to do more, to build more, to explore more. The difficulty changes according to the player's strategy and play style. In a game where the tasks consist of linguistic annotation we think that this is the best model. Rewards are primarily of power-ups, equip items, new mechanics and new areas to explore. However, as players advance, we plan to give them the possibility to annotate more ambiguous sentences, that is, sentences that have received mixed interpretations and are thus more difficult to classify.

5.2. Genre and setting

Choosing the right genre is important since it has an impact on how text is presented during game play. Role-playing games (RPGs) are a viable option when it comes to moderately high amounts of text since they naturally present players with lots of messages from non-playing characters. Since the tasks that have been implemented are based on hate speech and the corpus was created by young students, we decided to set the game in a school. The architecture and aesthetics were inspired by Mt Tacoma High School in Washington, USA. The model of the school is under construction but it is intended to be fully explorable when it is finished, allowing a certain amount of free roam.

5.3. Graphics

The game environment is a 3D world rendered in a cartoon style (called cel shading or toon shading), which is quite common in commercial video games. Thanks to the versatility of Unity and Blender and their widespread documentation, it is relatively easy to create 3D environments, as long as the models are kept simple. To match the basic style of the 3D models, we implemented a cel shader with black outlines. The final result was achieved by modifing an existing shader available for free on the Unity Asset Store. This choice was also influenced by the fact that some of the most successful commercial games of the last decade, and 3D games by Nintendo in general, use colorful graphics: *Fortnite* by Epic Games, *The Legend of Zelda: Breath of The Wild*, the *Super Mario* franchise and more independent experimental games like *Untitled Goose Game*, to name a few.

Figure 3: A view of the school yard.

5.4. Player representation

A core feature of many RPGs is the avatar customizability (especially in massive mutiplayer online RPGs, but also in traditional RPGs to a lesser extent). In our game the player is represend as a customizable 3D character. At the beginning of the game, players have the opportunity to create a character with the appearance they prefer. The game lets the players customize their avatar without asking for their gender: it is sufficient to choose the preferred hair style and clothes.

It is worth noticing that this feature is not limited to RPGs and recently there have been attempts to bring character customization even to genres where the player appearance is of minimum importance in terms of gameplay experience, like driving games (see *Forza Horizon 4* or even *Farming Simulator 2019*). This feature in particular seems to drive user motivation remarkably. It is not infrequent to see users online reporting having spent hours just in the character creation interface screen. Customization improves our sense of control over the game outcomes and makes it more likely that we continue playing (Turkay and Adinolf, 2015). Overall, the freedom to modify one's own avatar contributes to the sense of agency and autonomy, which is one of the three psychological needs theorized in

self-determination theory: autonomy, competence and relatedness (Ryan et al., 2006).

5.5. Development tools

The game is currently being developed in Unity[2], in C#, relying on Blender for the 3D modeling. Both programs boast huge online documentation and Unity has many build options, including mainstream gaming consoles and WebGL, allowing easy multi-platform releases. Most importantly they are free to use, at least within a certain amount of profit in the case of Unity, and Blender is open source.

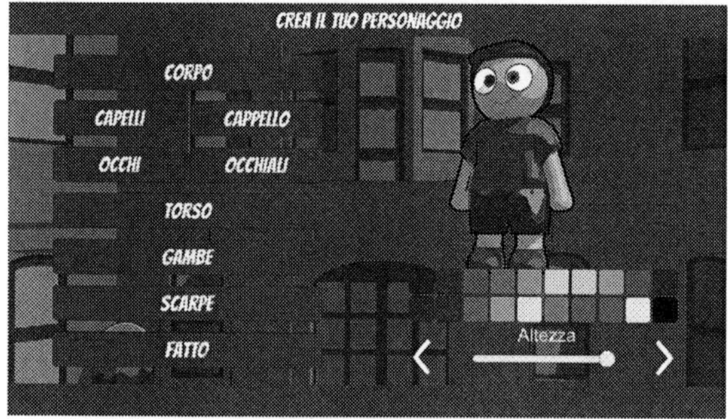

Figure 4: Character customization interface.

6. Conclusion and Future Work

In this paper we have presented a work-in-progress 3D roleplaying video game for abusive language annotation that uses disjoint design as its core design strategy. This feature allows the designer to hide a task making the whole experience more gameful. This project aims at being a first step towards the use of disjoint design in a gamified application for sentence-level linguistic annotation. While we did not devise this game with a particular educational purpose in mind, it is certainly a welcome byproduct to be able to raise awareness about the topic of abusive language and cyberbullying.

One of our next steps will be to study a method to let players add their own content to be annotated later by other players. The exact way this will be made possible has not been defined yet. Some commercial games have already tried to gather text input by the players. An example from commercial games is *Kind Words*[3], where people are free to exchange supportive messages with each other, a mechanism that presents an obvious occasion for collecting corpora.

We are also planning a pilot study to evaluate the overall playability of the game and the task intrusiveness. A questionnaire to probe intrinsic motivation is being redacted, based on self-determination theory, to assess this aspect. An evaluation in terms of quality and cost of the annotations will also be made comparing our approach with the quality, time and cost of human annotation.

7. References

Basile, V., Bosco, C., Fersini, E., Nozza, D., Patti, V., Pardo, F. M. R., Rosso, P., and Sanguinetti, M. (2019).

---

[2]Unity Technologies, https://unity.com/.

[3]Popcannibal, https://www.popcannibal.com/wp/

Semeval-2019 task 5: Multilingual detection of hate speech against immigrants and women in twitter. In *Proceedings of the 13th International Workshop on Semantic Evaluation, SemEval@NAACL-HLT 2019, Minneapolis, MN, USA, June 6-7, 2019*, pages 54–63.

Cowley, B., Charles, D., Black, M., and Hickey, R. (2008). Toward an understanding of flow in video games. *Computers in Entertainment*, 6(2):1, July.

Csikszentmihalyi, M. (1997). *Finding flow: The Psychology of Engagement with Everyday Life.* Finding flow: The psychology of engagement with everyday life. Basic Books, New York, NY, US.

Fort, K., Guillaume, B., and Chastant, H. (2014). Creating Zombilingo, a Game with a Purpose for Dependency Syntax Annotation. In *Proceedings of the First International Workshop on Gamification for Information Retrieval - GamifIR '14*, pages 2–6, Amsterdam, The Netherlands. ACM Press.

Fortuna, P. and Nunes, S. (2018). A survey on automatic detection of hate speech in text. *ACM Comput. Surv.*, 51(4):85:1–85:30, July.

Habernal, I., Hannemann, R., Pollak, C., Klamm, C., Pauli, P., and Gurevych, I. (2017). Argotario: Computational Argumentation Meets Serious Games. In *Proceedings of the 2017 Conference on Empirical Methods in Natural Language Processing: System Demonstrations*, pages 7–12, Copenhagen, Denmark. Association for Computational Linguistics.

Jamieson, P., Hall, J., and Grace, L. (2012). Research Directions for Pushing Harnessing Human Computation to Mainstream Video Games. In *Meaningful Play 2012*, East Lansing, MI.

Joubert, A., Lafourcade, M., and Brun, N. L. (2018). The JeuxDeMots Project is 10 Years Old: What We have Learned. In *Proceedings of the 2018 LREC Workshop "Games and Gamification for Natural Language Processing (Games4NLP)"*, pages 22–26, Miyazaki, Japan.

Jurgens, D. and Navigli, R. (2014). It's All Fun and Games until Someone Annotates: Video Games with a Purpose for Linguistic Annotation. *Transactions of the Association for Computational Linguistics*, 2:449–464, December.

Krause, M., Takhtamysheva, A., Wittstock, M., and Malaka, R. (2010). Frontiers of a paradigm: exploring human computation with digital games. In *Proceedings of the ACM SIGKDD Workshop on Human Computation - HCOMP '10*, pages 22–25, Washington DC. ACM Press.

Öhman, E. and Kajava, K. (2018). Sentimentator: Gamifying Fine-grained Sentiment Annotation. In *Proceedings of the Digital Humanities in the Nordic Countries 4th Conference (DHN 2019)*, volume 2084, pages 98–110, Helsinki, Finland, February.

Poesio, M., Chamberlain, J., Kruschwitz, U., Robaldo, L., and Ducceschi, L. (2013). Phrase detectives: Utilizing collective intelligence for internet-scale language resource creation. *ACM Transactions on Interactive Intelligent Systems*, 3(1):1–44, April.

Robertson, M. (2010). Can't Play, Won't Play. https://kotaku.com/cant-play-wont-play-5686393.

Ryan, R. M., Rigby, C. S., and Przybylski, A. (2006). The Motivational Pull of Video Games: A Self-Determination Theory Approach. *Motivation and Emotion*, 30(4):344–360, December.

Seaborn, K. and Fels, D. I. (2015). Gamification in theory and action: A survey. *International Journal of Human-Computer Studies*, 74:14–31, February.

Sprugnoli, R., Menini, S., Tonelli, S., Oncini, F., and Piras, E. (2018). Creating a WhatsApp Dataset to Study Pre-teen Cyberbullying. In *Proceedings of the 2nd Workshop on Abusive Language Online (ALW2)*, pages 51–59, Brussels, Belgium. Association for Computational Linguistics.

Tuite, K. (2014). GWAPs: Games with a Problem. In *Proceedings of the 9th International Conference on the Foundations of Digital Games*.

Turkay, S. and Adinolf, S. (2015). The effects of customization on motivation in an extended study with a massively multiplayer online roleplaying game. *Cyberpsychology: Journal of Psychosocial Research on Cyberspace*, 9(3).

Vannella, D., Jurgens, D., Scarfini, D., Toscani, D., and Navigli, R. (2014). Validating and Extending Semantic Knowledge Bases using Video Games with a Purpose. In *Proceedings of the 52nd Annual Meeting of the Association for Computational Linguistics (Volume 1: Long Papers)*, pages 1294–1304, Baltimore, Maryland. Association for Computational Linguistics.

Venhuizen, N. J., Evang, K., Basile, V., and Bos, J. (2013). Gamification for word sense labeling. In *Proceedings of the International Conference on Computational Semantics (IWCS)*, pages 397–403.

Proceedings of the LREC 2020 Workshop Games and Natural Language Processing, pages 44–48
Language Resources and Evaluation Conference (LREC 2020), Marseille, 11–16 May 2020
© European Language Resources Association (ELRA), licensed under CC-BY-NC

Designing a GWAP for Collecting Naturally Produced Dialogues for Low Resourced Languages

Zulipiye Yusupujiang, Jonathan Ginzburg

Université de Paris, CNRS, Laboratoire de Linguistique Formelle

zulipiye.yusupujiang@linguist.univ-paris-diderot.fr, yonatan.ginzburg@univ-paris-diderot.fr

Abstract

In this paper we present a new method for collecting naturally generated dialogue data for a low resourced language, (specifically here—Uyghur). We plan to build a games with a purpose (GWAPs) to encourage native speakers to actively contribute dialogue data to our research project. Since we aim to characterize the response space of queries in Uyghur, we design various scenarios for conversations that yield to questions being posed and responded to. We will implement the GWAP with the `RPG Maker MV` Game Engine, and will integrate the chatroom system of the game with the Dialogue Experimental Toolkit (DiET). DiET will help us improve the data collection process, and most importantly, make us have some control over the interactions among the participants.

Keywords: GWAPs, Response Space, DiET, Low Resource Languages

1. Introduction

There are many tasks such as data and text annotation, and image labeling, which challenge even the most high-performing computational algorithms or computer programs, but which are actually very easy to handle for humans. This motivated (Von Ahn and Dabbish, 2008) to propose a method called "games with a purpose" (GWAPs), in which players produce a large amount of useful data and perform tasks which are difficult for computer systems while they are entertaining with interesting online games. As a result, players make considerable contributions towards providing a sufficient amount of annotated data for training and developing computational algorithms. GWAPs have been used successfully in many tasks such as *the ESP Game* for image labeling (Von Ahn and Dabbish, 2004), *Peeka-boom* (Von Ahn et al., 2006) for locating objects within images, and also the *FoldIt* (Cooper et al., 2010; Khatib et al., 2011) for protein folding. GWAPs have also been used for solving NLP problems, for instance the *Phrase Detectives* (Poesio et al., 2013) for creating anaphorically annotated resources, and also the *Puzzle Racer* and the *Ka-Boom!* GWAPs for word sense disambiguation.

The main objective of our project is to characterize the response space for queries across languages. A question can be responded to in many ways. (Łupkowski and Ginzburg, 2016) studied one significant component of the response space of questions, which is responding to a question with a question. They used the British National Corpus (BNC corpus) and three other more genre-specific corpora in English, and classified the range of question responses using 7 classes (Clarification requests, dependent questions, questions about the form of the answer, requests for underlying motivation, indirect question responses, and two classes of evasion questions), and showed how to model these 7 classes within the framework of Conversation Oriented Semantics (KoS in short), which is based on the formalism of Type Theory with Records (TTR) (Ginzburg, 2012). Furthermore, (Ginzburg et al., 2019) offered a characterization of the entire response space for English and Polish. Based

on these works, we aim to take the challenge of characterizing the response space of questions in low resource languages that have yet to be studied in this regard. However, most low resourced languages have very little or even no digital language resources available for conducting scientific research. In particular, a sufficient amount of naturally produced dialogue data is rare to find. Therefore, constructing a dialogue corpus for such low resourced languages is the first essential step of our project. In this project we focus on collecting dialogue data and analyzing the response space of questions in Uyghur since it is a low resourced language under threat. In addition, conducting field work for collecting Uyghur dialogue data is not possible given the current difficult situation of the target area. Thus, we propose a new method for collecting natural dialogue data using a GWAP.

Inspired by current work on GWAPs, we plan to design and create a Massively multiplayer online role-playing game (MMORPG), using the **RPG Maker MV Game Engine**.[1] Since MMORPG involves a large number of online players and their active interactions with each others, through text or voice, we hope to collect the naturally produced dialogues that take place during each game.

In this paper, we aim to present our initial design and further plan for this GWAP for collecting dialogue data. In the following section, we introduce the initial design for how to get players to produce a large variety of natural dialogues while playing the game; we then introduce the chatroom system of our GWAP and the data collection process; subsequently, we give the overall rules and conventions of the game, and also the reward system; finally, we draw some brief conclusions and offer some ideas for future work.

2. Integrating Task-oriented Dialogue with GWAP

Since our project is about characterizing the response space of questions, we hope to collect a varied corpus of questions and answers. Therefore, we have to pay much attention to enticing the participants to produce different

---

[1]https://store.steampowered.com/app/363890/RPG_Maker_MV/

types of questions and answers during the game. Consequently, our primary goal is to ensure that the players chat extensively on a wide range of topics. To achieve this, we plan to design some task oriented dialogues inside the GWAP so that players will participate in dialogues with more specific guidelines and certain aims. The spoken part of The British National Corpus (BNC), which is used in (Łupkowski and Ginzburg, 2016; Ginzburg et al., 2019), was collected in different contexts, including formal business meetings, government meetings and also radio shows and phone-interviews. To evaluate the difference between the data collected by our method and the BNC corpus, we will also use our GWAP for collecting English dialogue data so that we can conduct a comparative study on two different English dialogue corpora.

To achieve our goal, we plan to design and implement an MMORPG using the RPG Maker MV Game Engine. We will create a virtual world in our GWAP, so every player of the game has several options for choosing a character class and role-playing class in the virtual world. Virtual worlds (Bartle, 2004) are computer systems or applications which imitate a real environment. They can be simultaneously affected by an enormous numbers of players, and can exist and develop internally. Thus, virtual worlds are said to be *shared* or *multi-user*, and also *persistent* (Bartle, 2004).

The game *Ring Fit Adventure*,[2] is a game in which players accomplish their fitness exercises while being entertained with an adventurous and fun game. It is a Role Playing Game in which there is a big world to explore, monsters to beat, and also bonus items to collect. Players can freely choose the level of exercises and manage to accomplish different work-out exercises during their journey in the virtual world. Since the main objective of this game is to encourage or force the players to do more exercises, it is designed in a way that players have to do different exercises in order to battle various monsters they come across on their way, otherwise they cannot continue their journey. This game has become very popular since it is a very new and fun way to keep one motivated to reach a fitness goal.

Inspired by the *Ring Fit Adventure*, we have come up with a similar idea which encourages or in a sense "forces" the players to have a discussion on various topics with other players during the game. Players will be given several topics to choose, or sometimes will be randomly assigned to a specific topic, and they will have a free chat according to the instruction within a time limit. In what follows, we sketch the initial design of scenarios for various tasks in the game:

- **Role-playing:** in this task, you will be role playing one of the characters in the following story: There was a severe public attack yesterday on the main street of your city. The police has successfully arrested one of the assailants, who is currently being interrogated.

    - If you are the police: you should ask various questions from the suspect to obtain a confession, and try to let him admit his crime, and also force him to disclose his accomplices;

    - If you are the criminal suspect: you should try your best to deny your crime, and make the police believe that you are innocent.

- **Planning a given task:** you are invited to participate in a real-life TV show, and you are paired up with a stranger (who is also here to participate in the TV show). Your task is to plan a trip together to a totally unfamiliar place. The two of you should work together on planning the entire two week trip. The trip is self-funded so you may want to discuss your financial situation and how to arrange the budget for the trip. Since you will travelling together for the entire two weeks you should start by getting to know your partner well, including his/her basic information, family situation, hobbies etc.

- **Direction giving:** in this task you will be chatting with your partner in order to find out how to get to his/her current address. You should pay close attention to the details and draw a travel plan to your partners's place. This task should be done in two rounds, with each of you playing both roles.

- **Real open discussions:** in this task, you and your partner/partners in the chatroom should freely and openly discuss a topic, you may discuss an issue happening around the world, or a news item, politics, comedies, education, or anything you may interested in. During the discussion, you should ask each other various questions about the topic.

- **Future ideal society:** in this task you and your partner/partners in the chatroom should discuss the ideal future society you want to live in. You should tell your partner how is your ideal future society, and your partner should ask questions about that ideal society. You can talk about the social system, education, medical, transportation, and any other aspect of that ideal society.

- **Interviewing:** in this task, you will be role-playing an interviewer or an interviewee.

    - If you are the interviewer, you should ask various questions of the person you are interviewing, including basic information, private information, their current mission, their opinion about some topics, or even their further plans.

    - If you are the interviewee (you will role-play one of the famous people randomly assigned to you from our list), you may choose quite freely how to respond, you may want to answer correctly, or lie to the interviewer, you can refuse to answer or change the topic.

---

[2] https://www.nintendo.com/games/detail/ring-fit-adventure-switch/

- **Guessing other person's current location:** in this task, you will guess the current location of your partner according to the description of their surrounding environment. You can also ask some questions to verify your partner's location, such as, *'Is there a desk nearby?'*. You should ask as many questions as you need to correctly guess the current location of your partner. For the safety reason, the current location does not have to be the players' real location so they can make up or just imagine a place and let the others to guess.

3. Design of the Chatroom in the Game

All conversational tasks above will take place in the chatroom system which is implemented in the game. Each time the players are assigned to perform a task, they will be able to choose chat-rooms with different numbers of participants. We will have chat-rooms with only two players, with 4 5 players, and also with 6 10 players. This will enable us to make comparisons of dialogical behaviour across 2 person dialogue, small group multi-party, and larger group (Carletta et al., 2000; Ginzburg and Fernández, 2005). Players are randomly assigned to the chat-rooms to prevent cheating, and they should actively participate in the discussion until the time expires. To guarantee a successful dialogue flow, players will be informed at the beginning about the conversation rules and typing conventions, such as adding a question mark after each question and the minimal number of turns they should take during the conversation. In the end, after using a text mining technique, an overall assessment of the conversation will be sent to all participants of the conversation. They will be rewarded if they fulfill the requirement, otherwise they have to participate in another conversation. Since we are interested in various types of questions and answers with different word using, sentence making and speaking style, players will have freedom of speech so they are able to discuss any social issue or topic without restriction. This can be rather intriguing for people who used to live in a society where the government strictly controls their speech and actions. The real-world private information of the players will not be provided during the game, therefore, players should feel safe and free to discuss.

Furthermore, in order to collect conversational data in a more efficient way, we will adapt the Dialogue Experimental Toolkit (DiET)[3] (Healey et al., 2003) to be usable on the internet and link it with the chatroom system of our game. DiET is in its original form a text-based chat-tool which allows utterances of particular types to be artificially introduced into natural dialogues in a controlled and synchronous manner, and unknown to the dialogue participants. DiET lead to novel findings about dialogue interaction (Healey et al., 2003; Eshghi and Healey, 2016). This methodology has been approved by several ethics committees (e.g., at Stanford), as long as the subjects are debriefed after participation, similarly for online GWAPs [4].

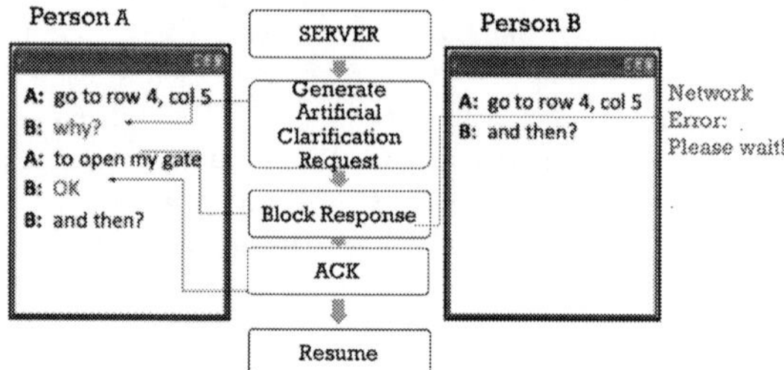

Figure 1: Example of the workflow of DiET chattool

The DiET chatool can automatically record all activities of the participants including key-presses, words and turns, typing notifications, read receipts, number of edits, typing speed, typing overlap. All dialogue data is immediately saved in various formats so it can be loaded into different data analysis tools such as Excel, SPSS, R, MATLAB, etc. Therefore, there is no need for transcription and post-processing of the data. Integrating the chatroom system of our GWAP with DiET helps us improve the data collection accuracy and efficiency.

Another key strength of DiET is that it can manipulate the interactions between participants. As seen in 1, DiET can send artificial clarification requests such as "why?", "what?", some fake feedback "Ok", "yeah", and also some artificial hesitations such as "umm", "uhh". This interactions are unknown to the participants so it can assist participants in producing more dialogues and various types of question responses which we are interested in. Thus, DiET's integration with our chattool system can help us reduce the problem of data sparseness.

4. Gameplay and Mechanics

Since the Uyghur diaspora outside China who are above 16 years old are the primary target audience of this game, we would like to attract more Uyghurs to participate through designing the game to their taste. Therefore, we will use some famous Uyghur fairy tales as narratives of the game and also use the original names in these stories as some characters' names in the game. Since most of the Uyghurs are familiar with those fairy tales, it will hopefully be intriguing for them to play the game. In addition, we will develop the game in English and in Uyghur, so Uyghur can also be the operating language of the game. To the best of our knowledge, there is almost no game which has Uyghur as the operating language. Having a game in their mother tongue would be novel and interesting for the target audience, so there will be more people attracted, especially people who are not familiar with the main world languages, and will give the game a try. Most importantly, the Uyghur diaspora are well aware that their language is under threat and they have to make a great effort to keep it alive. Thus, participating in such a game with a scientific purpose will potentially impress members of this community.

We will build a MMORPG with a linear story structure and the game moves on as the improvement of player's lev-

---

[3] https://dialoguetoolkit.github.io/chattool/

[4] https://www.scienceathome.org/legal/game-consent-form/skill-lab-science-detective-terms-of-service/

els and skills. There will be several game sections separated by the difficulty levels, so the players should gain enough experience points and skills to move to the next higher game section. To begin with, players should create a character for themselves once they register for the game. They will be able to choose the class, race, and also gender for their character. Every novice starts the game with *Level 1*, and their levels increase as they gain more experience points, `Experience Points`. The player improves in levels when their character reaches a certain `Experience Points`. As the level goes up, their character will have better attributes, more advanced skills, become more resistant and will have greater choices for more powerful equipment. There are three different points in the game, `Experience Points`, `Battle Points`, and `Health Points` to measure the overall quality of the players.

Each player has various quests to accomplish along with their journey in the game. First of all, there will be the `Player versus Environment Combat(PvE)` in which players will have battle with monsters in the virtual world in order to become stronger and increase their level. In addition, players will be given freedom of choice between the `Player versus Player Duel(PvP)` and `conversations on different topics` as a challenge. If players choose a PVP duel, the winner will be rewarded with `Experience Points`, `Battle Points` (for purchasing some unique and powerful items they usually cannot buy with gold coins), and also `Gold Coins`; whereas the failed one will be debuffed so their movement speed and vitality will decrease dramatically by 70%. To recover their original game stats, players should chat with other players about a topic under a time limit (usually 10-15 minutes), otherwise, they have to wait for two hours to be recovered automatically. However, if players opt for having conversations on different topics voluntarily rather than having a PVP duel, all participants of the conversation will be rewarded with the same amount of `Experience Points` and `Gold Coins` as the winner of PVP duel, but obtain relatively less `Battle Points`.

Players will be given clear guidance on how to move freely in the virtual world. For instance, giving them instructions on how to use different keypads for walking, running, and jumping etc. We will give them absolute direction commands, such as North, northeast, west, and so on. Besides, contextual and landmark directions are also provided for them as reference points and help them identify their current location and target place. We will have an in-game virtual economy in the game. Players will have a welcome bonus as a starting point and earn more gold coins as they are involved in playing. Gold coins can be earned in different ways: if the players win in a PVE combat and kill a monster, they will get gold coins as a reward or a loot from the monster; players can also gain equipment as loots from monsters so they can use these loot equipment or sell it for gold coins. Players accumulate gold coins and buy more advanced equipment in order to achieve more success and improve their levels in the game. A frail economy leads to a very few purchase options so that the players will not be able to buy more powerful equipment. As a result, there will be less chance for them to win in a battle. Apart from gold coins, the `Battle Points` can serve as another in-game currency. There will be some unique powerful equipment which are purchasable only with `Battle Points`, so the players will be motivated to have more PVP duel since `Battle Points` are given more if they win in PVP duel. In result, it will facilitate conversations among players since the failed players from PVP duel are asked to take part in a conversation.

5. Conclusion

We have presented the ultimate goal of our project and proposed a new method for collecting dialogue data for a low resource language, Uyghur. We have introduced the initial design of this method, namely via implementing games with a purpose (GWAPs) for collecting naturally produced dialogues from the game players. We plan to design and implement a MMORPG using the `RPG Maker MV` Game Engine in which the players will have the ability and the freedom to explore the virtual world according to their levels, and they are given opportunities to accomplish some missions or challenges during the game such as `Player versus Environment Combat(PvE)`, `Player versus Player Duel(PvE)`, and `conversations on different topics`. Apart from this, players who fail in a PvP battle can recover their original game stats by chatting with others in the chatroom, otherwise, they will be waiting for two hours to be recovered automatically. In this way, we can encourage and motivate players to participate in the conversations. We also plan to integrate the Dialogue Experimental Toolkit (DiET) with the chatroom system of the game so that we can have some control over the interactions of participants, and can improve the data collection process as well. At the same time we can also save our time and costs for transcribing and post-processing the data with DiET.

We will continuously improve the design of the game and start implementing it with the `RPG Maker MV` Game Engine. After completing the first version of the game, we will test it by recruiting some players and get feedback from them for further improvements.

References

Bartle, R. A. (2004). *Designing virtual worlds*. New Riders.

Carletta, J., Garrod, S., and Fraser-Krauss, H. (2000). Placement of authority and communication pattern in workplace groups. *Small Group Research*, 29:531–559.

Cooper, S., Khatib, F., Treuille, A., Barbero, J., Lee, J., Beenen, M., Leaver-Fay, A., Baker, D., Popović, Z., et al. (2010). Predicting protein structures with a multiplayer online game. *Nature*, 466(7307):756–760.

Eshghi, A. and Healey, P. G. (2016). Collective contexts in conversation: Grounding by proxy. *Cognitive science*, 40(2):299–324.

Ginzburg, J. and Fernández, R. (2005). Scaling up to multilogue: some benchmarks and principles. In *Proceedings of the 43rd Meeting of the Association for Computational Linguistics*, pages 231–238, Michigan.

Ginzburg, J., Yusupujiang, Z., Li, C., Ren, K., and Łupkowski, P. (2019). Characterizing the response space of questions: a corpus study for english and polish. In *Proceedings of the 20th Annual SIGdial Meeting on Discourse and Dialogue*, pages 320–330.

Ginzburg, J. (2012). *The interactive stance*. Oxford University Press.

Healey, P., Purver, M., King, J., Ginzburg, J., and Mills, G. (2003). Experimenting with clarification in dialogue. In R. Alterman et al., editors, *Proceedings of the 25th Annual Conference of the Cognitive Science Society*, pages 539–544. Mahwah, N.J.: LEA.

Khatib, F., DiMaio, F., Cooper, S., Kazmierczyk, M., Gilski, M., Krzywda, S., Zabranska, H., Pichova, I., Thompson, J., Popović, Z., et al. (2011). Crystal structure of a monomeric retroviral protease solved by protein folding game players. *Nature structural & molecular biology*, 18(10):1175–1177.

Łupkowski, P. and Ginzburg, J. (2016). Query responses. *Journal of Language Modelling Vol*, 4(2):245–292.

Poesio, M., Chamberlain, J., Kruschwitz, U., Robaldo, L., and Ducceschi, L. (2013). Phrase detectives: Utilizing collective intelligence for internet-scale language resource creation. *ACM Transactions on Interactive Intelligent Systems (TiiS)*, 3(1):1–44.

Von Ahn, L. and Dabbish, L. (2004). Labeling images with a computer game. In *Proceedings of the SIGCHI conference on Human factors in computing systems*, pages 319–326.

Von Ahn, L. and Dabbish, L. (2008). Designing games with a purpose. *Communications of the ACM*, 51(8):58–67.

Von Ahn, L., Liu, R., and Blum, M. (2006). Peekaboom: a game for locating objects in images. In *Proceedings of the SIGCHI conference on Human Factors in computing systems*, pages 55–64.

Proceedings of the LREC 2020 Workshop Games and Natural Language Processing, pages 49–58
Language Resources and Evaluation Conference (LREC 2020), Marseille, 11–16 May 2020
© European Language Resources Association (ELRA), licensed under CC-BY-NC

CALLIG: Computer Assisted Language Learning using Improvisation Games

Luis Morgado da Costa ♠[iD], **Joanna Ut-Seong Sio** ♡[iD]

♠ Nanyang Technological University, Singapore
♡ Palacký University, the Czech Republic
lmorgado.dacosta@gmail.com
joannautseong.sio@upol.cz

Abstract

In this paper, we present the ongoing development of CALLIG – a web system that uses improvisation games in Computer Assisted Language Learning (CALL). Improvisation games are structured activities with built-in constraints where improvisers are asked to generate a lot of different ideas and weave a diverse range of elements into a sensible narrative spontaneously. This paper discusses how computer-based language games can be created combining improvisation elements and language technology. In contrast with traditional language exercises, improvisational language games are open and unpredictable. CALLIG encourages spontaneity and witty language use. It also provides opportunities for collecting useful data for many NLP applications.

Keywords: improvisation; computer-assisted language learning; language games; creativity; divergent thinking; remote association

1. Introduction

The system introduced in this paper is part of a larger project entitled iTELL – a suite of applications looking into applying deep computational parsers to intelligent Technology Enhanced Language Learning environments. iTELL includes several applications, for both English and Mandarin Chinese, exploring how to leverage the broad linguistic knowledge available to deep computational parsers and apply it to pedagogical settings. In particular, this paper focuses on CALLIG (Computer Assisted Language Learning using Improvisation Games). CALLIG comprises a series of fun language games, integrating the principles of improvisation comedy with grammatical error detection and other language technologies in order to create a fun language learning environment.

The main motivation for this project was to create a platform where we could explore improvisation principles as a dimension to gamify certain aspects of second language learning for advanced learners of English. In addition, we were also enticed by the ability to collect new kinds of data that are extremely rare, which can facilitate research in certain niche fields of linguistics and psychology, such as humor and creativity.

The remainder of this paper is structured as follows: Section 2 provides a brief introduction to improvisation, as well as some anchors between improvisation and the rest of the paper; Section 3 discusses some aspects of gamification of learning, followed by Section 4, which discusses the current state of Computer Assisted Language Learning; Section 5 discusses Grammatical Error Detection (GED) in CALLIG; Section 6 provides an overview of the games currently available in CALLIG, followed by a more descriptive description of how we simulate certain aspects of these games in Section 7; Section 8 discusses our current plans for future work; Section 9 discusses some applied usages of the data collected by our system; Section 10 provides release notes; Section 11 provides some concluding remarks and Section 12 contains the ackowledgements.

2. Improvisation

Improvisation is a type of performance where performers create the content of the performance as it is performed. There is no predetermined content. Everything is made up on the spot. Such performances can be of music, theater or dance, to name a few possibilities.

Improvisational comedy is a branch of improvisational theatre. There are two main types of improvisational comedy: long form and short form. Long form improvisational comedy consists of a sequence of improvised scenes. A few suggestions would be elicited from the audience for inspiration, which act as the launching pad for the show. These scenes are often related. The thread that links them is discovered and developed as the performance progresses. Short-form improvisational comedy consists of games (generally a few minutes in length). Each game has its own built-in constraints. For example, in the game "Numbers", players can only speak in sentences with a given number of words. Every game requires inputs from the audience, e.g., an occupation, a location, an emotion, a number, etc.. These suggestions would be used in the scene. We have been using the term "improvisational comedy", but in fact one of the rules in improvisation is that improvisers do not try to be funny in a performance, contrary to what one would expect. The comic effect produced is a side-effect. In improvisational comedy, the suggestions and the constraints in the games are often incongruous and the comedy often comes from the unexpected connections that improvisers make to link seemingly unrelated ideas together. This, we believe, is one of the sources of humour in improvisational comedy. The popular American TV show "Whose line is it anyway?" is a well-known performance of short-form improvisational comedy. The show consists of a panel of four performers who engage in a number of games where they create characters, scenes, and songs on the spot.

Improvisation promotes, among other things, collaboration, spontaneity, risk-taking and creative language use. The applied value of such an art form hasn't gone unnoticed. The techniques, the principles, tools, practices, skills and mindsets developed in improvisation have been used for non-performance purposes, such as language learning and corporate training. Many of the major players in tertiary education have improvisation programs for business schools or for communication training (e.g., UCLA [1],Stony Brook University [2], and MIT [3]).

2.1. Improvisation elements in CALLIG

Improvisation games are regularly performed as theatre performances, involving not just witty language use, but also physicality and most often than not, collaboration with multiple players. For CALLIG, only verbal improvisation is relevant. At this stage, we are only building single-user games, though collaboration is an implementation on our agenda. There are a lot of online resources for improvisation games, though such games might not not be directly usable and need to be adapted or designed anew due to the aforementioned reasons.[4]

Excluding physicality and collaboration (for the time-being), both existing and future games of CALLIG (will) contain the following improvisation elements: (i) spontaneity; (ii) random suggestions; (iii) creativity. We discuss each item in turn below.

Improvisation performances are spontaneous. In a performance, improvisers have to react and respond on the spot. Any delay in response due to over-thinking is considered bad improvising. In CALLIG, spontaneity is attained by having a time limit within which the user must finish the task. The time limit differs in different games depending on the difficulty level. We tested multiple time limits with multiple users to decide on a length that is long enough to create tension but not too short to finish the task at hand.

In an improvisation performance, suggestions are elicited from the audience and are incorporated into the performance to highlight both the unscripted nature of the performance and the skills of the performers. In CALLIG, each game begins with a randomly generated prompt to guide the user's input. The prompts could be random words, phrases, numbers, etc. In an improvisation performance, the performers can ask for many suggestions and select among them. In CALLIG, users can also refresh and get a new prompt if they don't like the one they are given.

Improvisation activities are celebrated for their creativity. Creativity contains many aspects. For our purposes, we focus on two cognitive processes, which exist in a lot of improvisation games: remote association and divergent thinking. Creative thinking is the process of putting associative elements into new combinations which either meet specific requirements or are in some way useful (Mednick, 1962). The more mutually remote the elements of the new combination, the more creative the process or solution. Divergent thinking is the process of generating multiple related ideas for a given topic or solutions to a problem. (Guilford, 1967). Divergent thinking occurs in a spontaneous, free-flowing, "non-linear" manner. In improvisation training, improvisers are told to stop filtering themselves. This inhibition of self-judgment enhances the ability to generate a large number of ideas. All our current and future games (will) require remote association and divergent thinking. Users have to connect words/phrases in an unusual way, forcing them to generate uncommon ideas.

2.2. Improvisation in language learning

The most effective learning occurs when the learners are free to explore and discover with the support of scaffolds (the learning paradox) (Sawyer, 2011a). Similarly, in teaching, teachers must allow themselves the freedom to explore within plans, routines and structures (the teacher paradox) (Sawyer, 2011b). This makes improvisation an excellent tool in teaching and learning. Improvisation contrasts with the traditional way of teaching as transmission of knowledge and skills. Instead of a prescribed curriculum and a fixed execution plan, improvisation celebrates openness and unpredictability (Kurtz, 2011). On the other hand, improvisation is never completely free, it occurs within a network of structures, rules and frameworks (Sawyer, 2011b). Each short-form improvisational comedy game comes with its own set of rules and restrictions, these constraints provide a nice platform to anchor and scaffold teaching and learning. Furthermore, improvisational comedy games are highly malleable. The constraints can be customized for various training programs, especially those pertaining to language. In addition to providing contexts for witty language use, improvisation games also provide possibilities of testing particular language skills, for instance, they can be adapted for the teaching of linguistics, covering areas in phonetics, syntax, semantics and pragmatics (Sio and Wee, 2012). Improvisation activities provide varied contexts of language use that do not appear in traditional language classrooms. The entertaining nature of such games makes language learning less repetitive and more enjoyable. CALLIG can thus function as a useful complement to regular classroom teaching and learning.

3. Gamification of Learning

Despite being a relatively young topic, gamification of learning has become a trending topic in recent years. As the number of papers published on gamification of learning is fastly growing (Hamari et al., 2014), so is general public awareness and peer scrutiny of its effectiveness.

Gamification is broadly understood as the *use of game design elements in non-game contexts* (Deterding et al., 2011). These can include game mechanics, game dynamics, and frameworks, such as badge or point reward systems, time constraints, limited resources, turn taking, interaction, competition, roleplaying, etc. – integrated in a way that encourages users to achieve some desired learning goals (Tu et al., 2015; Deterding et al., 2011).

An extensive literature review presented by Hamari et al., aiming to answer the question *Does gamification work?* (Hamari et al., 2014), suggests that gamification works,

---

[1] http://www.npr.org/2012/12/05/166484466/it-s-improv-night-at-business-school

[2] http://www.centerforcommunicatingscience.org/improvisation-for-scientists/

[3] http://tll.mit.edu/design/improv-workshops

[4] http://improvencyclopedia.org/

despite also suggesting that more rigorous methodologies ought to be used to further research on gamification. Moreover, gamification can be used for multiple domains of learning, including declarative knowledge, conceptual knowledge, rule-based knowledge, and procedural knowledge (Kapp, 2012).

The inherent benefit of gamification is often deemed to come from a positive, intrinsically motivating, "playful" experience – an experience that relate well with improvisation games.

4. Computer Assisted Language Learning

The field of Computer Assisted Language Learning (CALL) had its birth around the 1980s and has been gaining momentum ever since. Throughout the last four decades, Artificial Intelligence's contributions to CALL applications have been mainly focused on problems like error classification and correction, user modeling, expert systems, and Intelligent Tutoring Systems (Schulze, 2008; Gamper and Knapp, 2002). Individual systems differ immensely. Some focus on one basic language skill (e.g., reading, writing, listening, or speaking), while others look for broader coverage. Some systems have a larger focus on grammar, others on vocabulary, dialogue interaction, pronunciation, etc.

Within the written dimension, the tasks of automated Grammar Error Detection (GED) and Correction (GEC) have attracted much attention from the field in recent years. This is especially true for English, where a myriad of shared-tasks periodically compare and attest the impact of the latest available technology (Dale and Kilgarriff, 2011; Dale et al., 2012; Ng et al., 2013; Ng et al., 2014; Daudaravicius et al., 2016; Bryant et al., 2019).

Gamification in CALL, even though not entirely new, is still widely unexplored. Nevertheless, a few CALL platforms must be acknowledged due to their popularity. Duolinguo[5] is one of such applications. Duolinguo is a free mobile and web-based platform, where users can learn dozens of different languages through vocabulary and translation-based exercises (Garcia, 2013). It presents gamification elements such as badges, point systems, leaderboards, a skill tree for users to progress through, to name a few. Two other systems, very similar in nature, are Memrise[6] and Quizlet[7]. These two are free mobile and web-based platforms focusing on learning through digital flashcards. Learning through flashcards is widespread in language learning, though in and on its own, it is not specific to language learning. This kind of learning method has been acknowledged concerning the benefits to vocabulary retention (Kornell, 2009), which has undoubtedly contributed to their popularity. Both platforms also include gamification elements such as point systems, leaderboards, time constraints, along with a few different games to explore and learn the content of the flashcards. In addition to these applications, a great number of other similar applications could also be made reference to, with some minor differences. Most language learning platforms available today share, in great part, a lot of the mechanics and goals of the applications mentioned above.

Platforms like Duolinguo, Memrise or Quizlet focus on language learning at earlier stages of second language acquisition, in particular vocabulary and simple sentence structures. Our system has different goals. We aim at the training of language skills in the domain of semantics and pragmatics, with unrestricted language, which are more suitable for advanced second language learners. These skills include but are not limited to the understanding of lexical semantics, semantic association, conceptual retrieval, different registers of language use and witty language use. Our system is built based on improvisational principles so it also enhances spontaneity, flexibility and potentially creativity. Improvisational games are also engaging and fun to play because of the accidental generation of humour. All these provide users strong intrinsic motivation to use CALLIG for language learning.

5. Grammatical Error Detection (GED) in CALLIG

CALLIG uses symbolic parsers, such as computational grammars, to perform GED. Symbolic parsers take a long time to develop before being able to compete against statistical parsers on coverage aspects. When coverage is acceptable, however, symbolic parsers generally provide much higher quality and richer analyses of the language. Our system takes advantage of this rich semantic and syntactic information to perform error detection and select feedback based on a concept known as *mal-rules*.

Mal-rules, as first proposed by (Schneider and McCoy, 1998), extend descriptive grammars in order to allow specific ungrammatical phenomena, while reconstructing structures that were violated. Although the design of *mal-rules* is time consuming, they can enable fine-tuned error distinctions that statistical parsers would have a hard time dealing with. Consider example (1), below:

(1)   * *This cats like ball.*

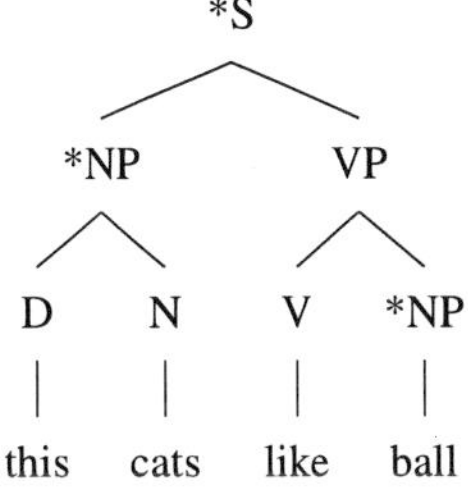

Diagnosing (1) as ungrammatical is just the first step. The subsequent decision of how to correct this sentence is a much harder task. Without context, at least four corrections (2 to 5) should be considered (but more exist).

(2)   *These cats like the ball.*

(3)   *These cats like balls.*

(4)   *This cat likes the ball.*

(5)   *This cat likes balls.*

From a pedagogical point of view, each of these corrections should elicit different kinds of corrective feedback. While

---

dealing with this ambiguity might seem daunting for some statistical systems, a few *mal-rules* would allow this sentence to be parsed while reconstructing all of the meanings shown above. Describing the inner workings of *mal-rules* is outside the scope of this paper – a fuller account of how *mal-rules* and semantic reconstruction can be used in Computer Assisted Language Learning can be found in Morgado da Costa et al. (2016).

However, the important aspects of using *mal-rules* is that they can apply to syntactic and semantic structures, as well as individual lexical items. This enables *mal-rules* to be used for both error detection and error correction.

From a pedagogical perspective, however, providing a corrected form for an ungrammatical sentence is not enough to engage students in active learning. Because of this, within CALLIG we perform only grammatical error detection. Detected error can then be used to provide feedback messages and guide students towards a successful correction of a problematic sentence.

CALLIG's error detection technology is mostly inspired by and builds on previous work by Suppes et al. (2014) and Flickinger and Yu (2013), who have showed that the use of computational parsers, such as the English Resource Grammar (Copestake and Flickinger, 2000; Flickinger, 2000), to evaluate the grammatical correctness of the written work of individual students yields significant positive results. The use of this kind of technology can be used to reduce the workload of teachers in their attempt to evaluate written sentences produced by each of their students in a timely manner.

6. Improvisation Games in CALLIG

CALLIG's ultimate goal is to build a collection of fun improvisation games, explore language learning contexts and provide opportunities for spontaneous and witty language use. We currently have four implemented games. We will give an account of each of these games below.

6.1. Sex with Me

Sex with Me is a one-liner game. The player will be given a prompt with the form: *"Sex with me is like a/an [object]!"* The object is randomly generated by the system. For words that we consider not common, definitions would be provided. The player can read the definition by hovering the cursor over the word.

The goal of the game is to justify why *sex with me* is like the randomly generated object. The player has to come up with a justification and type it in the answer box within 40 seconds.

Some examples are given below:

Prompt: *Sex with me is like legos...*
Answer: *You need to be imaginative to make it fun.*

Prompt: *Sex with me is like depression...*
Answer: *It makes you want to sleep.*

This game, though a bit risqué, is fun and challenging. It requires the player to quickly find features shared by both sex and the object. The output is often humorous due to the unlikely combination.

There are many similar one-liner games which will likely be added to CALLIG in the future – **Famous Last Words** and **Pick up Lines** are some examples. In **Famous Last Words**, the prompt would be the name of a famous figure (dead or alive; real or fictional), and the input would be the last line that the figure utters before dying, making use of common knowledge of such figures. In **Pick up Lines**, the prompt would be an occupation, and the input would be a pick-up line uttered by someone with that occupation, playing with stereotypes of different occupations..

6.2. Haiku on Demand

Haiku is a short form of Japanese poetry, containing 3 lines and comprising 17 syllables: 5 (1st line), 7 (2nd line) and 5 (3rd line). The 3rd line often contains an observation about a fleeting moment in nature. It is simple, direct and intense. It focuses on the juxtaposition of images and a sudden revelation at the end with a sense of enlightenment. In this game, a random poem title is generated by the system. The generation of title follows one of multiple predefined patterns using a mix of parts-of-speech and frequency information. For example, one of such patterns is the combination of a determiner, an adjective and a noun into a noun phrase (e.g., *"my oversized urinal"*, *"the hysterical assumption"*). Another of such patterns is a modified verb phrase, comprised of a uninflected verb and an adverb (e.g., *"conjugate cold-bloodily"*, *"internalize pungently"*).

After the random title is generated, the user is then prompted to input the three lines of the haiku. A custom-made syllable-checker is ran after the Haiku is completed to confirm that the input has the desired number of syllables. The user has to come up with a haiku of the given title within 90 seconds. Here is an example:

Prompt: *The rude bug*
Answer: *Small and poisonous*
It lies on the floor, panting
And the light turns green

In the future we would like to explore some variations to this simple setting. These variations include, for example, in addition to a randomly-generated title, there would be a randomly generated word that needs to be placed at the last line of the haiku to force an unexpected ending. Yet another variation could be to reduce the allocated time with every completed Haiku – making it increasingly harder to complete the game.

6.3. Wicked Proverbs

A proverb is a well-known piece of wisdom that advises you on how to live properly, for example *"The squeaky wheel gets the grease."* (intended meaning: those who complain will get attention). Proverbs exist in all languages, but are often language/culture specific (e.g., similar messages are often expressed using different concepts).

The goal of this game is to invite the user to create a proverb-style piece of wisdom using randomly generated *must-use* words and provide an explanation. Some examples include:

Prompt: *Must use: "chocolate" and "chopsticks"*

Proverb: *Sex is like eating chocolate with chopsticks*
Explanation: *if it gets too hot you have a mess*

Proverb: *A good marriage is like chocolate chopsticks.*
Explanation: *always a sweet pair*

The game is timed at 90 seconds per proverb plus explanation, which is deemed to be enough for the user to come up with an idea without allowing the users to think too much about it (which would be undesirable).

Interesting variations of this game could include a randomized required length for the Wicked Proverb (e.g., a number from 5 to 20), which would also influence the number of *must-use* words generated. There could also be a repetition mode, where users are prompted to provide three Wicked Proverbs using the same constraints.

6.4. Forced Links

Forced Links is an association game. The user is given two unrelated words as a prompt (e.g., *tea* and *koala*), and is asked to come up with a chain of words that would connect the two given words within 20 seconds (e.g., *tea, England, Australia, koala*). It is essentially a game based on semantic association. It reveals patterns of relatedness among different words among different speakers. The two related words given as the prompt can be nouns or adjectives. There is no restriction on the part of speech of the linking words nor on the number of linking words.

7. The System

CALLIG is still under development, and it is mainly developed on top of existing open-source platforms. At its core, it is a modular web system developed using Python, Flask[8] and Bootstrap.[9] The system is fully open-source, and easy to expand in scope. The use of flexible web technologies such as Bootstrap also ensures that it can easily be played on mobile devices.

Each game in CALLIG has an introduction page with instructions on how the play the game, as well as a randomized sample of responses by previous players on the top of the page. These responses include information about the author (username) and the time it took them to complete that particular game, which can be used as a competitive measure among players (i.e., being able to come up with a funny response under time pressure can be seen as an achievement). Figure 1 shows the introduction page for the game **Wicked Proverbs**.

The game page differs for each game, but generally include a prompt (e.g., the title, in the case of **Haiku on Demand**; or words that must be used, in the case of **Wicked Proverbs**), some input boxes for the answers and a timer. The duration of this timer varies from game to game, and the user will lose the ability to submit an answer once the timer runs out. Examples of how the user plays these games can be seen in Figures 2 and 3.

7.1. Simulation of Audience Suggestions

In an improvisation performance, suggestions are elicited from the audience. In CALLIG, suggestions are randomly

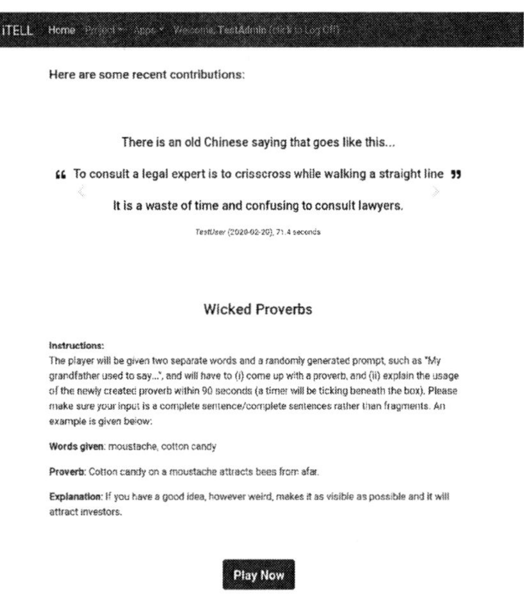

Figure 1: Introduction page for **Wicked Proverbs** game

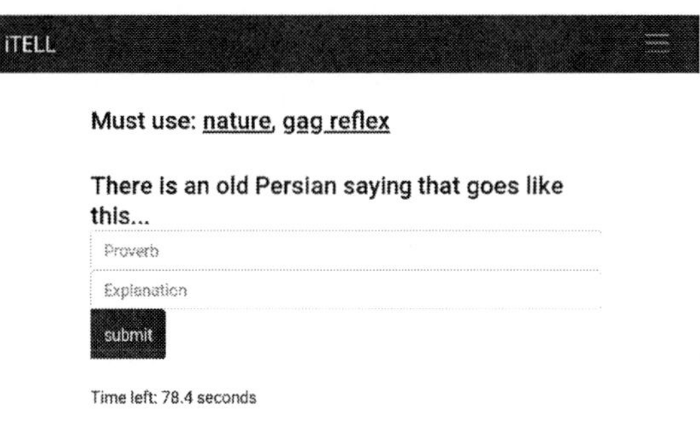

Figure 2: Example of **Wicked Proverbs** being played

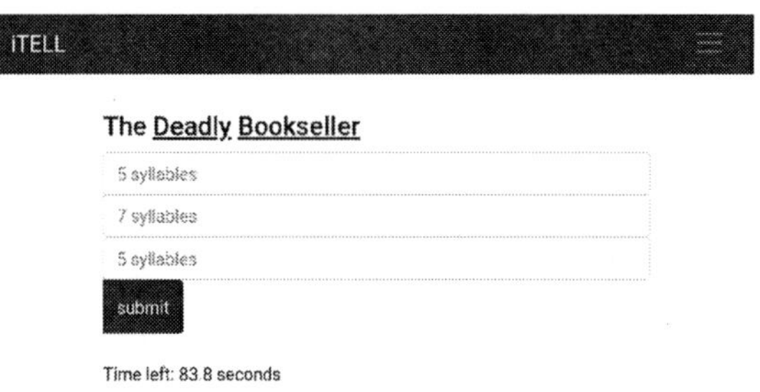

Figure 3: Example of **Haiku on Demand** being played

generated by the system. These two types of suggestions are not identical. Suggestions elicited from an audience are almost always interesting (and potentially amusing) since audience members suggest ideas they want to see developed on stage. Furthermore, the host of the game has the option of choosing a suggestion among the many given. This also gives the option of getting rid of undesirable suggestions. Within CALLIG, audience suggestions (e.g., for the title of the Haiku, or for must *use words* in other games) are gener-

---

[8]http://flask.pocoo.org/

[9]https://getbootstrap.com/

ated with the help of the Princeton English Wordnet (Fellbaum, 1998), which is accessed using the API provided by the Natural Language Toolkit (Bird, 2006).

Wordnets are often large lexical databases, where open class words (i.e., nouns, verbs, adjectives and adverbs) are grouped by sets of synonyms into semantic concepts. These concepts are linked to each other by semantic relations, such as hyponymy (i.e., *a type of*) and meronomy (i.e., *part-whole*). This rich semantic graph also allows the encoding of some measure of semantic distance, which is useful for certain games (i.e., **Forced Links**).

The Princeton English Wordnet is used in tandem with curated wordlists designed specifically for each game. While the wordnet is able to provide a level of true randomness, curated lists of words and expressions are used to maintain a level of familiarity and humor that would be expected from a real-life audience. It should be noted that the system can function perfectly without such curated lists. True randomness sometimes generates concepts that are infrequent, and possibly unknown to the user. Concepts like this come with a definition, provided by the wordnet, that is accessible to users by hovering the mouse on top of the suggested words. This can also be used as a way to introduce new vocabulary to second language learners. The mixture of randomized items from Wordnet and curated wordlists ensure that users won't be given too many unfamiliar words consecutively, which might lead to frustration.

Despite our attempts to control these simulated suggestions the best we can, there is no guarantee that all suggestions are meaningful or sensible. For examples, in **Haiku on Demand**, the system has generated titles like "the weak pisha paysha" and "the handsewn welterweight". The generation of this kind of nonsensical titles often has to do with semantic mismatch that is too far apart for the user's interpretative accommodation. The current way to address this is to allow users to refresh the game and get a new prompt if they don't like the one they are given. These infelicitous suggestions are kept by the system, and can be used to prevent similar suggestions in the future.

7.2. Linguistic Adequacy and Feedback

Whenever appropriate, CALLIG tries to enforce certain degrees of linguistic adequacy. This is the pedagogical dimension of the system. It tries to use each game to enable "learnable moments" throughout the user experience. The system tries to be as precise as possible, ignoring problems when it isn't prepared to provide useful feedback.

This linguistic adequacy takes different forms in different games. In the **Haiku on Demand** game, for example, only answers that respect the syllable count for each line are accepted as a valid answer. If the user fails to follow the 5-7-5 syllable constraint, then they will be notified and prompted to try again. Our hope is that this will raise the user's awareness of how to count syllables, a skill that can help with pronunciation and fluency in a foreign language.

Given **Haiku on Demand**'s poetic nature, there would not be much sense to perform strict grammatical checks in this game. For other games, however, such as **Sex with Me** and **Wicked Proverbs**, grammatical checks are appropriate. Following the discussion presented in Section 5, CALLIG

is able to identify around 50 different classes of grammatical errors using a special version of the English Resource Grammar (Copestake and Flickinger, 2000; Flickinger, 2000) expanded with *mal-rules*. The selection of these error classes was done using corpora that identified common grammatical errors among undergraduate student population, such as the NTU (Nanyang Technological University) Corpus of Learner English (Winder et al., 2017) and the NUS (National University of Singapore) Corpus of Learner English (Dahlmeier et al., 2013). Our system is currently able to detect a wide variety of common errors. These error classes include: problems with subject-verb agreement; the omission of articles for singular count nouns; the use of indefinite articles with mass nouns; and the use of the wrong form of the indefinite article "a/an"; "their/there" confusion; "its/it's" confusion; irregular forms of past tense, etc.. More than one error can exist in each sentence. And for each error identified in a sentence, the system will generate a constructive feedback message that aims to explain the error and help the user to avoid it in the future. When the system is unsure what is wrong with a sentence, then the error is completely ignored. This is done with the user's experience in mind, as flagging too many ungrammatical sentences might be demotivating for the user. The available error checks and constructive feedback messages present in CALLIG were adapted from the work presented in Morgado da Costa et al. (2020).

Similar to what happens with **Haiku on Demand**, after submitting and answer to **Sex with Me** or **Wicked Proverbs**, the user's answer is checked for grammaticality. Figure 4 shows an example of an answer that was deemed ungrammatical by the system. In this case, the system is able to correctly identify the lack of a determiner before the noun "jungle".

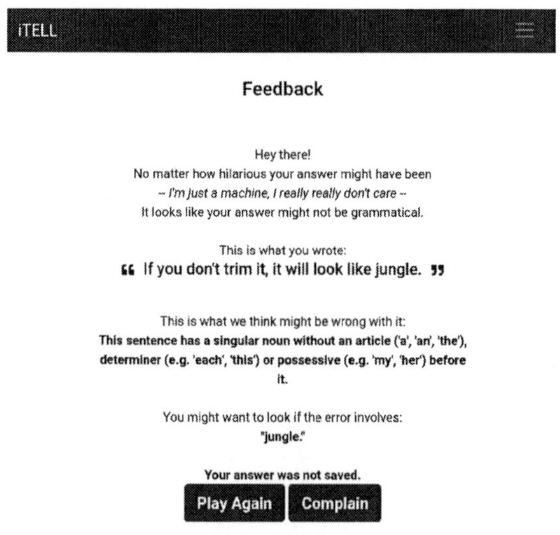

Figure 4: Example of constructive feedback provided for an ungrammatical answer in **Sex with Me**

8. Future Extensions

As mentioned before, CALLIG is still very much under development. As such, in this section we will outline the main dimensions we would like to expand our system to cover in the near future.

8.1. Future Games

As the central aspect of CALLIG, we are constantly researching possible games to adapt and make available through our system. In principle, games must satisfy at least one of two requirements: a) they must be able to focus on some aspect of language learning that CALLIG is able to control and diagnose; or b) they must produce relevant linguistic data related to creativity or humour that can be used in further research on creativity, humour or language learning. In addition to variations of already existing games, we are currently considering the implementation of the following games:

Give Me Ten

This is a game where the user is asked to produce a list of 10 items. This game takes a few forms, for example: a) *"10 ways to describe a/an entity"*; b) *"10 things you cannot do in a structure or geographical location"*; or c) *"10 things you cannot say to a/an person"*

Each pattern contains a semantic category, namely *entity*, *structure* or *geographical location* and *person*. To generate prompts, the system needs only to randomly extract a hyponym of the semantic category in the given pattern, for example: *"10 things to describe a banana"*, *"10 things you cannot do in a church"*, *"10 things you cannot do in China"*, *"10 things you cannot say to a priest"* (etc.).[10]

A potential variation for this game, likely increasing its difficulty, would be to have a pattern containing two slots for randomly drawn items belonging to the same category, for example, *"10 things you can do in France but not in China"*; or *"10 things you can say to Jesus not to but Buddha"*.

Reverse Trivial Pursuit

In this game, the system prompt should be interpreted as an answer. The goal of the game is for the user to provide as many possible questions as possible. For example, if the answer generated is *"my intellect"*, some potential questions would be *"What is your most valuable possession?"*, *"What is the sharpest thing in the world?"*, *"What is the thing that makes you unattractive?"*, etc. The system can generate single words or phrases as prompts. As usual, a timer would be used to create pressure and the user would try to input as many questions as possible.

This game would be especially interesting to test and help with the formation of questions, as all the user answers should be in the form of a question.

Famous Conversations that Never Existed

---

[10]This is similar to the challenge "Scenes we'd like to see" in the British panel show "Mock the Week" where comic contestants take turn coming up with witty one-liners on different given scenarios, except that in our game, 10 answers are needed consecutively.

Dialogues introduce different language registers that contrasts greatly with poetic or narrative styles introduced by other games. Dialogues are often casual, and elicit the use of linguistic constructions that are more frequent in this style of writing (e.g., questions, orders, interjections, etc.) The goal of this game is for the user to create a dialogue between two characters meeting in a specific location. Both characters and locations should be randomly generated. These characters can be fictional characters or famous people (e.g., Batman, Shrek, Jesus, Gandhi) or regular occupations (e.g., plumber, doctor). The location can be geographical locations (e.g., China) or structures (e.g., a submarine, a closet, etc.).

A random number of lines for each character would be generated, and the user would then be prompted to fill the empty lines with a coherent dialogue between the two characters based on possible relations between the characters and their current location. This game tests the user's ability to relate randomly selected items (characters and location) and weave all the elements into a sensible whole (the dialogue). Ideally, this game would be played line-by-line, and once submitted a line would be irreversible. As usual users would have a timer to complete each line (e.g., 15 seconds). This game allows a great number of variations, which would resort to restricting the users' input in some way: e.g., disallowing all questions, allowing only wh-questions, providing sentence length restrictions (e.g., minimum, maximum or exact number of words), and provision of *must-use* words for a given line.

8.2. Advanced Linguistic Constraints

With the use of the English Resource Grammar (ERG), CALLIG is also able to impose and check for certain classes of advanced linguistic constraints. For example, similar to what happens with **Haiku on Demand**, where the system is checking the number of syllables per line of input, using the ERG would allow our system to check if specific syntactic phenomena had been used. For example, the system could request and check if a passive construction or a definite noun phrase was used in a specific input. These specific linguistic requirements can also be incorporated in game design, e.g., an improvisational language game that focuses on question formation (see **Reverse Trivial Pursuit**). In other words, we would like to further explore the full range syntactic and semantic information provided by the ERG to improve our game design and to more tightly relate our games with certain aspects of language structure and fluency.

8.3. Social and Collaborative Gaming

Despite being hosted online, where users can see other people's answers, the current implementation of our games focuses on a single player environment.

Currently, the system takes the role of the host and the audience in an improvisation game, providing instructions as well as suggestions for the games. Nevertheless, adding social features to it would enable us to dwell deeper into performance style improvisation games, as well as allow meaningful interaction between users. We would like to extend the social and collaborative setting of CALLIG in two ways:

1. We would like to build a social platform that will enable users to save, post and share the results of their interaction with the system. This platform would allow users to publish the writings they feel the most proud of, and share them on social media. The published works will be accessible to all, and registered users will be able to upvote or downvote other users' writings (possibly even on a scale).

2. Improvisation, as a performance, is generally collaborative in nature, resorting to the use of a "group mind" to create something unpredictable. In the future, we would like to have spaces to explore this "group mind" by introducing collaborative gaming (i.e., chat-room style gaming). Different users can be playing the same game where multiple users are required to work together to create a coherent whole, and each active user takes turns in guiding the development of the narrative. Having this feature would allow us to add games that have been left out because they only make sense in a collaborative setting, as well as different variations of already implemented games. An example of this would be a variation of the game **Famous Conversations that Never Existed**, where instead of having a single user writing the dialog between two characters, we can have two users taking the role of each character and build a dialogue together. This brings in the element of unpredictability and requires flexibility on the user to adjust depending on what the other user has contributed.

8.4. Multilingual Support

Given the mostly language agnostic design of our games, we believe that most of the games currently implemented in CALLIG could easily be supported in other languages. With some exceptions (e.g., the syllable counter for *Haiku on Demand*), most of the language technology we use revolves around the semantic hierarchy provided by a WordNet. Fortunately, resources such as the Open Multilingual Wordnet (Bond and Foster, 2013) include parallel semantic data for hundreds of languages, facilitating this process.

The first language we would like to experiment with is Mandarin Chinese. Mandarin Chinese is a fairly well-resourced language including, for example, the Open Chinese Wordnet (Wang and Bond, 2013) – also integrated in the OMW. Also, despite being a completely optional resource within CALLIG, Mandarin Chinese also has computational grammar – ZHONG (Fan et al., 2015) – which is also being used to build an error CALL (Morgado da Costa et al., 2016). The existence of both a wordnet and a computational parser enhanced with *mal-rules* make Mandarin Chinese an ideal candidate to test CALLIG's ability to support other languages.

9.   Applied Usages

The creative outcomes (different formats of spontaneous writings) produced by users' interaction with CALLIG will generate a lot of spontaneously written data (e.g., semantic association, humour ranking of different forms of creative writings, etc.). This in turn can serve as a rich resource for both creativity studies and linguistic studies. For instance, games that require complete sentence input (when Grammatical Error Detection is performed) can generate data on grammatical errors, the game **Forced Links** provides association data between words, **Give Me Ten** can be used to derive commonsense knowledge, or to enrich semantic hierarchies, such as wordnets, by generating definitions and semantic associations for different entities. Games like **Give Me Ten** can potentially also provide data relevant for studies on phenomena such as the Serial Order Effect (Beaty and Silvia, 2012), by confirming whether remote associations are, as expected, reached later than obvious associations.

Improvisation often generates humour. However, improvisation performances are not generally transcribed, humour studies based on improvisation data are rare, if they exist at all. In CALLIG, we hope to have, in the near future, improvisation data with funniness ranking readily available for humour research. The data can then be subject to different kinds of text analysis, or repackaged for experimental use.

10.   Release Notes

This application is released as part of a larger project entitled iTELL. All its components, including CALLIG, are released under under an MIT License. The project is available on Github at `https://github.com/lmorgadodacosta/iTELL`.

11.   Conclusions

In this paper, we introduced the on-going development of CALLIG (Computer-Assisted Language Learning using Improvisational Games), a system that uses language technology to create online games with elements of improvisation. We have presented four available games, and discussed how we are integrating CALL technology to perform grammatical error detection and are able to provide timely feedback to advanced learners of English.

Improvisation provides opportunities to exercise the muscles of creativity, especially in the area of divergent thinking and remote association. Improvisation games have been used in second language teaching and learning due to its openness and flexibility. Improvisation allows the co-existence of *structure* and *freedom to explore* for both teachers and students, and is deemed an excellent tool for language training. Improvisation exercises in language classrooms, as of now, require the physical presence of a group of people. And despite its possible benefits, it is fair to state that there are people who do not feel comfortable physically performing these games (in public on in a classroom). CALLIG provides a platform for playing language games in a more private and less labour-intensive setting. It can be useful to build confidence before leaping to physical performances, or as training ground for important skills such as spontaneity, collaboration, and risk-taking.

Despite being in its early stages of development, CALLIG is now fully functional, and it has started to generate data in a closed beta environment. We hope this data will soon be useful to multiple lines of research – including but not limited to research on second language learning, lexical semantics, common sense reasoning, humor and creativity.

12. Acknowledgements

Even though CALLIG is not yet a public platform at this moment, we have opened it for a selected group of people for testing purposes. This includes, but not limited to, students and staff of the improvisation team from Palacký University, a few linguistic colleagues around the world as well as a few improvsation and stand-up comedians from Singapore. Even though it won't be possible to thank them all individually here due to space, we would like to thank them as a group and we are very grateful for their help and input.

An earlier version of this system was discussed at the 8th International Biennial Conference of the French Association for Cognitive Linguistics (AFLiCo) - "Language, Cognition, and Creativity" in Mulhouse, France (5-7 Jun 2019). We would to thank the Department of English and American Studies at Palacký University and the Interdisciplinary Graduate School at Nanyang Technological University for their financial support.

13. Bibliographical References

Beaty, R. E. and Silvia, P. J. (2012). Why do ideas get more creative across time? an executive interpretation of the serial order effect in divergent thinking tasks. *Psychology of Aesthetics, Creativity, and the Arts*, 6(4):309.

Bird, S. (2006). NLTK: the natural language toolkit. In *Proceedings of the COLING/ACL on Interactive presentation sessions*, pages 69–72. Association for Computational Linguistics.

Bond, F. and Foster, R. (2013). Linking and extending an Open Multilingual Wordnet. In *51st Annual Meeting of the Association for Computational Linguistics: ACL-2013, Sofia*, pages 1352–1362.

Bryant, C., Felice, M., Andersen, Ø. E., and Briscoe, T. (2019). The bea-2019 shared task on grammatical error correction. In *Proceedings of the Fourteenth Workshop on Innovative Use of NLP for Building Educational Applications*, pages 52–75.

Copestake, A. and Flickinger, D. (2000). An open source grammar development environment and broad-coverage English grammar using HPSG. In *In proceedings of LREC 2000*, pages 591–600.

Dahlmeier, D., Ng, H. T., and Wu, S. M. (2013). Building a large annotated corpus of learner English: The NUS corpus of learner English. In *BEA@ NAACL-HLT*, pages 22–31.

Dale, R. and Kilgarriff, A. (2011). Helping our own: The HOO 2011 pilot shared task. In *Proceedings of the 13th European Workshop on Natural Language Generation*, pages 242–249. Association for Computational Linguistics.

Dale, R., Anisimoff, I., and Narroway, G. (2012). HOO 2012: A report on the preposition and determiner error correction shared task. In *Proceedings of the Seventh Workshop on Building Educational Applications Using NLP*, pages 54–62. Association for Computational Linguistics.

Daudaravicius, V., Banchs, R. E., Volodina, E., and Napoles, C. (2016). A report on the automatic evaluation of scientific writing shared task. In *Proceedings of the 11th Workshop on Innovative Use of NLP for Building Educational Applications*, pages 53–62.

Deterding, S., Dixon, D., Khaled, R., and Nacke, L. (2011). From game design elements to gamefulness: defining gamification. In *Proceedings of the 15th international academic MindTrek conference: Envisioning future media environments*, pages 9–15. ACM.

Fan, Z., Song, S., and Bond, F. (2015). An hpsg-based shared-grammar for the chinese languages: Zhong [—]. In *Proceedings of the Grammar Engineering Across Frameworks (GEAF) Workshop*, pages 17–24.

Fellbaum, C. (1998). *Wordnet: An electronic lexical database*. MIT Press Cambridge.

Flickinger, D. and Yu, J. (2013). Toward more precision in correction of grammatical errors. In *Proceedings of the Seventeenth Conference on Computational Natural Language Learning: Shared Task, CoNLL 2013, Sofia, Bulgaria, August 8-9, 2013*, pages 68–73.

Flickinger, D. (2000). On building a more effcient grammar by exploiting types. *Natural Language Engineering*, 6(01):15–28.

Gamper, J. and Knapp, J. (2002). A review of intelligent CALL systems. *Computer Assisted Language Learning*, 15(4):329–342.

Garcia, I. (2013). Learning a language for free while translating the web. does duolingo work? *International Journal of English Linguistics*, 3(1):19.

Guilford, J. P. (1967). *The nature of human intelligence*. McGraw-Hill.

Hamari, J., Koivisto, J., and Sarsa, H. (2014). Does gamification work?–a literature review of empirical studies on gamification. In *2014 47th Hawaii International Conference on System Sciences*, pages 3025–3034. IEEE.

Kapp, K. M. (2012). *The gamification of learning and instruction: game-based methods and strategies for training and education*. John Wiley & Sons.

Kornell, N. (2009). Optimising learning using flashcards: Spacing is more effective than cramming. *Applied Cognitive Psychology*, 23(9):1297–1317.

Kurtz, J. (2011). Breaking through the communicative cocoon: Improvisation in secondary school foreign language classrooms. *Structure and improvisation in creative teaching*, pages 133–161.

Mednick, S. (1962). The associative basis of the creative process. *Psychological review*, 69(3):220.

Morgado da Costa, L., Bond, F., and Xiaoling, H. (2016). Syntactic well-formedness diagnosis and error-based coaching in computer assisted language learning using machine translation. In *Proceedings of the 3rd Workshop on Natural Language Processing Techniques for Educational Applications (NLPTEA2016)*, pages 107–116, Osaka, Japan. The COLING 2016 Organizing Committee.

Morgado da Costa, L., Winder, R. V. P., Li, S. Y., Liang, B. C. L. T., Mackinnon, J., and Bond, F. (2020). Automated writing support using deep linguistic parsers (in print). In *Proceedings of the 12th Conference on Language Resources and Evaluation*, Marseille, France, may. European Language Resources Association (ELRA).

Ng, H. T., Wu, S. M., Wu, Y., Hadiwinoto, C., and

Tetreault, J. (2013). The CoNLL-2013 shared task on grammatical error correction. In *Proceedings of the Seventeenth Conference on Computational Natural Language Learning: Shared Task*, pages 1–12, Sofia, Bulgaria, August. Association for Computational Linguistics.

Ng, H. T., Wu, S. M., Briscoe, T., Hadiwinoto, C., Susanto, R. H., and Bryant, C. (2014). The CoNLL-2014 shared task on grammatical error correction. In *CoNLL Shared Task*, pages 1–14.

Sawyer, R. K. (2011a). *Structure and improvisation in creative teaching*. Cambridge University Press.

Sawyer, R. K. (2011b). What makes good teachers great? the artful balance of structure and improvisation. *Structure and improvisation in creative teaching*, pages 1–24.

Schneider, D. and McCoy, K. F. (1998). Recognizing syntactic errors in the writing of second language learners. In *Proceedings of the 17th International Conference on Computational Linguistics - Volume 2*, COLING '98, pages 1198–1204, Stroudsburg, PA, USA. Association for Computational Linguistics.

Schulze, M. (2008). AI in CALL – artificially inflated or almost imminent? *Calico Journal*, 25(3):510–527.

Sio, U. S. J. and Wee, L. H. (2012). Teaching linguistics using improvised comedy. In *Language Arts in Asia: Literature and Drama in English, Putonghua and Cantonese*, pages 283–302. Cambridge Scholars Publishing.

Suppes, P., Liang, T., Macken, E. E., and Flickinger, D. P. (2014). Positive technological and negative pretest-score effects in a four-year assessment of low socioeconomic status k-8 student learning in computer-based math and language arts courses. *Computers & Education*, 71:23–32.

Tu, C.-H., Sujo-Montes, L. E., and Yen, C.-J. (2015). Gamification for learning. In *Media Rich Instruction*, pages 203–217. Springer.

Wang, S. and Bond, F. (2013). Building the Chinese Open Wordnet (COW): Starting from core synsets. In *Proceedings of the 11th Workshop on Asian Language Resources, a Workshop at IJCNLP-2013*, pages 10–18, Nagoya.

Winder, R. V. P., MacKinnon, J., Li, S. Y., Lin, B., Heah, C., Morgado da Costa, L., Kuribayashi, T., and Bond, F. (2017). NTUCLE: Developing a corpus of learner English to provide writing support for engineering students. In *Proceedings of the 4th Workshop on NLP Techniques for Educational Applications (NLPTEA 2017)*, Taipei, Taiwan. (IJCNLP 2017 Workshop).

Proceedings of the LREC 2020 Workshop Games and Natural Language Processing, pages 59–67
Language Resources and Evaluation Conference (LREC 2020), Marseille, 11–16 May 2020
© European Language Resources Association (ELRA), licensed under CC-BY-NC

Bringing Roguelikes to Visually-Impaired Players by Using NLP

Jesús Vilares, Carlos Gómez-Rodríguez, Luís Fernández-Núñez, Darío Penas, Jorge Viteri

Universidade da Coruña, CITIC, LyS Research Group, Dept. of Computer Science & Information Technologies
Facultade de Informática, Campus de Elviña, 15071 – A Coruña, Spain
{jesus.vilares,carlos.gomez,j.viteri.letamendia}@udc.es {fernandezn.luis,dariosoyyo}@gmail.com

Abstract

Although the roguelike video game genre has a large community of fans (both players and developers) and the graphic aspect of these games is usually given little relevance (ASCII-based graphics are not rare even today), their accessibility for blind players and other visually-impaired users remains a pending issue. In this document, we describe an initiative for the development of roguelikes adapted to visually-impaired players by using Natural Language Processing techniques, together with the first completed games resulting from it. These games were developed as Bachelor's and Master's theses. Our approach consists in integrating a multilingual module that, apart from the classic ASCII-based graphical interface, automatically generates text descriptions of what is happening within the game. The visually-impaired user can then read such descriptions by means of a screen reader. In these projects we seek expressivity and variety in the descriptions, so we can offer the users a fun roguelike experience that does not sacrifice any of the key characteristics that define the genre. Moreover, we intend to make these projects easy to extend to other languages, thus avoiding costly and complex solutions.

Keywords: Natural Language Generation, roguelikes, visually-impaired users

1. Introduction

One of the main factors for the huge growth of the video game industry has been the radical improvement of the graphic quality of video games. Paradoxically, this fact significantly hinders the access to these products by users with severe visual impairments such as blindness. Aware of this situation, some members of our Natural Language Processing (NLP) research group[1] decided to do our small part to help. Within this initiative, named TOP PLAYER LYS,[2] we have been offering to our students the chance of developing specially adapted roguelike games as their Bachelor's or Master's theses. These games should be accessible to both sighted and visually-impaired players by using NLP techniques (Jurafsky and Martin, 2009; Manning and Schütze, 1999). To do this, the games offer, apart from the standard game mode, a *descriptive mode* intended for visually-impaired users. In this game mode, the classic graphic representation of the dungeon and its elements is replaced by automatically generated natural language descriptions.

The choice of this particular genre is intentional and is due to several factors: the fact of being a game genre yet to adapt to this type of users; the existence of a large and well organized fan community, including both players and developers; and the relatively low value given to the graphic quality in these games. This allows us to ignore accessory aspects and focus on generating an accurate description.

This initiative of ours presents different aspects of interest, both at the social and academic levels. From a social point of view, we are not only concerned with how to extend the current offer of this type of entertainment to this sector of the population, but also with favoring their integration, since both sighted and visually-impaired users can play the same game and, thus, share common experiences. By helping draw students' attention to accessibility concerns, students will be aware of them when they go on to become software developers. Finally, from an academic point of

view, this type of final-year projects allow us to introduce the student to NLP in a practical and engaging way. This is not a minor issue for us since no NLP course is currently available in our Computer Engineering Degree.

Regarding the rest of the paper, Section 2. describes the tools available to visually-impaired users and the relation of these users with video games. Next, Section 3. introduces the roguelike genre, its main features, and why this genre was chosen for this initiative. Section 4. makes a detailed analysis of the pre-requisites to be taken into account. Section 5., the core of this document, describes the games we have developed until now, their architecture, the linguistic levels involved and the solutions applied. Finally, Section 6. outlines our conclusions and future work.

2. Visually-Impaired Users

Tiflotechnology is a type of assistive technology that enables the practical use of high-tech devices to people who are blind or with low vision (Hersh and Johnson, 2008). Regarding computers, some of the proposed solutions involve the use of screen reader software (e.g. JAWS,[3] NVDA[4] and ORCA[5]), screen magnifiers (either software or hardware), OCR software and refreshable braille displays, among others. In the case of Web navigation, a careless design of a website may prevent screen readers from working properly on it. To avoid this, it is very important to follow basic accessibility guidelines, such as the WCAG 2 (W3C, 2018), to create a user-friendly website for blind people.

Another interesting issue is the fact that most software developers, even when designing accessible software, do not take into account that, when operating a computer, blind users often work in pairs with a sighted partner to help them in the event of a problem. Therefore, an accessible interface should make the same updated information available

---

[1] http://www.grupolys.org/
[2] http://www.grupolys.org/~jvilares/topplayerENG.html

[3] http://www.freedomscientific.com/Products/software/JAWS/
[4] http://www.nvaccess.org/
[5] http://wiki.gnome.org/Projects/Orca

to both the visually-impaired user and their sighted partner in every moment.

Concerning computer games, paradoxically, technological advances have made them less and less accessible to this sector of society. *Interactive text adventures*, for example, were a big part of the early days of gaming back in the 70s and part of the 80s (Barton, 2008). In this game genre, gameplay consists in reading brief text passages describing the current state of the game. In response, the player types a brief command describing the action to be taken by the main character of the story which, in turn, results in a new state. These input commands consist in simple phrase constructions, mainly directions and VERB+OBJECT structures. Their origin dates back to 1975, when Will Crowther, a professional programmer, designed and distributed the game *Colossal Cave Adventure* on the ARPANET, becoming a very popular title. By not containing graphics, except perhaps some static graphic as a supplement to the setting, they could be played by blind gamers by using text-to-speech synthesizers.

However, the progressive improvements of computers in terms of computing power and graphic capabilities, together with the availability of better and cheaper video terminals, made mainstream computer games progressively more focused on graphical aspects. As a result, games became less and less accessible for the blind, who were relegated to more mundane and simple games, such as board or card game adaptations. This led some developers to adapt certain computer games for the blind by modifying their sound effects and, subsequently, creating games based solely on audio. These so-called *audio games* focus on the possibilities of game immersion through audio. The appearance of 3D positional sound in the 2000s made it possible to somehow represent the position of elements in space through sound. This allowed audio game developers to approach new genres (Urbanek and Güldenpfennig, 2019).

3. The Roguelike Genre

The origin of this genre is in the computer game *Rogue*, created by two enthusiasts, Michael Toy and Glenn Wichman, in the early 80s (Craddock, 2015). Originally developed for UNIX mainframes, it became very popular after being included with BSD UNIX, thus making it virtually available at universities all over the world and giving birth to the *Rogue*-like genre.

Influenced by sword-and-sorcery tabletop role-playing games, in *Rogue* the player controls a hero who explores a dungeon complex. As the player's character defeats lurking monsters, avoids traps and discovers treasures, they will be awarded with *experience points*. As the character gains experience, they become stronger, so they can face greater challenges. The dungeon also hides a multitude of items such as weapons, armors, amulets, etc., which may give extra bonuses or penalize the actions of the adventurer.

Among the main features of this first game and, by extension, of the genre, we remark the following:

- *Random environment generation.* The dungeon and its elements (enemies, traps, items, etc.) are randomly generated for every new game by using procedural

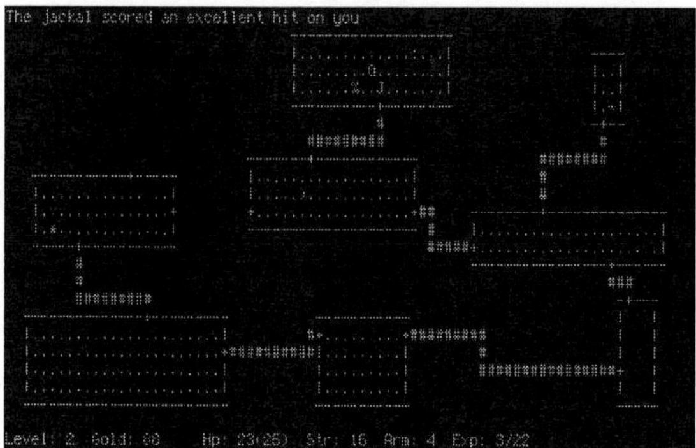

Figure 1: Gameplay screenshot of a *Rogue* UNIX clone. The dungeon map is drawn using '−' and '|' for room walls, '.' for room floors, '+' for doors, '#' for passageways between rooms, and '%' for stairs connecting dungeon levels. Regarding other characters and elements, the player's character (the hero/adventurer) is represented as an '@', an enemy monster (a jackal) as a 'J', gold coins as '*' and weapons as ')'.

content generation algorithms (Shaker et al., 2016), thus favoring replayability.

- *Random outcomes.* As with tabletop games, the calculation of the result of tactical actions, such as attacks or spells, includes a random component to add certain degree of variability and tension.

- *Permanent consequences.* Saves are only permitted between gameplay sessions and are automatically deleted after loading. This also implies that the player's character has a single life (*permadeath*).

- *Turn-based.* Each command corresponds to a single action which, in turn, takes a single turn with no time limit. This allows the player to take their time to assess the situation and decide what to do.

- *Grid-based.* The dungeon is represented by a uniform grid of orthogonal tiles, where every element (adventurer, monsters, items, etc.) takes up a single tile. Movement between tiles is atomic.

- *ASCII (pseudo-)graphics.* Although modern roguelikes, mainly commercial ones, usually have a true graphical display, classic roguelikes were played on text terminals using a text-based display instead. As depicted in Figure 1,[6] the dungeon map and its elements are drawn from a top-down view by using ASCII characters. This allows to reduce the computer requirements of the game and favors portability. Even nowadays, many roguelike fans prefer to play them, if possible, using ASCII graphics: a good roguelike should be judged according to its game mechanics and the player experience, not by its graphics.

---

[6]Obtained from *Retro Rogue Collection*: `https://github.com/mikeyk730/Rogue-Collection`

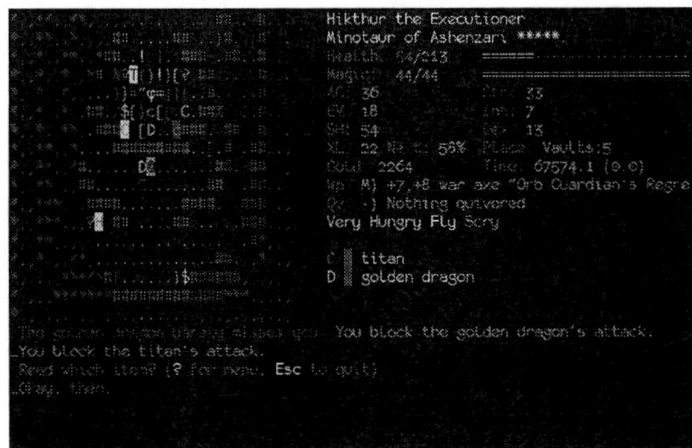

Figure 2: Gameplay screenshot of the game *Dungeon Crawl Stone Soup*, where we can see the complexity of these text-based interfaces.

Nowadays, these features may not be impressive to many current gamers but, back then, they were innovative and have had a great influence in subsequent games of all genres (Craddock, 2015).

Today, roguelike games count on a large group of enthusiastic fans, both players and developers, either amateur or professional. They are well-organized around webs such as *RogueBasin*[7] and *Temple of the Roguelike*,[8] where they share their experiences. At the commercial level, apart from the influence they had (and still have) in other genres, roguelikes are in good shape, particularly among indie developers. In the last years, the genre has even given rise to a new subgenre, the *roguelite* or *roguelike-like* games: a less strict interpretation of the genre that tries to bring it closer to the general public (Craddock, 2015).

3.1. Why Roguelikes

There are several reasons for having chosen the roguelike genre for our initiative of developing games adapted to visually-impaired players by using NLP techniques.

The very first motive was that, even having wide experience as both players and amateur developers of these games, as far as we knew no specifically adapted roguelike was available. Furthermore, our previous contacts with blind gamers supported that assumption. As one of them, who was a fan of the genre, explained to us, the only way he could play these games was by using a Braille display. This means that, every turn, he had to read the screen contents, line by line, using the gadget. In parallel, he had to form in his mind some kind of mental representation of the map, its elements and his stats, so he could make a decision about what to do next. As can be guessed by looking at Figure 2, corresponding to the popular roguelike *Dungeon Crawl Stone Soup (DCSS)*,[9] the time and mental effort needed for such a task must be noteworthy. It is not easy for a blind player to discern (and then remember) the required information about the current state of the game in such a jumble.

The second reason for our choice was the existence of an active and well-organized community of players and developers. This fact guaranteed the availability of freely-available resources (such as tutorials, code libraries, discussion forums, etc.) which should reduce the effort of implementing the core game itself, allowing us to focus on our NLP problem. Moreover, with such a wide and dedicated fan community, the chances of our work to be improved or extended to new languages increased.

Finally, as explained above, many roguelike players pay little attention to the game graphics, instead focusing on the core playing experience. This means that we do not need to worry about creating state-of-the-art graphics and, again, can mainly focus on the language generation issues.

4. Pre-Requisites

Our goal was to develop roguelike games specially adapted to visually-impaired players as Final-Year Projects (i.e., Bachelor's and Master's Theses) of a Bachelor's and Master's degree in Computer Engineering. These games should provide visually-impaired players, using natural language, with an accurate description of the dungeon and its elements, in such a way that they can assess what action to take next. This *descriptive mode* would require the use of NLP techniques (Jurafsky and Martin, 2009; Manning and Schütze, 1999). In the case of sighted players, they can keep playing the game using the standard ASCII-based *graphic mode*. However, we should also take into account a major limitation: that the curriculum of said degrees includes no NLP courses. Therefore, before launching our idea, it was necessary to establish clear prerequisites that were compatible with this context:

- It should be conceived as an introduction to NLP, since this field is not covered by the curriculum.

- The difficulty and scope of the project must fit the workload assigned to these projects: 12 ECTS credits (300 hours).

- Therefore, the main effort should focus on the development of the description generator module. The game itself should be simple, as it acts only as a "demonstration platform". Issues such as graphic quality, variety of enemies and items, creature AI, etc., should be secondary.

- The system must be designed with *multilingualism* in mind. Thus, it should be able to generate descriptions in at least two languages: English and Spanish. The reason for this is twofold. The number of potential English-speaking users is much higher, as is the availability of NLP tools and resources. On the other hand, Spanish, apart from being the native language for our students and hence an easy starting language, is also the first language of an important number of potential users and, after consulting in specialized forums, we could confirm that a good portion of them have problems with English. Furthermore, with a more complex morphology and syntax than English, it can provide an idea of the scalability of our solutions.

- At the same time, the system should be flexible and easily extensible and modifiable by third parties.

---

[7]http://www.roguebasin.com
[8]https://blog.roguetemple.com/
[9]https://crawl.develz.org/

Thus, they could improve aspects of the basic game or add new languages to the description module.

- To do this, we should avoid complex solutions. Although there is a wide community of amateur developers, we know nothing about their competence level. Our intention is that any person with basic programming skills and high-school linguistic skills should be able to extend the system, at least in part, to a new language.

- Additionally, our experience with low-resource languages suggested that the number and complexity of the linguistic resources to be used should be low. Therefore, they should be simple to obtain or build, if needed. Note that the free availability of these types of resources is often limited (Rehm and Uszkoreit, 2011).

- The collaboration of beta-testers is mandatory in a project like this, including not only sighted players but, above all, visually-impaired ones. Their perspectives are different but complementary, and reliable feedback from both sides was needed. The help obtained from specialized forums and from trainers from the National Organization of Spanish Blind People,[10] was invaluable.

- The game should allow either blind or sighted users to play the same game. This has a triple effect: (1) it makes debugging much easier; (2) when working in pairs, as described in Section 2., it makes the work of the sighted partner easier; and (3) if the same game can be played by either visually-impaired or sighted users, they will be sharing the same experience (a very similar one, at least), thus favoring integration.

- Special attention should be paid to *usage licenses*. The games should be made freely available in the Web under a non-commercial open source license. This means that third-party resources used must be compatible with such a license.

5. Game Development

Until today, we have been developed three games with different approaches to the problem. All of them are freely available under a GNU General Public License v3 at our website:

1. *The Inner Eye*, by Luis Fernández-Núñez;

2. *The Accessible Dungeon*, by Darío Penas;

3. and *Hamsun's Amulet*, by Jorge Viteri.

As an example, Figure 3 shows one screenshot of *The Accessible Dungeon*. In what follows, instead of describing them separately, we will analyze the different solutions adopted in their design and implementation together.

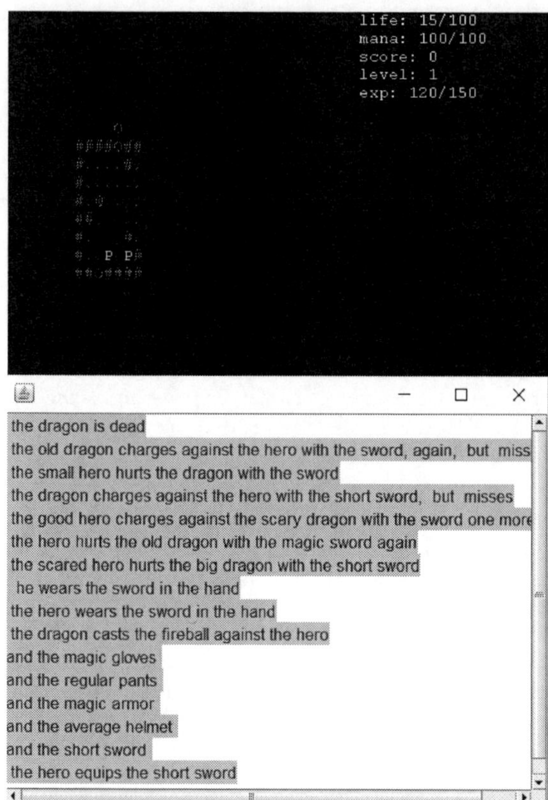

Figure 3: Gameplay screenshot of *The Accessible Dungeon* with its double display: the classic ASCII graphics (top) and the output of the description module (bottom). Note than, following a suggestion of our beta-testers, the content of this later text window must be read in reverse order (from bottom to top).

5.1. System Architecture

Figure 4 shows the general architecture of our games. The main difference with respect to regular roguelikes is the addition of a so-named *Text Description Engine* module. This new component takes as input the (current) world model and, together with the information provided by the game logic in response to the commands of the user, it generates a textual description of the dungeon and what is happening within the game. Such description is generated according to the linguistic resources available and the language selected. Regarding this new module, it follows the classic architecture of a Natural Language Generation (NLG) system. It is composed of three stages (Reiter and Dale, 2000):

- *Content planning*. Determines the content and structure of the description.

- *Microplanning*. Selects the words and syntactic structure to be used to express such content.

- *Surface realisation*. Integrates all this information and transforms the abstract representation of the message into actual text to be presented to the user.

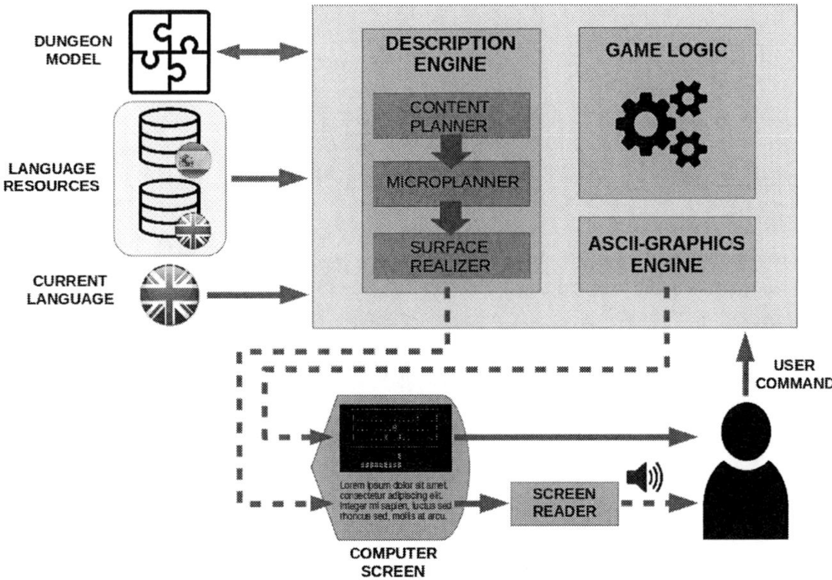

Figure 4: General architecture of the system.

Especial attention has been paid to the microplanner, seeking expressivity and variety. For this purpose, we intend to take advantage of the so-called *linguistic variation* (a.k.a. *linguistic flexibility*): the ability of our languages to express the same message in very different ways (and vice versa) (Arampatzis et al., 2000).

5.2. Linguistic Processing

The various solutions adopted cover different levels of linguistic processing, from the lexical to the pragmatic level, without losing sight of multilingualism. At this point, the languages that have been addressed are: English, Spanish, Galician and Dutch. Preliminary work has been made for Japanese, too.

5.2.1. Lexical and Morphological Levels

Firstly, it is necessary to rely on a *system vocabulary* that includes every element, action and situation that may occur or appear within the game. The terms of this vocabulary also need to be complemented with their corresponding morphosyntactic information; for example, its word category, its Part-Of-Speech (POS) tag, etc.

Each of these terms must be conveniently indexed with an external identifier. This key must be conveniently referenced in the corresponding program entities or processes with which it is involved. For instance, if the user gives the order to attack a goblin, the text generator receives from the program logic the information that the *player's character* (ID_hero) is performing an *attack action* (ID_toAttack) in which the target is a *goblin* (ID_goblin) and the instrument used is a sword (ID_sword) —the weapon they currently have equipped. In our particular case, the use of the English word lemmas as identifiers yielded good results, being both meaningful and manageable. Once obtained, the generator module can now retrieve the actual terms corresponding to those key identifiers in the currently-selected language. This procedure is very similar to the way in which assets are organized and managed during game localization (Chandler and Deming, 2011), and the way in which synsets from different languages corresponding to the same meaning are interlinked through the Interlingual Index (ILI) in the case of WordNet-like lexical resources (McCrae and Cimiano, 2015).

Finally, the system also needs to be able to obtain the inflectional variants of a term due to changes in gender, number, person, etc. To do this, one option was the use of inflectional generators (Jurafsky and Martin, 2009, Ch. 3). Taking as input the word lemma (e.g. "glorioso", Spanish for "glorious") and the required inflection (e.g. the feminine plural form), a tool of this type would generate the corresponding inflected term ("gloriosas"). However, we decided not to use these tools, at least initially. Otherwise, this would imply the need to either find an inflectional generator meeting our criteria (i.e. freely available for each of the given languages) or to build one from scratch. Both cases were problematic if we wanted to allow third parties to extend the system to new languages easily. On the one hand, this resource may not be available for every language; on the other hand, building a tool of this type from scratch requires NLP knowledge that an amateur would not have. Thus, we decided to adopt a simpler, albeit somewhat cumbersome, solution: to hold in the dictionary not only the lemma of the word, but also its inflectional variants.

These dictionaries have been implemented as JSON files because of their simplicity and flexibility. They are just text files with a structured and human-readable format, so they can be easily extended and modified even with a simple text editor. As an example, we show below the entry corresponding to the adjective "glorious" in the English dictionary of the game *The Accessible Dungeon*:

```
{
  "ADJ": {
    ...
    "glorious":
    [
        {"num": "sing"},
        {"translation": "glorious"},
        {"numopposite": "glorious"},
        {"gender": ""}
    ],
    ...
  }
}
```

as well as the entries corresponding to its translation in the Spanish dictionary,[11] also indexed by their common key identifier (i.e. the original lemma in English):

```
{
  "ADJ": {
    ...
    "glorious":
    [
        {"num": "sing"},
        {"translation": "glorioso"},
        {"numopposite": "gloriosos"},
        {"genopposite": "gloriosa"},
        {"gen": "mas"}
    ],
    "gloriosa":
    [
        {"num": "sing"},
        {"translation": "gloriosa"},
        {"numopposite": "gloriosas"},
        {"genopposite": "glorious"},
        {"gen": "fem"}
    ],
    "gloriosos":
    [
        {"num": "plural"},
        {"translation": "gloriosos"},
        {"numopposite": "gloriosas"},
        {"genopposite": "gloriosas"},
        {"gen": "mas"}
    ],
    "gloriosas":
    [
        {"num": "plural"},
        {"translation": "gloriosas"},
        {"numopposite": "gloriosa"},
        {"genopposite": "gloriosos"},
        {"gen": "fem"}
    ],
    ...
  }
}
```

As can be seen, it is a redundant format where, for each term, we have available its inflectional features and, for each of them, the term obtained by varying only that single feature with respect to the current one (e.g. masculine vs. feminine for gender, and singular vs. plural for number). This scheme allowed a simple navigation through the different inflected forms of the term when applying agreement restrictions such as, for example, the gender-number agreement between a noun and its adjectives in Spanish.

These dictionaries were created manually taking the English one as a reference, since it contains the minimum vocabulary to cover all the elements currently in the game.

In contrast, in the case of the game *Hamsun's Amulet*, a semi-automatic approach was chosen instead. The content word lemmas (nouns, verbs, adjectives and adverbs) of the basic game vocabulary still have to be selected manually. This first manual phase is mandatory in any game, since it is dependent on the design and implementation of the roguelike itself: the game developers are the ones that decide which elements, situations and actions are implemented and how they are related. However, given a lemma, its inflected forms were automatically extracted from an external corpus of the language.[12] Any annotated text corpus containing the POS tag and lemma of its terms would be suitable for the task. In this case, the corpus used was Wikicorpus (Reese et al., 2010), a freely available trilingual corpus (English, Spanish and Catalan) that contains large portions of a 2006 Wikipedia dump. The texts forming this corpus, over 750 million words, were automatically enriched with linguistic information including POS tags and lemmas. The format chosen for the resulting dictionaries, one for each language and word category, was also simpler and similar to the classic *(word, POS tag, lemma)* lexicon format, as we show here:

```
{
    ...
    "glorioso":{
        "type": "qualificative",
        "sing_m": "glorioso",
        "plu_m": "gloriosos",
        "plu_f": "gloriosas",
        "sing_f": "gloriosa"
    },
    ...
}
```

5.2.2. Syntactic Level

Until now, we have described how the game vocabulary is managed by the system. In this way, the description module is able to retrieve those terms corresponding to the elements and actions involved in a given gameplay event. However, these individual words have yet to be arranged to form a meaningful message describing said event. For that purpose, a *generation grammar* has been developed for every available language. In turn, this main grammar has been structured into *subgrammars* according to the syntactic structures generated (e.g. noun phrases) and the different contexts in which they are used: combat, use of magic, movement, generic actions, etc. This makes their management and maintenance easier. For example, if the developer intends to make a complete upgrade to the game's magic system, the possible changes to be made in the grammar will be restricted to that subgrammar.

As in the case of individual terms, the various subgrammars of the system and their rules are identified using an external identifier or key. This key is used to link each subgrammar with the events it describes, independently of the specific language being used at a given time.

These grammars are defined using context-free rules and kept in the form of JSON files. The notation employed for its specification, properly adapted to JSON format, is inspired by the one employed to specify the set of restrictions in feature structure-based grammars (Carpenter, 1992). We show as an example the definition of a simple noun phrase structure for English in the game *The Accessible Dungeon*:

```
"GENERAL": {
    "GM_3": {
        "S":
            [
                {"DET_1": ""},
                {"ADJ_1": ""},
```

---

[11]Translated as "glorioso", "gloriosa", "gloriosos" or "gloriosas" depending on the gender and number of the modified noun.

[12]Those inflected forms not appearing in the corpus, a minority, still had to be completed manually.

```json
        {"N_1": ""}
    ],
    "restrictions": [
        {"DET_1.num": "N_1.num"},
        {"N_1.num": "ADJ_1.num"}
    ]
  }
}
```

GENERAL is the key identifier corresponding to the current subgrammar and GM_3 is a rule identifier for internal use. We can distinguish two sections: S (for the classic start symbol), that describes the structure (i.e. the "right-hand side" of the rule); and restrictions, where we specify the morphosyntactic restrictions applicable to the elements of the structure. In this case, the grammatical structure corresponds to a sequence formed by a single DETerminer (DET_1), followed by an ADJective (ADJ_1) that modifies a Noun (N_1) (proper or common), as in the case of "a red potion", for example.

Regarding the restrictions of the example above, they specify that the number (feature num) of the determiner must be the same as that of the noun, and that the number of the noun must be the same as that of the adjective. In other words, we are informing the generator module about the well-known *number agreement* of a noun with its determiners and modifiers.[13] Thus, we will be avoiding the generation of ungrammatical phrases such as "a red potions".

Given a game event to be described, the generator engine will choose a random rule to be used among those of the subgrammar corresponding to that situation. By doing this, the generator module is taking advantage of *syntactic flexibility*, that is, using different syntactic structures to express the same message in a different way (Ferreira, 1996). Again, we are favoring variety and expressivity. For example, for the same attack action, we might obtain a brief description such as "The hero attacks the dragon", or an epic version such as "The mighty hero attacks the fierce dragon with his sword". So, by extending the grammars and/or subgrammars, any user can improve the quality and variety of descriptions.

5.2.3. Semantic Level

On this matter, it is interesting to take a look to the approach taken in *Hamsun's Amulet*. In this game, the terms forming the system vocabulary were not selected and organized individually, but at a *synset* level instead. For this purpose, its creator used the *Multilingual Central Repository (MCR) 3.0* (González-Agirre et al., 2012) as source. The MCR is a freely available WordNet-like resource that integrates in the same framework WordNets from six different languages: English, Spanish, Catalan, Basque, Galician and Portuguese. It also contains an Inter-Lingual-Index (ILI) that connects words in one language (actually synsets) with their equivalent translations (again, a synset) in any of the other languages.

Therefore, in this case the system vocabulary is composed not of a list of words corresponding to the different elements, actions and situations in the game, but of a list of synonym sets. As an example, and continuing with the one

---

[13]Noun-adjective agreement is unnecessary in English (as adjectives don't inflect for number), but essential in languages like Spanish.

previously used in Section 5.2.1., the entries corresponding to the English adjective "glorious" and the rest of terms of its synonym set are these:

```json
{
    ...
    "glorious":[
        "brilliant",
        "glorious",
        "magnificent",
        "splendid"
    ],
    ...
}
```

while their corresponding entries in the Spanish dictionary ("glorioso" and its synonyms) are:

```json
{
    ...
    "glorious":{
        "glorioso":{
            "type": "qualificative",
            "sing_m": "glorioso",
            "plu_m": "gloriosos",
            "plu_f": "gloriosas",
            "sing_f": "gloriosa"
        },
        "brillante":{
            "type":"qualificative",
            "sing_m":"brillante",
            "plu_m":"brillantes",
            "plu_f":"brillantes",
            "sing_f":"brillante"
        },
        "magnifico":{
            ...
        },
        "esplendido":{
            ...
        }
    },
    ...
}
```

Again, an external identifier has been used to identify and link the entries between languages. This time, one of the lemmas of the original English synset is used as key. We could have just employed ILI-based keys but, in this context, the lemmas proved again to be more flexible and manageable with respect to a meaningless alphanumeric code.

The basic generation process of this synset-based game vocabulary did not differ too much from the regular one. After defining an initial word-level English vocabulary, its corresponding synsets were identified by means of an automatic matching at the lemma level followed by a manual revision to filter out incorrect senses. The use of Word-Sense Disambiguation techniques was immediately discarded because of its high cost and complexity, which were incompatible with our requirements (see Section 4.). Once the synsets to be used were delimited, their inflected forms were obtained as described in Section 5.2.1..

With respect to the description generation process, the only difference with respect to the regular one is that the specific term to be used at a given moment is selected randomly among those in the synset.

5.2.4. Discourse and Pragmatic Levels

Given the time and complexity restrictions associated to these projects, previously described in Section 4., little progress were made at these levels.

One of the features integrated consisted in changing the adjectives used to describe a character taking into account their current state, thus introducing a subjective point of view. For example, if the number of hit points of an enemy creature is very low with respect to those of the adventurer, the generator module will reflect this fact by describing that enemy as "small", "insignificant", etc. If the situation is the opposite, adjectives such as "huge", "powerful", etc. will be used instead. Therefore, the enemy will be seen differently depending on the context. This mechanism gives the system more expressivity, while also improving the player experience by enhancing his empathy for the character.

To take into account persistence over time is another way of improving the player experience. For example, after having defeated an enemy, we have taken it into account for subsequent descriptions. Thus, for example, when the adventurer crosses again a room where they have fought and killed a goblin, the description should reflect this by automatically making reference to the dead body of the defeated enemy.

5.3. Other Relevant Features

Some extra accessibility-related features were added according to the comments and suggestions of our beta-testers and other members of the community.

The first one was the possibility of selecting how certain aspects of the game are described: in a qualitative or a quantitative way. For instance, in the case of hit points and other player statistics, some players preferred to be given an exact numeric value, but others preferred the use of fuzzy terms such as "high", "low", "enough", etc. A similar suggestion was made to describe the current position of the adventurer within a room, for example. Some players required the use of X-Y coordinates, while others were happy with approximate descriptions with respect to the elements of the room. Another one was the configuration of other aspects of the interface, such as to enable the change of font size, the reassignment of command keys or the use of different color palettes in the case of color-blind users.

Finally, we were also asked to make a sound every time the player moves within the game, since sometimes this is the only feedback the player has about whether the action has been performed or not.

6. Conclusions and Future Work

Throughout this paper we have described the development of a description generator module to adapt roguelike games to visually-impaired users. This NLP-based module describes, in the form of text, what is happening within the game, enabling a blind person to play the game using a screen reader. Expressivity and variety are achieved by taking advantage of linguistic flexibility at diferent levels. With regard to design and implementation, our premises were simplicity, flexibility and extensibility, so that, once made available to the public, any user with basic knowledge of programming and linguistics could extend the game to other languages. Several languages have been successfully tried until now: English, Spanish, Galician and Dutch.

With respect to the future, now that we have achieved a certain amount of critical mass, we can extend this initial work in several possible ways, specially at the discourse and pragmatic levels. The management of temporal aspects such as the elimination of unnecessary repetitions with respect to recent events or considering other aspects of persistence, would be of interest. Another possibility is the addition of a "summary mode" that, taking as input the sequence of events that happened during the gameplay and their corresponding descriptions, could generate as output a story about the adventures of the player. However, the possible need for applying *storytelling* (Salen-Tekinbas and Zimmerman, 2004) and *narrative modeling* (Mani, 2012) techniques may be too much of a challenge given our present context. Other less obvious aspects of linguistic variation (Pérez L. de Heredia and de Higes Andino, 2019) such as to modify the tone of the description according to the psychological condition of the adventurer (e.g. injured and hungry vs. victorious and satisfied) or their career (e.g. a rude barbarian vs. a cultured wizard), for example, would also be worthy of time.

There are also other interesting features to add, but not so directly related to NLP. For example, improving and making the game configuration mechanisms more flexible, allowing individual features to be activated and deactivated. In the case of the descriptive mode for visually-impaired users, we are considering to split it in two: a *verbose mode*, with more detailed and extensive descriptions; and a *brief mode*, with minimalist descriptions for experienced players who want to streamline the gameplay. Finally, we also intend to improve the evaluation process through questionnaires for users.

Acknowledgements

The work of Profs. Vilares and Gómez-Rodríguez was partially funded by MINECO (through project ANSWER-ASAP TIN2017-85160-C2-1-R) and Xunta de Galicia (through grants ED431B 2017/01, ED431G/01 and ED431G 2019/01).

We also want to thank the reviewers for their helpful comments. Finally, we also want to express our gratitude to the roguelike and blind gaming community, specially to members of *Tiglo-juegos* Google group, and to Juan Carlos Buño-Suárez, trainer from the National Organization of Spanish Blind People (ONCE), for their help in sharing their needs, suggesting improvements and betatesting.

7. Bibliographical References

Arampatzis, A., van der Weide, T. P., van Bommel, P., and Koster, C. (2000). Linguistically-motivated information retrieval. In *Encyclopedia of Library and Information Science*, volume 69, pages 201–222. Marcel Dekker, Inc, New York-Basel.

Barton, M. (2008). *Dungeons and Desktops: The History of Computer Role-Playing Games*. A K Peters, Ltd, Wellesley, MA, USA.

Carpenter, B. (1992). *The Logic of Typed Feature Structures*. Number 32 in Cambridge Tracts in Theoretical Computer Science. Cambridge University Press, Cambridge/New York/Melbourne.

Chandler, H. M. and Deming, S. O. (2011). *The Game Localization Handbook*. Foundations of Game Development. Jones & Bartlett Learning, USA, 2nd edition.

Craddock, D. L. (2015). *Dungeon Hacks: How Nethack, Angband, and other Roguelikes Changed the Course of video Games*. Press Start Press, Canton, OH, USA.

Ferreira, V. S. (1996). Is it better to give than to donate? syntactic flexibility in language production. *Journal of memory and language*, 35(5):724–755.

Marion A. Hersh et al., editors. (2008). *Assistive Technology for Visually Impaired and Blind People*. Springer, London.

Jurafsky, D. and Martin, J. H. (2009). *Speech and Language Processing: An Introduction to Natural Language Processing, Computational Linguistics, and Speech Recognition (2nd ed.)*. Pearson–Prentice Hall, Upper Saddle River, New Jersey, 2 edition.

Mani, I. (2012). *Computational Modeling of Narrative*. Synthesis Lectures on Human Language Technologies. Morgan & Claypool Publishers.

Manning, C. D. and Schütze, H. (1999). *Foundations of Statistical Natural Language Processing*. The MIT Press, Cambridge (Massachusetts) and London (England).

McCrae, J. P. and Cimiano, P. (2015). Guidelines for linguistic linked data generation: Wordnets. Draft Community Group Report 29, Best Practices for Multilingual Linked Open Data (BPMLOD) Community Group, World Wide Web Consortium (W3C). Available online at: `https://www.w3.org/community/bpmlod/` (visited on Feb. 2020).

Pérez L. de Heredia, M. and de Higes Andino, I. (2019). Multilingualism and identities: New portrayals, new challenges. In María Pérez L. de Heredia et al., editors, *Special Issue on Multilingualism and Representation of Identities in Audiovisual Texts*, volume 4 of *MonTI: Monografías de Traducción e Interpretación*, pages 9–31. Available online at: `http://hdl.handle.net/10045/96908` (visited on Feb 2020).

Georg Rehm et al., editors. (2011). META-NET White Paper Series. Springer. Available online at `http://www.meta-net.eu/whitepapers`.

Reiter, E. and Dale, R. (2000). *Building Natural Language Generation Systems*. Cambridge University Press, New York, NY, USA.

Salen-Tekinbas, K. and Zimmerman, E., (2004). *Rules of Play: Game Design Fundamentals*, chapter Games as Narrative Play. MIT Press.

Shaker, N., Liapis, A., Togelius, J., Lopes, R., and Bidarra, R. (2016). Constructive generation methods for dungeons and levels. In Noor Shaker, et al., editors, *Procedural Content Generation in Games: A Textbook and an Overview of Current Research*, chapter 3, pages 31–55. Springer.

Urbanek, M. and Güldenpfennig, F. (2019). Celebrating 20 years of computer-based audio gaming. In *Proceedings of the 14th International Audio Mostly Conference: A Journey in Sound*, AM'19, page 90–97, New York, NY, USA. Association for Computing Machinery.

W3C. (2018). Web content accessibility guidelines. Available at: `https://www.w3.org/WAI/standards-guidelines/wcag/` (visited on February 2020).

8.   Language Resource References

González-Agirre, A., Laparra, E., and Rigau, G. (2012). Multilingual central repository version 3.0: upgrading a very large lexical knowledge base. In Christiane Fellbaum et al., editors, *Proceedings of the Sixth Global WordNet Conference (GWC 2012). Matsue, Japan*. Tribun EU. Resource available at: `https://adimen.si.ehu.es/web/MCR` (visited on Feb. 2020).

Reese, S., Boleda, G., Cuadros, M., Padró, L., and Rigau, G. (2010). Wikicorpus: A word-sense disambiguated multilingual Wikipedia corpus. In *Proceedings of the Seventh International Conference on Language Resources and Evaluation (LREC'10)*, Valletta, Malta, May. European Language Resources Association (ELRA). Resource available at: `https://www.cs.upc.edu/~nlp/wikicorpus/` (visited on Feb. 2020).

Demonstration of a Serious Game for Spoken Language Experiments — GDX

Daniel Duran[1] **& Natalie Lewandowski**[2]
[1] Albert-Ludwigs-Universität Freiburg, Germany
[2] High Performance Computing Center Stuttgart (HLRS), Germany
daniel.duran@germanistik.uni-freiburg.de, natalie.lewandowski@hlrs.de

Abstract

Increasing efforts are put into gamification of experimentation software in psychology and educational applications and the development of serious games. Computer-based experiments with game-like features have been developed previously for research on cognitive skills, cognitive processing speed, working memory, attention, learning, problem solving, group behavior and other phenomena. It has been argued that computer game experiments are superior to traditional computerized experimentation methods in laboratory tasks in that they represent holistic, meaningful, and natural human activity. We present a novel experimental framework for forced choice categorization tasks or speech perception studies in the form of a computer game, based on the Unity Engine – the Gamified Discrimination Experiments engine (GDX). The setting is that of a first person shooter game with the narrative background of an alien invasion on earth. We demonstrate the utility of our game as a research tool with an application focusing on attention to fine phonetic detail in natural speech perception. The game-based framework is additionally compared against a traditional experimental setup in an auditory discrimination task. Applications of this novel game-based framework are multifarious within studies on all aspects of spoken language perception.
Keywords: spoken language, gamification, categorization tasks, speech perception

1. Introduction

We present an experimental framework designed as a *computer game*[1] for auditory categorization and perception studies. We demonstrate its utility as a research tool with an application focusing on attention to fine phonetic detail in natural speech perception.

Increasing efforts are put into *gamification* of experimentation software in psychology and educational applications and the development of *serious games* or *games with a purpose* in natural language processing, computational linguistics and other related research disciplines. Computer game paradigms have been applied in studies with adult subjects, children and even monkeys (Berger et al., 2000; Keil et al., 2016; Washburn and Gulledge, 1995). Regarding the tested skills, computer games have been developed for research on cognitive skills (Donchin, 1995; Lindstedt and Gray, 2015), cognitive processing speed (McPherson and Burns, 2007; McPherson and Burns, 2008), working memory (Washburn and Gulledge, 1995), attention (Berger et al., 2000), learning (Nelson et al., 2014), problem solving (Quinn, 1991), or group behavior (Hawkins, 2015; Keil et al., 2016), etc. They have also been developed for computer-assisted language learning (Peterson, 2010). The body of work with applications of computer games as research tools to study some aspects of human language processing, however, is still comparably small.

In this paper we present a novel experimental framework for forced choice categorization tasks or speech perception studies, designed in the form of a computer game – the *Gamified Discrimination Experiments* engine (GDX). The remainder of this paper is structured as follows. First we give a brief overview of related work which comes primarily from research fields other than natural language processing. We also briefly discuss classic experimental approaches which are employed in the study of the mechanisms of human language understanding in psycholinguistics and cognitive sciences. GDX, our novel experimental framework, is described in detail in section 3. along with a first use case in a study on speech perception. In section 4., we compare the application of GDX with a classical test scenario. Finally, we discuss our findings in the context of gamified spoken language experiments.

2. Related work on serious games

Gamification of experimentation software and *serious games* or *games with a purpose* have been employed in various human behavior and language related research disciplines like psychology, cognitive sciences, computational linguistics or natural language processing. Usually, such computer games are custom made for the purpose of a specific study or data acquisition task. Using existing off-the-shelf computer games for research may be possible for some research questions. For example, *Tetris* has been used to study cognitive skills (Kirsh and Maglio, 1994; Maglio and Kirsh, 1996). The commercial games *The Sims* or *World of Warcraft* have been employed for computer-assisted language learning (Peterson, 2010). However, this is in general not possible with all tasks or experimental designs. Donchin (1995), for example, points out: "A game is useful as a research tool if, and only if, the investigator can exercise systematic control over the game's parameters." The researcher needs to know the internal workings of a game in order to develop appropriate empirical procedures and gather the required data from the participants and their interaction with the game (Porter, 1995). One very important aspect is detailed logging of user ac-

---

[1] A note on terminology: We use the term *computer game* throughout this paper to refer to interactive software programs which represent some sort of game. Most of the general discussion is applicable irrespective of the fact whether it is a competitive or cooperative game, whether it is a single-player or multiplayer game or whether it is made for PC, smartphones or dedicated gaming hardware (i.e. a video game console). The term *video game*, thus, is treated as synonymous with *computer game*. Furthermore, we do not discuss the differences between *serious games* and *games with a purpose*.

tions and game events, which is usually not possible with proprietary computer games (Järvelä et al., 2014; Lindstedt and Gray, 2015).

Apart from experimental research, gamification is also often employed in educational applications (Gruenstein et al., 2009; Habernal et al., 2018; Mayer et al., 2014; McGraw et al., 2009). Picca et al. (2015) review various serious games which employ some NLP techniques with applications in: tutoring systems, computer-assisted foreign language learning, risk management training, communication skills training, conflict resolution training, cognitive-behavioral therapy or scientific and academic education.

Serious games are not only an effective alternative to classic experimentation frameworks – e.g. with respect to participant motivation and naturalness of the gathered data. They are also valuable tools in crowdsourcing and labeling scenarios – e.g. for language data annotations and manual classifications (von Ahn, 2006; Kicikoglu et al., 2019; Madge et al., 2019). Levitan et al. (2018), for example, present a gamification approach for annotation of deceptive speech.

2.1. The computer game paradigm in psychology and cognitive research

Most applications of computer game experiments can probably be found in experimental research in psychology and cognitive sciences. Järvelä et al. (2014) review the use of computer games as "experiment stimulus" and provide a practical guide for game selection and experimental set-up. *Space Fortress* is an example of a game developed in the early 1980s for research on skill acquisition (Donchin, 1995). Using the game *Tetris*, it was found that skilled players use more *epistemic actions*, e.g. rotating a piece physically instead of rotating it mentally in order to see if it fits (Kirsh and Maglio, 1994; Maglio and Kirsh, 1996). Later, Lindstedt and Gray (2015) presented *Meta-T*, a *Tetris*-like computer game for cognitive research. They discuss the use of computer games as a means to investigate complex, cognitive behavior of highly skilled experts (gamers) and novices. Other games are employed to study acquisition, categorization or learnability in psycholinguistics experiments (Wade and Holt, 2005; Lim and Holt, 2011; Kimball et al., 2013; Rácz et al., 2017)

2.2. Computer games in linguistics

Games are a well-established paradigm in speech production studies as an elicitation tool. One example is the well-known *Map Task* (Anderson et al., 1991). It provides a pen-and-paper framework to elicit quasi-spontaneous dialogs. In this task, two participants have to find a path on a printed map. Both participants receive a map of their own and they are not able to see the map of their dialog partners. However, the two maps contain different information and the only way to navigate through it is to exchange information verbally. The experimenter can influence the content of the dialog, to a certain extend, by the specific landmarks shown on the maps. Another example is the *Diapix* task (Baker and Hazan, 2011; Van Engen et al., 2010). It is similar to a map task but involves two pictures of various scenes with the task being to spot the differences.

In analogy to these pen-and-paper tasks, cooperative computer games are often used as an elicitation tool for research on human verbal interaction (Garrod and Anderson, 1987; Levitan et al., 2012; Ward and Abu, 2016).

2.3. Classic computerized experimentation methods

Commonly used experimental frameworks in language research are *DMDX* (Forster and Forster, 2003), *PsychoPy* (Peirce, 2007) or *Praat* (Boersma, 2001; Boersma and Weenink, 2020). Classic computerized experimentation methods like these involve explicit instructions for the participants. Their attention is drawn directly to the phenomenon under investigation such that each decision is made consciously. However, human language and speech processing is affected (among many others also) by cognitive factors like attention, distraction and memory (Duran and Lewandowski, 2018) cognitive resources which are likely to be employed in different ways in experimental settings or everyday situations. In addition to the inherently unnatural scenarios created by such experiments, they are most often carried out within an artificial laboratory setting. This raises questions about the validity and naturalness of the obtained data. Consequently, it has been argued that game experiments are superior to traditional experimentation methods. Porter (1995), for example, states: "To a much greater extent than most traditional laboratory tasks, computer games represent holistic, meaningful, and natural human activity."

Lumsden et al. (2016) carried out a simple Go/No-Go experiment where participants have to respond as quickly as possible to some stimuli (Go) but withhold their response to other stimuli (No-Go). They compared this task in different presentation forms: a traditional non-game version, a traditional version with an added scoring mechanism to reward participants for correct actions and a game version (a "cowboy shootout"). They found longer reaction times with the game version as well as lower accuracies. Note, however, that a ceiling effect of accuracy was observed on the non-game variants. It thus can be argued in favor of the game variant, if avoiding ceiling effects is considered desirable. It has to be mentioned, though, that higher visual complexity in the game variant may have contributed to the increased difficulty and the resulting lower performance. A questionnaire about enjoyment and engagement showed that the "non-game control was clearly rated as the least enjoyable and stimulating, the most boring and the most frustrating", and that "participants also reported putting less effort into this variant than others."

3. The GDX framework

In order to alleviate the known issues with classic computerized experimentation methods (mentioned above), we developed a computer-game based experimental framework for forced choice categorization tasks and speech perception studies: GDX – the *Gamified Discrimination Experiments* engine[2]. It was originally motivated by a study

---

[2]GDX is available for research purposes from the first author upon request. A freely-available version is being prepared for public release.

Figure 1: GDX screenshot: Beginning of a trial during the training phase with visual category information "human".

Figure 2: GDX screenshot: Feedback after the end of a trial with a correct classification as "alien".

on phonetic convergence (see section 4.2. below) to assess individual differences in attention to fine phonetic detail during speech perception in verbal interactions. However, within this study it was not *explicit* attention to fine phonetic detail which we wanted to assess. Explicit, i.e. consciously directed attention probably involves processes which are different from the processes leading to phonetic convergence in natural conversations. We therefore developed an experimental framework based on a gamification approach, where attention could be gauged in an implicit manner. GDX was first employed during the creation of the GECO2 database, which contains spontaneous dialog recordings (Schweitzer et al., 2015), The game was one task among many psychological, social and cognitive tests the subjects had to complete aside the main dialog recordings.

The setting of GDX is that of a first person shooter game with the narrative background of an alien invasion on earth (inspired by an earlier version implemented by Lange et al. (2015)). The remainder of this section describes technical details of the game.

3.1. Design and Implementation

GDX is implemented using the Unity game engine (Unity Technologies, 2016). This provides a state-of-the-art game engine for a high-quality 3D game. Subjects experienced with modern computer games may find this appealing. The game is designed such that experimental parameters are not hard-coded into the game but can be set through a simple configuration file which is loaded by the game at runtime. The game takes place in a virtual 3D environment through which the player has to navigate. Navigation in GDX is controlled via the WASD keys on the keyboard in combination with the computer mouse. This scheme is common in first-person action games of this type. The player encounters agents ("enemies") to which she/he has to react. In order to minimize interaction between experimenter and participants, all instructions are incorporated into the game and presented subsequently on screen within the game. This approach additionally facilitates the immersion of the participant with the virtual game environment and the background story. Screenshots are shown in Figure 1 and Figure 2.

The narrative of GDX is that of an alien invasion on earth from outer space. The player encounters agents of two categories – "humans" and "aliens". Within the story of the game, the aliens are disguised as humans. Only during an initial training phase are visual cues shown to indicate the category of an agent (Figure 1). After a few trials, visual cues disappear and the agents are visually indistinguishable. Once the player approaches a given agent, the agent becomes active and starts chasing the player. This starts an experimental trial. A sound stimulus is played once and an optional visual display next to the agent shows a color along with a descriptive text label. The player is equipped with two tools ("weapons"): one that freezes a hit agent in a block of ice and one which beams a hit agent away within a bundle of green light rays. The tools are associated with the left and right mouse buttons and correspond to the two response categories. After the end of a trial, feedback is provided to the player about the true category of an agent (also showing an *alien* figure instead of the default *human* figure in case the agent belonged to the *alien* category, cf. Figure 2). All player actions are logged and stored in a text file for post-processing and evaluation of reaction times and response accuracy.

3.2. Experimental control, logging and reaction time measurements

All game logic (like input handling, agent behavior, experiment control, logging, etc.) is implemented in C#. Experimental parameters are not hard-coded into the game but can be set through a plain text file which is loaded by the game at runtime. The structure of this configuration file corresponds to the familiar Java *.properties* format with key–value pairs. The configurable parameters include, a.o., time limits, trial specifications and also the texts displayed on screen. The actual sound files (using uncompressed wav format) are not compiled into the game, as well, but loaded at runtime from hard disk. This makes GDX very flexible, providing a language-independent framework for various experimental scenarios.

The player's location and rotation in world-space are logged at key events during the game, e.g. on all mouse clicks (firing one of the two weapons), the beginning of experimental trials, or upon reaching specific landmarks.

Accuracy of time measurements is an important issue in behavioral experiments, which has been discussed for several decades now (Babjack et al., 2015; Segalowitz and Graves,

1990). The DMDX software presented by Forster and Forster (2003), for example, allows running experiments on machines with the Windows operating system. It specifically aims at the minimization of both display timing errors (by keeping track of the system's refresh cycle time) as well as response timing errors, by supporting parallel port input. For high-precision time measurements, GDX relies on the C# `Stopwatch` class (in `System.Diagnostics`) and its property `ElapsedTicks` which refers to the smallest possible unit of time that this class can measure. The actual resolution depends on the underlying operating system and hardware, but it remains constant during experimental runs on the same machine. At the beginning of each session with GDX, the `Stopwatch` update frequency and the high-resolution flag are written to the log file. This aids later analysis of timing *precision*.

4. Game vs. classic perception test

In order to evaluate the utility of GDX, we compared it with a classic perception test in a follow-up study (Lewandowski and Duran, 2018).

4.1. Test case: the role of attention in phonetic convergence

To demonstrate the utility of GDX as a testing environment for auditory stimuli, or more broadly, within all kinds of forced choice categorization tasks and speech perception studies, data were collected in conjunction with a phonetic convergence study. Within the GECO2 project (Schweitzer et al., 2015), we gathered data of thirty adult subjects, who performed the GDX game in the scenario described below. The test set-up of GDX was targeted at measuring the attention given to fine phonetic detail in speech, when no explicit instructions are given to the players.

4.2. Background: a socio-cognitive model of phonetic convergence

Phonetic convergence (sometimes also called *accommodation*, *alignment* or *entrainment*[3]) is the phenomenon when two speakers become more alike in their speech productions within the course of a dialog. It occurs (1) in laboratory set-ups, e. g. in shadowing tasks or question-answer sequences (Bailly and Lelong, 2010; Delvaux and Soquet, 2007; Namy et al., 2002; Nielsen, 2011); (2) between native or non-native speakers in (quasi) spontaneous dialogs (De Looze et al., 2011; Kim et al., 2011; Lewandowski, 2012; Lewandowski and Jilka, 2019; Schweitzer and Lewandowski, 2013; Schweitzer et al., 2015); (3) between non-native speakers in a shared L2 (Trofimovich and Kennedy, 2014); and (4) even in human–machines interaction (Beňuš et al., 2018; Gessinger et al., 2019).

Previous attempts to explain convergence (not only at the phonetic level) can be categorized into two branches. Probably the most prominent one is a socio-linguistic model: the *Communication Accommodation Theory* (Cat) (Giles, 2016). It attempts to model the motives and evaluations of switching in terms of a balance of social psychological processes focusing on social integration and differentiation (Sachdev and Giles, 2006). The fundamental assumption is that individuals use communication, in part, to indicate their attitudes toward each other, and, as such, communication is a barometer of the level of social distance between them (Sachdev and Giles, 2006). According to this model, convergence is an expression of attitudes towards the interlocutor, and is affected by intentions, goals and knowledge of the involved speakers. Thus, convergence is essentially a conscious means of expression.

The second model is a mechanistic one, as proposed by Pickering and Garrod (2013), for example. The goal of interaction for speakers is to achieve mutual understanding or "common ground" (Trofimovich and Kennedy, 2014). At least one way of doing so is to align or coordinate language at several linguistic levels (lexical, syntactic, and phonological) (Trofimovich and Kennedy, 2014). According to this model, phonetic convergence is caused by the adoption of perceived phonetic details, based on psychological and cognitive processes which link perception and production – the *perception-production feedback loop*. Thus, convergence is modeled as an automatic process here, and potential (social or other) influencing factors are not discussed by Pickering and Garrod in their original model.

As Babel (2012) correctly points out, a crucial aspect has been left out of the discussion between the above models – the reasons for the lack of convergence, which is fairly often observed. She points to several possible solutions, including the incapacity to resolve perceptual details, production biases, or a lack of sufficient attention.

Research on convergence during the last years shows more and more that it is affected not only by social aspects (Schweitzer et al., 2017; Schweitzer and Lewandowski, 2014), but also by psychological (personality-related) and cognitive (processing skill-related) individual differences (Babel and McGuire, 2015; Lewandowski, 2013; Lewandowski and Jilka, 2019; Vais et al., 2015) as well. Amongst the cognitive factors, one feature seems to be especially involved – namely attention. As defined by Segalowitz (2007), attention control is the ability to focus and refocus attention on different semantic levels. The executive control part of attention might also operate beyond mere semantic levels, for instance, when switching between different levels/dimensions of the speech signal, e.g. between meaning vs. form. Lewandowski and Jilka (2019) also find attention skills (as tested by a mental flexibility task – the Simon Test (Craft and Simon, 1970)) to modulate the amount of convergence in their study, next to personality features such as, for instance, openness. The lower the switch costs in the Simon Test (i.e., the faster the subjects were able to switch between the dimensions in the test), the more phonetic convergence they displayed during the conversations. Another dimension which proved to be related to convergence in the study above was the Behavior Inhibition Scale (BIS). Results indicate that speakers displaying less behavioral inhibition (i.e., they are put off to a smaller degree by negative encounters or the fear of bad outcomes) again show more convergence. The authors conclude that some speakers (those showing more talent) seem

---

[3]Note on terminology: *Imitation* is not considered to be a synonym for phonetic convergence occurring in conversational speech. Compare, for instance, the discussion in (Lewandowski and Jilka, 2019).

to be more skilled in switching between different signal types (in their case: meaning vs. sound) and potentially giving more weight to their speaking partners' pronunciation, opposed to just focusing on transmitting information in the dialog (Lewandowski and Jilka, 2019). This in turn, is a phenomenon observable in its purest form within actual conversations, where attention towards certain communicative aspects usually arises (or does not) without any explicit instructions, just as it can be tested with the here presented serious game GDX. Therefore, the first described use case is a comparison of a test for attention to phonetic detail using our GDX engine (no explicit instructions necessary) and a classic perception test (inherently containing explicit instructions pointing the subject towards "areas of interest" in the speech signal).

4.3. Classic categorization experiment

The *classic experiment* is a categorization test with acoustic stimuli, designed in a way to maximally resemble the game scenario (involving the category labels "human" and "alien", just as in the game). All manipulated items belonged to the "alien" category, whereas the original recordings were used as the "human" samples. The nature of the manipulation was not communicated to the participants (neither in the perception test nor in the game). However, since the setting was an auditory categorization test, it was obvious to the participants that they were supposed to focus on cues in the sound of the stimuli. This is in stark contrast to the game scenario, where the target dimension of the signal was never explicitly nor circumstantially revealed to the participants. Similarly to the game, after a short training phase, subjects had to categorize the stimuli in three blocks, with one manipulation at a time (as in the three game levels).

4.4. Participants and method

Our subjects in the comparison study were 24 German native speakers (aged 20–31, 12 female) divided into two groups with 12 subjects each, which differed in testing order (game first vs. perception test first).

The test group – *Group 1 (G1)* – played the game first and then completed the classic perception test, the control group – *Group 2 (G2)* – took part in the classic perception test first and played the game afterwards. The two test sessions followed each other with a 3–7 days' break. Analyzed were accuracy and reaction times, as well as individual post-hoc questionnaires on the evaluation of the two methods. Two participants suffered from a mild case of cybersickness while playing the game (Frey et al., 2007; Rebenitsch and Owen, 2016). After a short break, however, they were able to continue with the experiment. Since the break occurred still within the training phase before any RTs were measured, the data did not have to be discarded but was included in the evaluation.

4.5. Post-hoc questionnaires

The first post-hoc questionnaire for every participant included sociodemographic information and questions on the usage of computers and other electronic devices, and the frequency and type of games played either on a computer, console or smartphone. The data was summarized in the following variables: *isGamer* (yes/no), *GamingFrequency* in days per week, *GamingScore* (i.e. How many types of games and on how many devices are usually played), and *ElectronicsUseScore* reflecting how many devices (smartphone, console, laptop, computer, tablet etc.) are being used on a daily basis. The second questionnaire was filled out directly after the respective experiment (game and perception test) and included a.o. questions on the difficulty and fun of the game/test (on a scale from 1–5), and also questions on the used "strategy" during the experiment in order to distinguish between aliens and humans.

4.6. Hypotheses

G1 (who started with the game) is expected to perform worse in their first task than G2, who began with the perception test. This difference should be the result of the explicitness of the instructions G2 received regarding the task at hand/ target to attend to. Furthermore, the classic design allows to focus solely on the experienced auditory stimuli, without any distractors present – thus differing considerably from the game. In consequence, we should also see G2 outperforming G1 in their second task, the game, since they already know which cue is essential (i.e., the sounds uttered within the game) and would not be held back by a false reliance on semantic or other unrelated cues.

4.7. Results

A full discussion of the results within the context of its original study (Schweitzer et al., 2015), the cognitive aspects in dialog situations, is beyond the scope of this paper. We present the results of the game vs. classic perception experiment and demonstrate the utility of the framework to collect reaction time and behavioral data.

The data sets were transformed and prepared for analysis using R version 3.4.3 (R Core Team, 2017) and the packages *tidyverse* (Wickham, 2017), *dplyr* and *stringr*. The statistical analyses were performed using *afex* (Singmann et al., 2018) and *lmerTest* (Kuznetsova et al., 2017), and visualized with *ggplot2* (Wickham, 2016). Raw reaction times (RT) were first log-transformed before supplying it to the model. Visual inspection of normality plots did not show any obvious deviations. Table 1 shows descriptive statistics. The best fitting linear mixed model (lmer) for predicting the variable *RT(log)* was obtained by maximum likelihood t-tests using Satterthwaite approximations to degrees of freedom (lmerMod) after fitting a large model first and applying an automatic stepwise reduction with the *step* procedure in the *lmerTest* package, which was manually overseen and double-checked with model comparison anovas.

The resulting model with the best fit contains random intercepts for *stimulus* and *subject*, and the fixed factors shown in Table 2 (model parameters: AIC 816.9, BIC 887.1, logLik -394.5, deviance 788.9, df.resid 1102). The number of *correct responses* in the two test scenarios was predicted by fitting a maximal generalized linear model (GLM) of type *binomial* and a subsequent reduction of factors to achieve the best fit (see Table 3).

The lmer shows that correct responses came hand in hand with shorter reaction times, and perceived *fun* in the ex-

Group	Test	Accuracy		reaction time	
		Mean	SD	Mean	SD
1	game	0.42	0.49	3.09	1.60
1	classic	0.69	0.46	3.96	1.22
2	classic	0.80	0.40	3.30	1.05
2	game	0.76	0.43	1.54	0.68

Table 1: Proportion correct responses (accuracy) and reaction times (sec) in both tests and groups, without the training phase. SD = standard deviation.

periments reduced RTs. Furthermore, there was an effect for the type of the acoustic manipulation of the stimuli and strong interactions between *test*group* and *test* and participants' *gaming score*, with more gaming experience actually prolonging reaction times in the game (see Table 2). Post-hoc pairwise comparisons with Tukey HSD Tests were performed on the factors in the fixed effects of the linear mixed model. For the interaction of *group* and *test* all between-group and within-group comparisons reached significance, indicating that subjects in both groups and tests responded to the stimuli with differing RTs.

The GLM for *accuracy* shows an effect for test type (i.e. a considerable negative effect for the *game*), and a main negative effect of perceived difficulty of the experiment. The subjective evaluation of the game's difficulty level seems to correlate with an actual decrease in accuracy for the classic test, which is, however, reversed for the game. The significant interaction of *group* and *test* confirms that G2 performed better in the game than G1. There also is a small bias for *fun* in favor of the game, mediated by group (post-hoc Tukey: game(g2)-classic(g1), diff 0.246735, p adj. = 0.005566).

A further analysis focused on the performance of both groups on their respective first test – *Time 1* – treating the game for G1 and the categorization test for G2 as two conditions of one variable, since the subjects had no knowledge as to the nature of the target cues prior to Time 1. The difference in accuracy on the first performed test per group was significant (compare Table 1, *Wilcoxon Rank Sum*: $W = 23705$, $p < 0.001$) – G2 was better able to correctly categorize the stimuli in the perception test than G1 was in the game. The same was true for Time 2 – G2 playing the game (76% correct) outperformed G1 completing the perception test with 69% correct ($W = 23705$, $p < 0.001$). For the logged RTs, the differences between both tests at Time 1 (*Tukey multiple comparisons of means*: diff. 0.156863, $p < 0.001$) and at Time 2 were significant (diff. -0.977677, $p < 0.001$). Figures 3 and 4 display the individual differences in performance of our subjects in both tests and groups.

5. Discussion and Conclusion

Our first validation study was designed as a comparison between a classical perception test, as used in speech perception research, and our gamified framework GDX. Several aspects have been found to speak in favor of using gamified testing environments. First, unsurprisingly, we have found a noticeable individual variation between our participants. Also, as expected in a scenario without any explicit instruc-

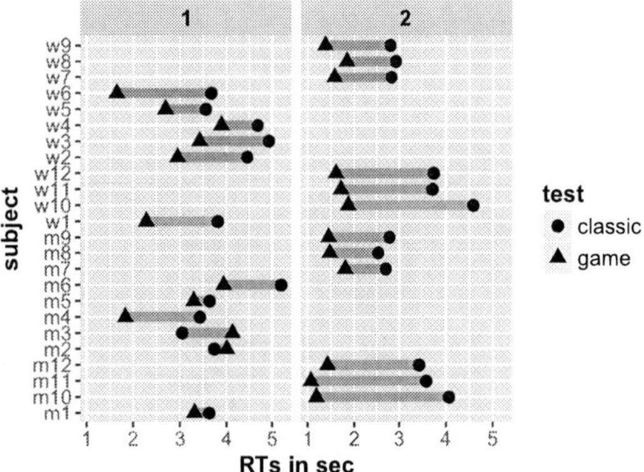

Figure 3: RTs in seconds in both tests per subject and group.

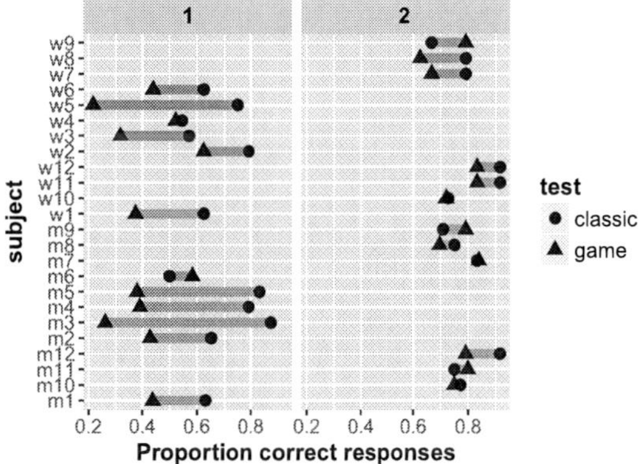

Figure 4: Proportion correct responses in both tests per subject and group.

tions, subjects have focused more on the (more salient) semantic content than on the acoustic information present in the game stimuli. Firstly, this seems to be a more genuine reflection of everyday communication, where meaning is the key, and the phonetic-acoustic part primarily serves as the means of transmission. Secondly, this casts doubt onto the validity of classical perception tests aiming at phonetic dimensions, or at the very minimum, onto the effect sizes observed in such tests. We presume that classic test designs might lead to exaggerated outcomes due to the explicit instructions subjects usually receive in these tasks (or, for example, in games like the one presented by Levitan et al. (2018)). Making participants aware which dimension they need to pay attention to, reduces task complexity considerably, and probably bypasses naturally occurring attention control or attention switching mechanisms, since the person already is focused on the "correct" task. In the reversed situation of the no-instruction gamified design, fewer subjects directed their attention towards the target dimension. Nevertheless, a number of participants in GDX were very successfully able to identify the task at hand (i.e. paying attention to the sounds) and reacted accordingly. These might be precisely those subjects who naturally pay more attention to sound properties in general, or, specifically in

	Estimate	Std. Error	df	t value	Pr(>|t|)
(Intercept)	1.82	0.17	44.12	10.90	0.00
testgame	-0.05	0.07	1081.66	-0.68	0.49
group	-0.14	0.08	24.47	-1.80	0.08
GamingScore	-0.05	0.03	24.63	-2.02	0.05
fun	-0.07	0.02	427.61	-3.29	0.00
manipulationF2	0.21	0.05	26.21	4.07	0.00
manipulationFRIC	0.11	0.05	31.66	2.26	0.03
manipulationOriginal	0.14	0.04	28.18	3.35	0.00
correct	-0.07	0.02	1091.13	-2.90	0.00
testgame:group	-0.47	0.04	1067.83	-11.69	0.00
testgame:GamingScore	0.07	0.01	1063.90	5.27	0.00

Table 2: Fixed factors in lmer: *RTlog ~test * (group + GamingScore) + fun + manipulation + correct + (1\stimulus) + (1\subject)*. Random effects: *stimulus (Intercept)*, var. 0.0032, SD 0.0564; *subject (Intercept)*: var 0.0324, SD 0.1801; *resid.*: var. 0.1100, SD 0.3317.

	Estimate	Std. Error	z value	Pr(> |z|)
(Intercept)	1.3275	0.4327	3.07	0.0022
test(game)	-3.2427	0.5900	-5.50	0.0000
group	0.3055	0.2127	1.44	0.1509
difficulty	-0.3399	0.0902	-3.77	0.0002
test(game):group	1.2073	0.2852	4.23	0.0000
test(game):difficulty	0.3622	0.1229	2.95	0.0032

Table 3: GLM output for the proportion of correct responses (accuracy) in both tests and groups. Model formula: *correct ~test * (group + difficulty)*; null deviance: 1416.5 on 1115 df, residual deviance: 1295.1 on 1110 df, AIC: 1307.1

situations where this becomes a relevant factor in communication (e.g., in L1–L2 encounters, in the presence of dialect, in order to allow situation-adequate style choices, or for the purpose of convergence in dialogs). We are at the same time aware of certain limitations of this first validation study. Most importantly, a third testing condition with participants knowing before starting the game that sound is important (however without knowing the exact acoustic-phonetic feature targeted) would bridge the current gap between the two experimental conditions and allow an even more refined conclusion on the ability to pay attention to fine phonetic detail.

There are two aspects of computer game-like experiments which are frequently discussed: (1) the appeal of the task or motivation of participants, and (2) the quality of the collected data.

Motivation of participants through game-like features has been mentioned repeatedly in the literature as desirable (Lindstedt and Gray, 2015; Nelson et al., 2014), although it has also been argued that this may not necessarily improve data (Hawkins et al., 2012). Howes (2017) points out that "games are so motivating that [...] people actively *choose* to engage with them and, today, action games are a significant and growing part of the fabric of everyday human experience" (emphasis in original). He compares game paradigms with "extremely simple paradigms" (Gray, 2017) where studies focus on isolated cognitive processes in order to build a big picture. Referring to Newell (1973), he emphasizes that "the pieces never seem to get put back together". Lindstedt and Gray (2015) point out the aspect of participant *motivation* as an advantage of using a Tetris-like game for psychological studies stating that it "is not a boring experimental paradigm, but a fascinating game that

has a life outside of academia".

Motivation is not only relevant in terms of engaging participants with the task during the experiment. It is also an important aspect in recruitment of participants for experiments, in the first place. Järvelä et al. (2014), for example, note that "the high penetration in the population serves to make games more approachable than abstract psychological tasks, which helps in recruiting participants." With computer games, social groups could be reached and recruited as subjects who usually do not find their ways into the labs of speech and language scientists. The kind of setup presented in this paper might not be suitable for all experiments or groups of subjects (e.g. taking into account the issue of cybersickness or different levels of experience with action games). Increased reaction times, as we find them (section 4.), for example, might indicate that the performance of (highly) experienced gamers is negatively affected by deviations from common game conventions. Further research is needed in order to asses the suitability of serious games in favour of classic experimental designs with participants beyond the usual subject group of undergraduate students.

Note also, that intrinsic motivation and *fun* may affect labeling and data annotation tasks. As a possible annotation tool, GDX exploits natural implicit judgments and does not require specially trained or skilled expert annotators. In comparison to common crowdsourcing methods (e.g. Amazon Mechanical Turk[4]), the gamification in GDX exploits intrinsic motivation of the participants in a more "natural environment". In comparison to explicit categorization tasks, the gamification in GDX thus allows for the elicitation of spontaneous behavioral (linguistic) data.

---

[4]https://www.mturk.com/

We would like to address the question, why we opt for conducting computer experiments in the lab rather than online via the internet. Online experiments face several issues which are easier to address in scenarios with local computer experiments, like control over test subjects (e.g. personal features like age, gender, language skills etc.) and how often they participate, or protection against malicious attacks on the system. Additionally, local experiments in the lab allow for control over the test situation and the used hardware and software equipment making results more consistent and comparable (Babjack et al., 2015). Other problems with web-based online experiments are: premature drop-out or loss of attention resulting in the participant's switching to other activities in the middle of an experiment as discussed, for example, by Hawkins (2015).

Another important issue in behavioral experiments which requires continued attention is the accuracy of time measurements. This has been discussed for several decades now (Babjack et al., 2015; Segalowitz and Graves, 1990). Experimentation software like DMDX specifically addresses timing issues by specific optimizations for operating systems and support of specific hardware Forster and Forster (2003). Babjack et al. (2015) observe that different configurations (operating system, sound card, API, etc.) introduce significant timing variability. They found mean sound onset latencies of approximately 25–35 ms on PC and 6–25 ms on laptops (running Windows 7 and 8). Often, such timing issues are tackled by the use of dedicated hardware for stimulus presentation and response detection. Within a game-like environment this is not feasible and also counters the goal of providing a low-cost, easy to use framework. Segalowitz and Graves (1990) strongly recommend external measurements of the timing accuracy of the employed computer systems and that "corrections of any systematic errors be made, and that such accuracy measurements and corrections be reported in published research articles". Unfortunately, timing *accuracy* is in general not easy to assess. It depends on various factors and may even change over time during running experiments. The timing mechanism implemented in GDX offers high precision time measurements which allow for analyses of reaction times. However, experimenters need to be aware of potential problems introduced by various combinations of hardware, operating system and other aspects of the experimental environment. In use cases where GDX is employed as a data annotation tool rather than a behavioral experiment framework, timing, of course, might not be of relevance.

In conclusion, we have demonstrated the utility of GDX for categorization tasks (within the scope of the described use case in the study of speech perception). We are positive that GDX offers a useful tool to researchers for experiments on human spoken language processing as well as categorization tasks such as data annotation.

6. Acknowledgements

The initial development of the game has been carried out at the Institute for Natural Language Processing at the University of Stuttgart within Project A4 of the Collaborative Research Center SFB 732 funded by the German Research Council (DFG), PI: Grzegorz Dogil and Antje Schweitzer. This work also benefitted from many discussions within the scientific network *Simphon.Net* (funded by DFG). We thank Jenny Krüwald who carried out some of the experiments within her Bachelor's thesis (Krüwald et al., 2018). We also thank the participants in our experiments and the anonymous reviewers for very helpful feedback.

7. Bibliographical References

Anderson, A. H., Bader, M., Bard, E. G., Boyle, E., Doherty, G., Garrod, S., Isard, S., Kowtko, J., McAllister, J., Miller, J., Sotillo, C., Thompson, H. S., and Weinert, R. (1991). The HCRC Map Task Corpus. *Language and Speech*, 34(4):351–366.

Babel, M. and McGuire, G. (2015). The effects of talker variability on phonetic accommodation. In *Proceedings of the 18th International Congress of Phonetic Sciences (ICPhS)*, pages 1–5, Glasgow, UK. Paper number 661.

Babel, M. (2012). Evidence for phonetic and social selectivity in spontaneous phonetic imitation. *Journal of Phonetics*, 40(1):177–189.

Babjack, D. L., Cernicky, B., Sobotka, A. J., Basler, L., Struthers, D., Kisic, R., Barone, K., and Zuccolotto, A. P. (2015). Reducing audio stimulus presentation latencies across studies, laboratories, and hardware and operating system configurations. *Behavior Research Methods*, 47(3):649–665.

Bailly, G. and Lelong, A. (2010). Speech dominoes and phonetic convergence. In *Proceedings of Interspeech*, pages 1153–1156, Tokio (Japan).

Baker, R. and Hazan, V. (2011). DiapixUK: task materials for the elicitation of multiple spontaneous speech dialogs. *Behavior Research Methods*, 43(3):761–770.

Beňuš, Š., Trnka, M., Kuric, E., Marták, L., Gravano, A., Hirschberg, J., and Levitan, R. (2018). Prosodic entrainment and trust in human-computer interaction. In *Proceedings of the 9th International Conference on Speech Prosody 2018*, pages 220–224.

Berger, A., Jones, L., Rothbart, M. K., and Posner, M. I. (2000). Computerized games to study the development of attention in childhood. *Behavior Research Methods, Instruments, & Computers*, 32(2):297–303.

Boersma, P. and Weenink, D. (2020). Praat: doing phonetics by computer. [Computer program]. Version 6.1.

Boersma, P. (2001). Praat, a system for doing phonetics by computer. *Glot International*, 5(9/10):341–345.

Craft, J. L. and Simon, J. R. (1970). Processing symbolic information from a visual display: Interference from an irrelevant directional cue. *Journal of Experimental Psychology*, 83(3, Pt.1):415–420.

De Looze, C., Oertel, C., Rauzy, S., and Campbell, N. (2011). Measuring dynamics of mimicry by means of prosodic cues in conversational speech. In *International Conference on Phonetic Sciences (ICPhS). Hong Kong*, page 1294–1297.

Delvaux, V. and Soquet, A. (2007). Inducing imitative phonetic variation in the laboratory. In *Proceedings of the 16th ICPhS*, pages 369–372, Saarbrücken.

Donchin, E. (1995). Video games as research tools: The

Space Fortress game. *Behavior Research Methods, Instruments, & Computers*, 27(2):217–223.

Duran, D. and Lewandowski, N. (2018). Untersuchung der kognitiven Beanspruchung durch Sprachassistenzsysteme. In André Berton, et al., editors, *Elektronische Sprachsignalverarbeitung 2018: Tagungsband der 29. Konferenz*, pages 159–166. TUDpress, Dresden.

Forster, K. I. and Forster, J. C. (2003). DMDX: A Windows display program with millisecond accuracy. *Behavior Research Methods, Instruments, & Computers*, 35(1):116–124.

Frey, A., Hartig, J., Ketzel, A., Zinkernagel, A., and Moosbrugger, H. (2007). The use of virtual environments based on a modification of the computer game Quake III Arena® in psychological experimenting. *Computers in Human Behavior*, 23(4):2026–2039, July.

Garrod, S. and Anderson, A. (1987). Saying what you mean in dialogue: A study in conceptual and semantic co-ordination. *Cognition*, 27(2):181–218.

Gessinger, I., Möbius, B., Fakhar, N., Raveh, E., and Steiner, I. (2019). A Wizard-of-Oz Experiment to Study Phonetic Accommodation in Human-Computer Interaction. In *Proceedings of the 19th International Congress of Phonetic Sciences*, pages 1475–1479.

H. Giles, editor. (2016). *Communication Accommodation Theory: Negotiating Personal Relationships and Social Identities Across Contexts*. Cambridge University Press.

Gray, W. D. (2017). Game-XP: Action Games as Experimental Paradigms for Cognitive Science. *Topics in Cognitive Science*, 9(2):289–307.

Gruenstein, A., McGraw, I., and Sutherland, A. (2009). A self-transcribing speech corpus: Collecting continuous speech with an online educational game. In *ISCA International Workshop on Speech and Language Technology in Education (SLaTE)*, pages 109–112.

Habernal, I., Pauli, P., and Gurevych, I. (2018). Adapting serious game for fallacious argumentation to German: Pitfalls, insights, and best practices. In *Proceedings of the Eleventh International Conference on Language Resources and Evaluation (LREC 2018)*, Miyazaki, Japan.

Hawkins, G. E., Rae, B., Nesbitt, K. V., and Brown, S. D. (2012). Gamelike features might not improve data. *Behavior Research Methods*, 45(2):301–318.

Hawkins, R. X. D. (2015). Conducting real-time multiplayer experiments on the web. *Behavior Research Methods*, 47(4):966–976.

Howes, A. (2017). Games for psychological science. *Topics in Cognitive Science*, 9(2):533–536.

Järvelä, S., Ekman, I., Kivikangas, J. M., and Ravaja, N. (2014). A practical guide to using digital games as an experiment stimulus. *Transactions of the Digital Games Research Association*, 1(2):85–115.

Keil, J., Michel, A., Sticca, F., Leipold, K., Klein, A. M., Sierau, S., von Klitzing, K., and White, L. O. (2016). The Pizzagame: A virtual public goods game to assess cooperative behavior in children and adolescents. *Behavior Research Methods*.

Kicikoglu, D., Bartle, R., Chamberlain, J., and Poesio, M. (2019). Wormingo: a 'true gamification' approach to anaphoric annotation. In *FDG '19: Proceedings of the 14th International Conference on the Foundations of Digital Games*, pages 1–7. Association for Computing Machinery. Article No.: 75.

Kim, M., Horton, W. S., and Bradlow, A. R. (2011). Phonetic convergence in spontaneous conversations as a function of interlocutor language distance. *Lab Phon*, 2(1).

Kimball, G., Cano, R., Feng, J., Feng, L., Hampson, E., Li, E., Christel, M. G., Holt, L. L., Lim, S.-j., Liu, R., and Lehet, M. (2013). Supporting research into sound and speech learning through a configurable computer game. In *IEEE International Games Innovation Conference (IGIC)*, pages 110–113.

Kirsh, D. and Maglio, P. (1994). On Distinguishing Epistemic from Pragmatic Action. *Cognitive Science*, 18(4):513–549.

Krüwald, J., Duran, D., and Lewandowski, N. (2018). Gamification in the phonology lab. Presented at: LabPhon16 – Variation, development and impairment: Between phonetics and phonology.

Kuznetsova, A., Brockhoff, P. B., and Christensen, R. H. B. (2017). lmerTest package: Tests in linear mixed effects models. *J. of Stat. Software*, 82(13):1–26.

Lange, L., Pfeiffer, B., and Duran, D. (2015). ABIMS – auditory bewildered interaction measurement system. In *Proceedings of the 16th Annual Conference of the International Speech Communication Association (Interspeech)*, pages 1074–1075.

Levitan, R., Gravano, A., Willson, L., Beňuš, Š., Hirschberg, J., and Nenkova, A. (2012). Acoustic-prosodic entrainment and social behavior. In *Proceedings of the Conference of the North American Chapter of the Association for Computational Linguistics: Human Language Technologies*, pages 11–19.

Levitan, S. I., Shin, J., Chen, I., and Hirschberg, J. (2018). LieCatcher: Game framework for collecting human judgments of deceptive speech. In Jon Chamberlain, et al., editors, *Games4NLP – Games and Gamification for Natural Language Processing. Proceedings*, pages 12–16.

Lewandowski, N. and Duran, D. (2018). Testing speech perception today and tomorrow: serious computer games as perception tests. In André Berton, et al., editors, *Elektronische Sprachsignalverarbeitung 2018: Tagungsband der 29. Konferenz*, pages 232–239. TUDpress, Dresden.

Lewandowski, N. and Jilka, M. (2019). Phonetic convergence, language talent, personality and attention. *Frontiers in Communication*, 4:18.

Lewandowski, N. (2012). *Talent in nonnative phonetic convergence*. Doctoral dissertation, Institut für Maschinelle Sprachverarbeitung, Universität Stuttgart.

Lewandowski, N. (2013). Phonetic convergence and individual differences in non-native dialogs. Montréal, Canada. Abstract presented at New Sounds.

Lim, S.-j. and Holt, L. L. (2011). Learning Foreign Sounds in an Alien World: Videogame Training Improves Non-Native Speech Categorization. *Cognitive Science*, 35(7):1390–1405, September.

Lindstedt, J. K. and Gray, W. D. (2015). Meta-T: Tetris as an experimental paradigm for cognitive skills research. *Behavior Research Methods*, 47(4):945–965.

Lumsden, J., Skinner, A., Woods, A. T., Lawrence, N. S., and Munafò, M. (2016). The effects of gamelike features and test location on cognitive test performance and participant enjoyment. *PeerJ*, 4:e2184.

Madge, C., Bartle, R., Chamberlain, J., Kruschwitz, U., and Poesio, M. (2019). Making text annotation fun with a clicker game. In *FDG '19: Proceedings of the 14th International Conference on the Foundations of Digital Games*, pages 1–6. Association for Computing Machinery. Article No.: 77.

Maglio, P. P. and Kirsh, D. (1996). Epistemic action increases with skill. In *Proceedings of the Eighteenth Annual Conference of the Cognitive Science Society*, pages 391–396.

Mayer, I., Bekebrede, G., Harteveld, C., Warmelink, H., Zhou, Q., van Ruijven, T., Lo, J., Kortmann, R., and Wenzler, I. (2014). The research and evaluation of serious games: Toward a comprehensive methodology. *British Journal of Educational Technology*, 45(3):502–527.

McGraw, I., Gruenstein, A., and Sutherland, A. (2009). A self-labeling speech corpus: Collecting spoken words with an online educational game. In *Proceedings of the 10th Annual Conference of the International Speech Communication Association (Interspeech)*, pages 3031–3034.

McPherson, J. and Burns, N. R. (2007). Gs Invaders: Assessing a computer game-like test of processing speed. *Behavior Research Methods*, 39(4):876–883.

McPherson, J. and Burns, N. R. (2008). Assessing the validity of computer-game-like tests of processing speed and working memory. *Behavior Research Methods*, 40(4):969–981.

Namy, L. L., Nygaard, C. L., and Sauerteig, D. (2002). Gender differences in vocal accommodation: The role of perception. *J Lang Soc Psychol*, 21:422–432.

Nelson, J. B., Navarro, A., and Sanjuan, M. d. C. (2014). Presentation and validation of "The Learning Game," a tool to study associative learning in humans. *Behavior Research Methods*, 46(4):1068–1078.

Newell, A. (1973). You can't play 20 questions with nature and win: projective comments on the papers of this symposium. Technical report, Carnegie Mellon University. Research Showcase at CMU.

Nielsen, K. (2011). Specificity and abstractness of VOT imitation. *Journal of Phonetics*, 39(2):132–142.

Peirce, J. W. (2007). PsychoPy—Psychophysics software in Python. *Journal of Neuroscience Methods*, 162(1-2):8–13, May.

Peterson, M. (2010). Computerized games and simulations in computer-assisted language learning: A meta-analysis of research. *Simulation & Gaming*, 41(1):72–93.

Picca, D., Jaccard, D., and Eberlé, G. (2015). Natural language processing in serious games: A state of the art. *International Journal of Serious Games*, 2(3):77–97.

Pickering, M. J. and Garrod, S. (2013). An integrated theory of language production and comprehension. *Behavioral and Brain Sciences*, 36(04):329–347.

Porter, D. B. (1995). Computer games: Paradigms of opportunity. *Behavior Research Methods, Instruments, & Computers*, 27(2):229–234.

Quinn, C. N. (1991). Computers for cognitive research: A HyperCard adventure game. *Behavior Research Methods, Instruments, & Computers*, 23(2):237–246.

R Core Team, (2017). *R: A Language and Environment for Statistical Computing*. R Foundation for Statistical Computing, Vienna, Austria.

Rácz, P., Hay, J. B., and Pierrehumbert, J. B. (2017). Social salience discriminates learnability of contextual cues in an artificial language. *Frontiers in Psychology*, 8.

Rebenitsch, L. and Owen, C. (2016). Review on cybersickness in applications and visual displays. *Virtual Reality*, 20(2):101–125.

Sachdev, I. and Giles, H. (2006). Bilingual Accommodation. In Tej K. Bhatia et al., editors, *The handbook of bilingualism*, pages 353–378. Blackwell Publishing, Malden, MA, USA.

Schweitzer, A. and Lewandowski, N. (2013). Convergence of articulation rate in spontaneous speech. In *Proceedings of the 14th Interspeech, Lyon*, pages 525–529.

Schweitzer, A. and Lewandowski, N. (2014). Social factors in convergence of f1 and f2 in spontaneous speech. In *Proceedings of the 10th International Seminar on Speech Production, Cologne*.

Schweitzer, A., Lewandowski, N., and Duran, D. (2015). Attention, please! Expanding the GECO database. In The Scottish Consortium for ICPhS 2015, editor, *Proceedings of the 18th International Congress of Phonetic Sciences (ICPhS)*, Glasgow, UK. Paper number 620.

Schweitzer, A., Lewandowski, N., and Duran, D. (2017). Social Attractiveness in Dialogs. In *Interspeech 2017*, pages 2243–2247.

Segalowitz, S. J. and Graves, R. E. (1990). Suitability of the IBM XT, AT, and PS/2 keyboard, mouse, and game port as response devices in reaction time paradigms. *Behavior Research Methods, Instruments, & Computers*, 22(3):283–289.

Segalowitz, N. (2007). Access Fluidity, Attention Control, and the Acquisition of Fluency in a Second Language. *TESOL Quarterly*, 41(1):181–186.

Singmann, H., Bolker, B., Westfall, J., and Aust, F., (2018). *afex: Analysis of Factorial Experiments*. R package version 0.19-1.

Trofimovich, P. and Kennedy, S. (2014). Interactive alignment between bilingual interlocutors: Evidence from two information-exchange tasks. *Bilingualism: Language and Cognition*, 17(04):822–836.

Unity Technologies. (2016). Unity. Computer program. Version 5.

Vais, J., Walsh, M., and Lewandowski, N. (2015). Investigating frequency of occurrence effects in l2 speakers: Talent matters. In The Scottish Consortium for ICPhS 2015, editor, *Proceedings of the 18th International Congress of Phonetic Sciences*, pages 1–5, Glasgow, UK. Paper number 723.

Van Engen, K. J., Baese-Berk, M., Baker, R. E., Choi, A., Kim, M., and Bradlow, A. R. (2010). The Wildcat Corpus of Native-and Foreign-accented English: Communicative Efficiency across Conversational Dyads with Varying Language Alignment Profiles. *Language and Speech*, 53(4):510–540.

von Ahn, L. (2006). Games with a purpose. *Computer*, 39(6):92–94.

Wade, T. and Holt, L. L. (2005). Incidental categorization of spectrally complex non-invariant auditory stimuli in a computer game task. *The Journal of the Acoustical Society of America*, 118(4):2618–2633.

Ward, N. G. and Abu, S. (2016). Action-coordinating prosody. In *Proc. Speech Prosody*, pages 629–633.

Washburn, D. A. and Gulledge, J. P. (1995). Game-like tasks for comparative research: Leveling the playing field. *Behavior Research Methods, Instruments, & Computers*, 27(2):235–238.

Wickham, H. (2016). *ggplot2: Elegant Graphics for Data Analysis*. Springer-Verlag New York.

Wickham, H., (2017). *tidyverse: Easily Install and Load the 'Tidyverse'*. R package version 1.2.1.

Aggregation Driven Progression for GWAPs

Doruk Kicikoglu,♣ Richard Bartle,♠ Silviu Paun,♣ Jon Chamberlain,♠ Massimo Poesio♣
o.d.kicikoglu@qmul.ac.uk, rabartle@essex.ac.uk, s.paun@qmul.ac.uk, jchamb@essex.ac.uk, m.poesio@qmul.ac.uk
♣Queen Mary Univ. Of London, United Kingdom
♠University Of Essex, United Kingdom

Abstract

As the use of Games-With-A-Purpose (GWAPs) broadens, their annotation schemes have increased in complexity. The types of annotations required within NLP are an example of labelling that can involve varying complexity of annotations. Assigning more complex tasks to more skilled players through a progression mechanism can achieve higher accuracy in the collected data while acting as a motivating factor that rewards the more skilled players. In this paper, we present the progression technique implemented in Wormingo , an NLP GWAP that currently includes two layers of task complexity. For the experiment, we have implemented four different progression scenarios on 192 players and compared the accuracy and engagement achieved with each scenario.

Keywords: GWAPs, player progression, Bayesian models, coreference annotation, citizen science

1. Introduction

The first GWAPs focused on simple tasks varying from text deciphering to image or sound labelling (von Ahn and Dabbish, 2004; Lafourcade et al., 2015; Barrington et al., 2009). Such GWAPs did not require their players to progress to more advanced tasks. However, modern GWAPs collecting more complex judgments, as in NLP, may require players to carry out annotations of varying complexity that may be harder to teach to entry-level players (Poesio et al., 2013). Such GWAPs may benefit from the practice, widely adopted within the gaming industry (Koster and Wright, 2004), of introducing a player to simpler tasks and proceeding to the more complicated ones once they have proven successful on the initial tasks. Such skill progression achieves higher motivation and engagement as the players are kept within flow (Csikszentmihalyi, 1991), meaning they face challenges corresponding to their improving competence. GWAPs can achieve a similar affect with this approach. In addition, this type of progression increases the quality of the data produced as players are assigned with more complicated tasks, only after they have reached a sufficient understanding of the annotation tasks within the system (Madge et al., 2019).

The fact that GWAP players vary in terms of competence makes it mandatory to assess the players by comparing to golden data, and proceed only when they reach a certain level of accuracy (Ipeirotis and Gabrilovich, 2015; Madge et al., 2019; Fort et al., 2014; Chamberlain et al., 2008). In addition to many GWAPs that utilize this method, Phrase Detectives and Zombilingo also implement progression techniques that assess the player accuracy based on the types of tasks that they are performing. These GWAPs include different types of tasks which vary in complexity. Players begin with simpler tasks, then move on to more complicated annotation tasks once they reached a certain level of success during the assessment period.

In addition to aligning the player progression along task complexity, another axis can be the difficulty of the labels; that can be defined as the difficulty of a label compared to the other labels within the same task i.e. some spans might be more ambiguous in Phrase Detectives, hence may be more difficult to resolve; creating more disagreement among the players. In a system where labels are identified and ranked by their difficulty, players can be assigned with more difficult tasks once they prove successful on the easier ones. Tile Attack and Quizz implement this technique, where players are assigned with labels matching their competence level (Ipeirotis and Gabrilovich, 2015; Madge et al., 2019).

Wormingo implements both of these approaches of progression. As players progress, they can advance to both more difficult documents (difficulty progression) and more complicated tasks (task progression). For difficulty progression, the documents in Wormingo are manually labelled into 5 levels of difficulty ranging from letter A to E. The documents in level A are considered as the easiest in terms of comprehension, while those in level E are the most difficult, that may include more sophisticated vocabulary or more complicated sentence structure. Wormingo uses a level-up mechanism which lets players reach higher levels (currently up to level 16) after collecting score points awarded for annotations. Players can play more difficult documents, only after reaching higher player levels (Figure 1).

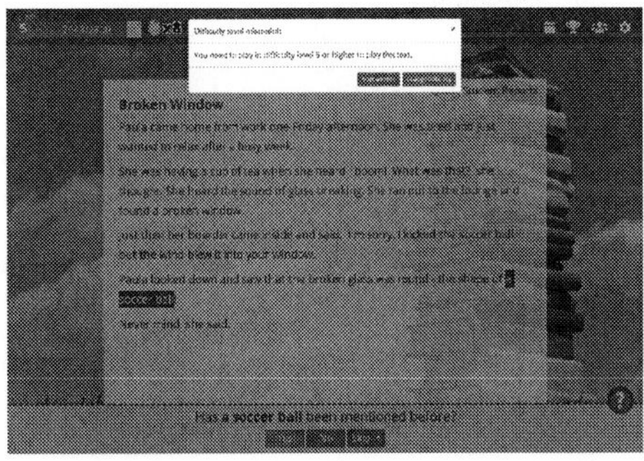

Figure 1: Player attempts to access a document that is too difficult for their level

Level-up mechanisms are widely used within games (Zichermann and Cunningham, 2011). Although they are proven effective for rewarding commitment to the game, they do not necessarily indicate that the player is more competent. A player who performs poorly in terms of accuracy can simply hoard points by playing longer and still reach the next player level. Therefore, when assessing the players' competence for more advanced tasks, their annotation accuracy can be a better indicator rather than the points they managed to hoard.

Comparing the players' annotations to the gold or aggregated data yields the player accuracy. However, cases in Phrase Detectives show that higher numbers of players can agree on a wrong annotation while fewer number of skilled players might contrarily have given the correct answer for a label (Paun et al., 2018). Relying solely on the number of annotators can be misleading in such cases. Therefore, Mention Pair Annotations model (MPA) builds a confidence-based model. MPA generates confidence scores for annotations, and players, via Bayesian models with the players' annotation accuracy taken into consideration. Players who have higher accuracy gain a higher confidence score from a range between 0 and 1. During data aggregation, the annotations of players with higher confidence scores are evaluated with higher weight. MPA also generates separate player confidence scores for each task, evaluating players' performance on individual tasks. This model overcomes the aforementioned problem and produces confidence ratings both for the aggregated data and the players. Wormingo uses the player confidence outcome when assessing their competence to progress to more complicated tasks.

2. Background

2.1. Annotation Tasks

Wormingo currently includes two types of annotation tasks, discourse-new and non-referring. The earlier versions of Wormingo already included the discourse-new task (Figure 2), which asks players if a label in the task has been mentioned before (Kicikoglu et al., 2019). In the current version of Wormingo , the non-referring task has been implemented as the second and more advanced task.

In the discourse-new task, the players annotate coreference chains. The game asks the players to annotate a label, such as the label "him" illustrated with purple colour in Figure 2. The player clicks "No" if this label was not mentioned in the text before, or "Yes" if it was mentioned. After clicking "Yes", clusters of phrases that we call "markables" are highlighted with colour yellow (Figure 3). The player chooses which of the markables that the label refers to in this interface.

In the non-referring task, labels such as "it" in the sentences "It is raining", "It is 3 o'clock" do not refer to a real object. Such occurrences should be labelled as non-referring (Chamberlain et al., 2009). However, this adds an extra layer to the discourse-new task implemented in the earlier versions of Wormingo , because in addition to the possibility of being a non-referring label, an occurrence of the word "it" can be a part of a coreference chain as well; such as in "I had a pizza, it was good!". Therefore,

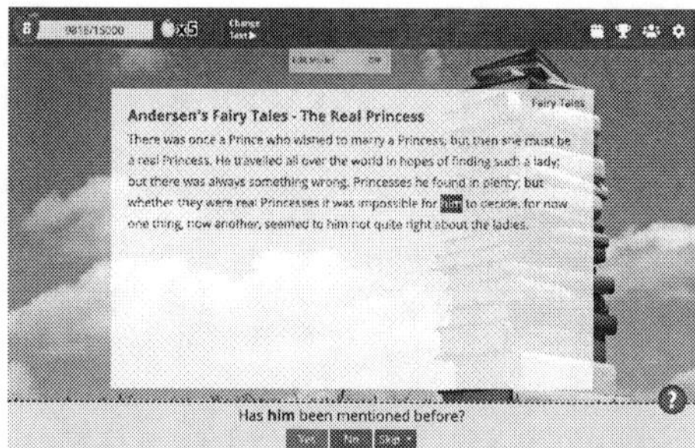

Figure 2: Discourse New Annotation Interface

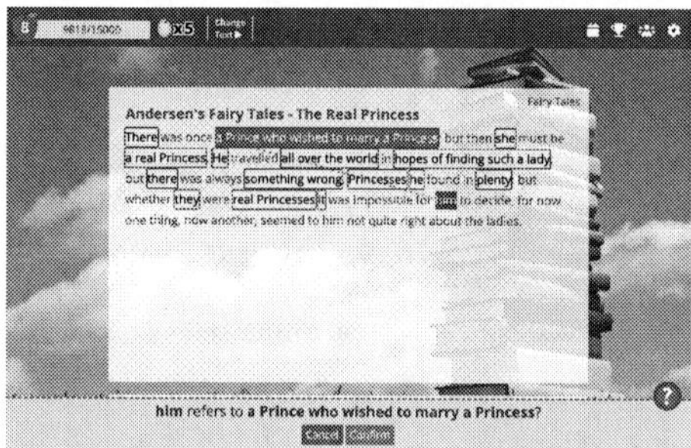

Figure 3: Discourse New Interface - Marking coreference

non-referring is considered as a more complicated task laid on top of the discourse-new task, as it includes the complexity of the discourse-new task with the non-referring option added on top. On the interface, non-referring task uses the same interface layout as the discourse-new task, but an additional "NR" button is added. Players who click this button annotate the given label as non-referring (Figure 4). Non-referring cases occur on expletive words "it" and "there", so only the labels with these string values were asked in the non-referring tasks.

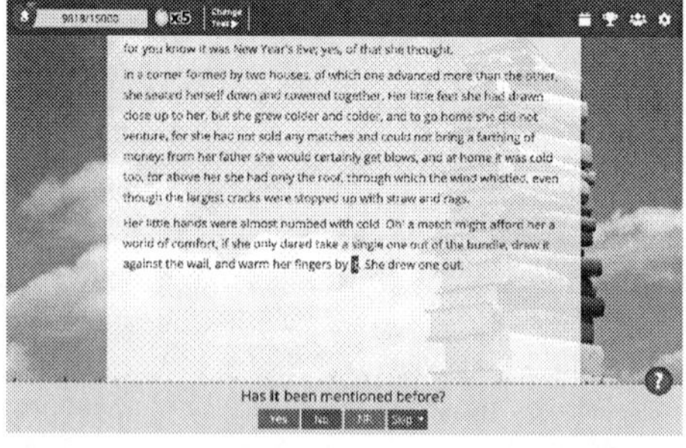

Figure 4: Non-referring Annotation Interface

2.2. Tutorials

Players are taught about the discourse-new task on their first annotation. This is done through freezing the interface and showing the player a message that explains the discourse new task. First an example whose correct answer is discourse-new (has not been mentioned before) is shown and the player can only continue by clicking the "No" button, which labels the annotation as discourse-new (Figure 5). On the following annotation, players are similarly shown a label that has been mentioned in the text before. Players can continue only by linking the label to one of its antecedents and clicking the "Confirm" button on this interface (Figure 6).

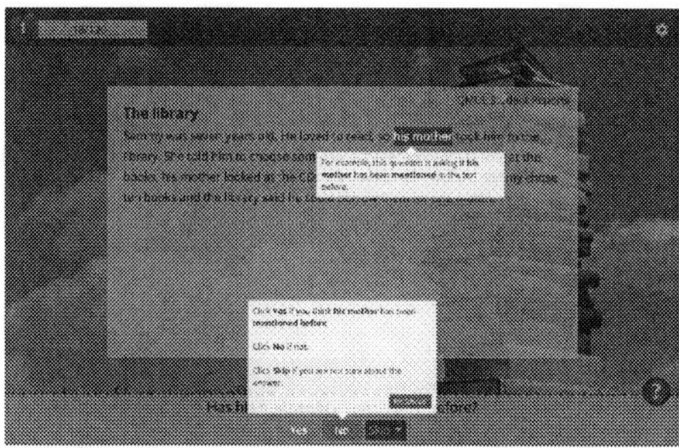

Figure 5: Tutorial for a discourse new label

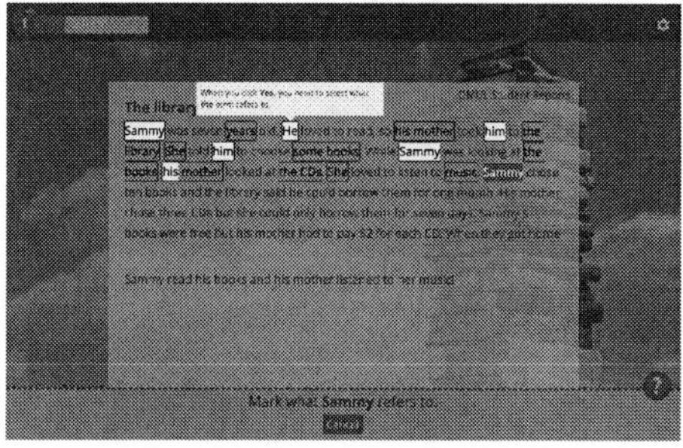

Figure 6: Tutorial for marking coreference

The case-selection algorithm of Wormingo chooses the next documents and labels to represent to the players from a selection of available items, where incomplete labels that received at least one annotation are prioritized (Chen et al., 2010). Labels that have received less than 7 annotations are considered incomplete.

Once a player has been assessed to qualify to the non-referring task, the case-selection algorithm starts including expletive labels as well. Expletive labels gain higher priority scores; however the final case selection happens with a random selection where higher priority items gain higher probability -meaning an item with less probability still has a chance to appear as the next task depending on the generated random value. The player may also qualify to the non-referring task while playing a document that contains no expletive expressions at all. Thus, the player may not immediately encounter a non-referring task after qualifying to the non-referring tasks. Once they do encounter a non-referring task for a first time, the tutorial interface appears (Figure 7) and the players are explained about the non-referring task and introduced with the "NR" button that allows the players to annotate labels as non-referring.

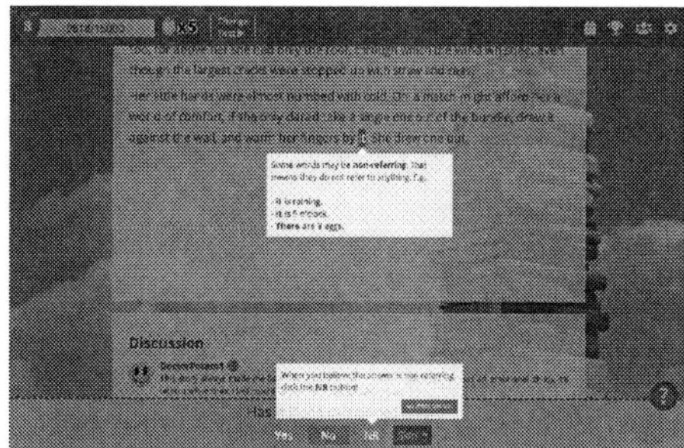

Figure 7: Tutorial for non-referring tasks

2.3. Methodology

In the experiment, we divided the players into 4 groups. Each group needed to accomplish a different scenario to advance to the non-referring tasks. Group A needed to earn 350 score points, which corresponds to reaching level 3 and an average of 16.77 discourse-new annotations (players gain 25 points for each correct discourse-new annotation and 50 points for each correct non-referring annotation). The accuracy of this group was not considered when evaluating; hoarding enough points was sufficient for Group A to qualify to the non-referring task.

Groups B, C and D needed to pass the 350 point barrier like Group A. On top of this, they needed to achieve certain MPA confidence scores for their discourse-new annotations. Group B needed to reach 0.8 MPA confidence score in order to progress. Group C needed to reach 0.85 confidence score and Group D needed to reach 0.9. Comparing Group A to the other groups allowed observing the difference between assessing players based solely on their score, versus assessing players based on their accuracy. Comparing Group B, C and D allowed observing how the value of the qualification threshold affects the data produced.

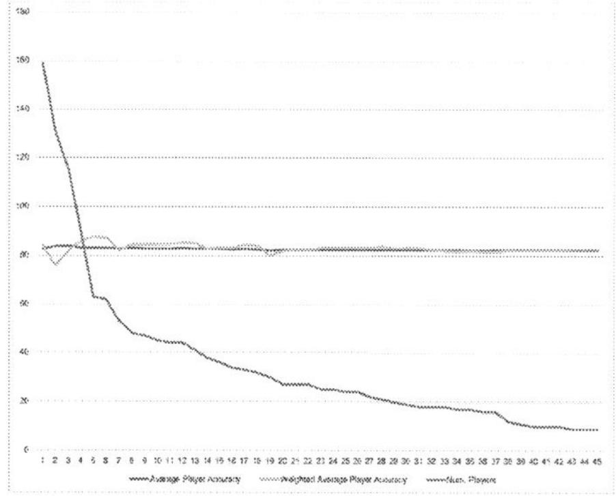

Figure 8: Average discourse new accuracy of players by number of annotations

Prior to the experiment, players were evaluated based on their discourse-new annotation accuracy over time. The yellow line in Figure 8 displays the average accuracy of players, varying by the number of annotations they have done. The red line is their weighted accuracy; calculated by comparing players' accuracy on each document to the average accuracy of all players on the respective document. The average weighted accuracy can vary on the first few annotations, but after players' 10th annotations, it reaches a plateau around 84% accuracy. Therefore, we took 10 annotations as the threshold -the number of discourse-new annotations a player must complete before being progressing to the non-referring tasks. Players who did annotations fewer than this threshold were not assigned to any of the observation group. The players who reached 350 points and did at least 10 annotations were assigned to an observation group.

3. Results

We analyze the data produced between 07 Feb 2020 and 17 Mar 2020. During this period, 192 Wormingo players did at least 1 annotation. The players came from the subreddits that we have posted on reddit.com and university e-mail groups with interest towards Computer Science and games.

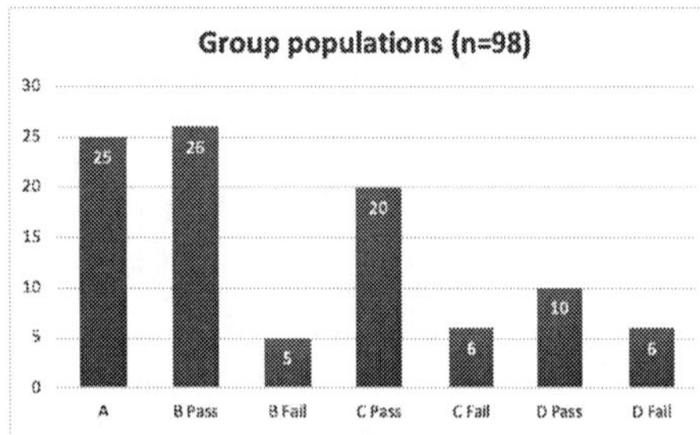

Figure 9: Number of players per group

Out of the 192 players, 98 completed the qualification requirements and were therefore assigned to a observation group. Figure 9 shows the number of players in each group. Groups B Pass, C Pass and D Pass are the groups of players who were originally in groups B, C and D respectively and have accomplished progression to the non-referring tasks. Similarly, groups B Fail, C Fail and D Fail contain the players who were in groups B, C and D respectively but failed to advance to the next task.

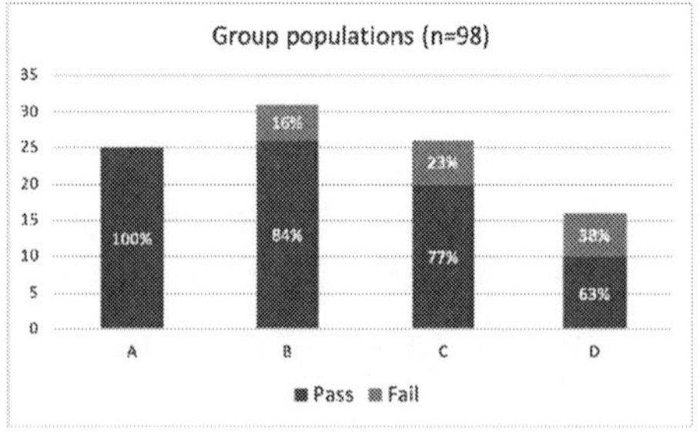

Figure 10: Pass/Fail percentages per group

Figure 10 shows each group's ratio of players who passed or failed progression to the non-referring task. The ratio of players increase as expected from Group B towards D;

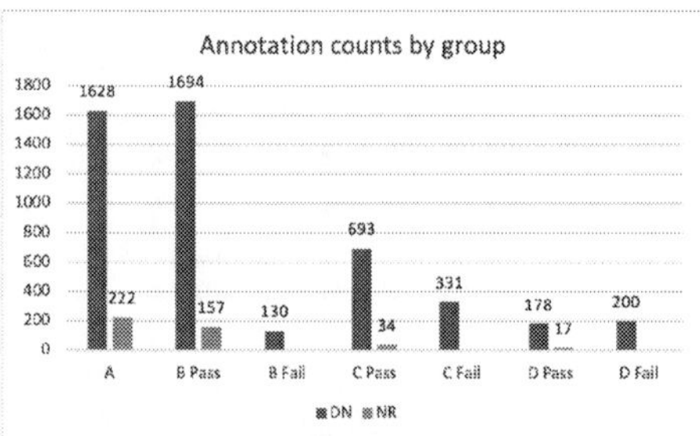

Figure 11: Total annotation counts per group

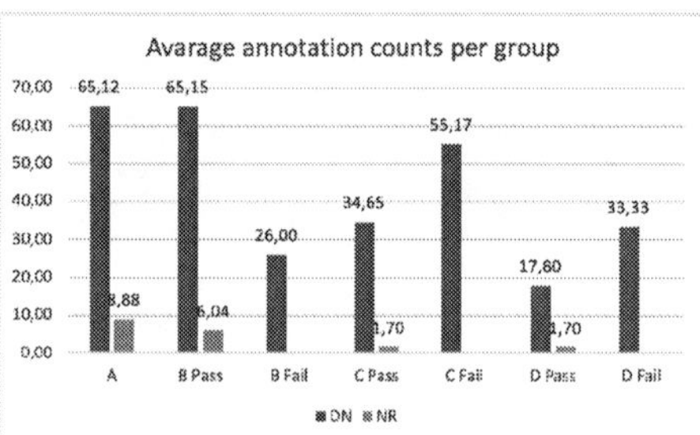

Figure 12: Average annotation counts per player

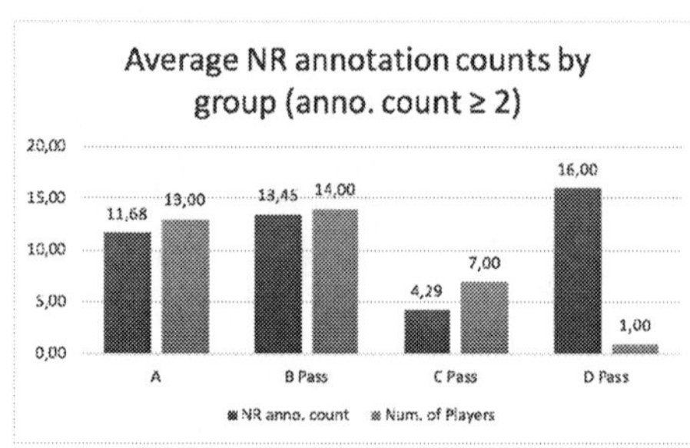

Figure 13: Average number of NR annotations and number of players who have done at least 2 NR annotations

as the threshold for progression also increases towards this direction.

Figures 11 and 12 display annotation counts per group and average annotations done by players within each group. Figure 12 includes players who have qualified to the NR task but have not done any non-referring annotations (since players may not immediately come across NR tasks after they qualify), hence the average annotation counts appear low. Figure 13 provides more meaningful average scores, as it displays values for players who have done at least 2 annotations. Groups A and B Pass contribute significantly higher number of annotations (DN and NR) in both total and average per player.

Figure 14 shows the groups' average accuracy and MPA confidence scores, wherein no significant difference in terms of NR accuracy is observed. However a significant difference is observed in D Pass group's NR MPA confi-

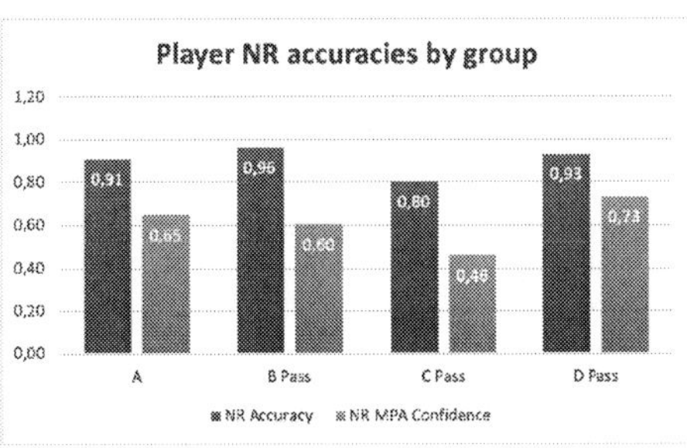

Figure 14: Average non-referring accuracy and MPA confidence scores per group

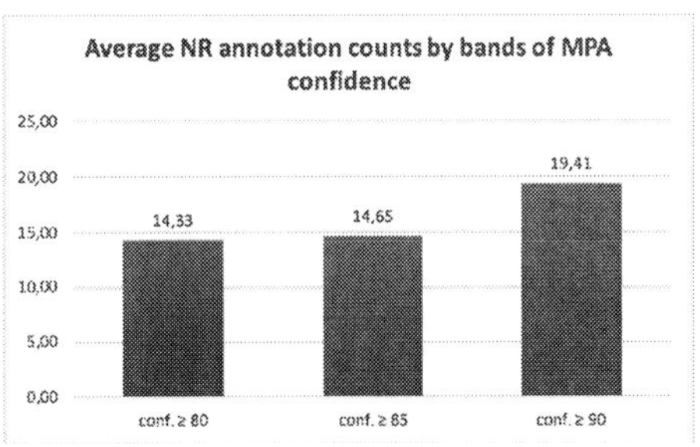

Figure 17: Average Non-referring annotation counts for each band of NR MPA confidence

dence value (p=0.01). Although it might seem like a good strategy to set the qualification threshold to D Pass group's value, 0.9, this would potentially lead to generation of too small data, as D Pass group has only generated 17 NR annotations. B-Pass group however generated much more data (157 annotation) with an average of 0.60 confidence.

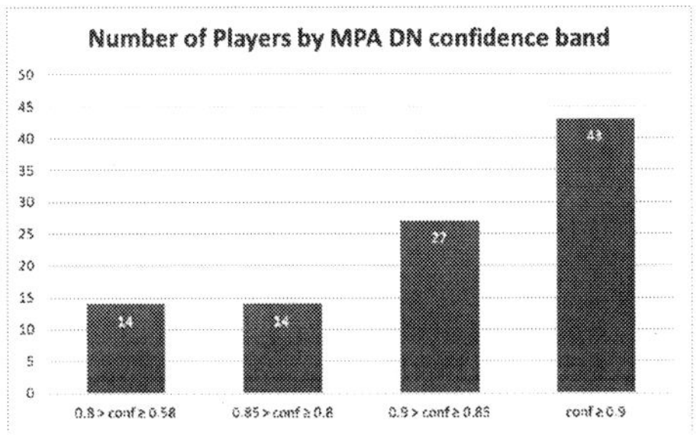

Figure 15: Number of players within each band of NR MPA confidence scores

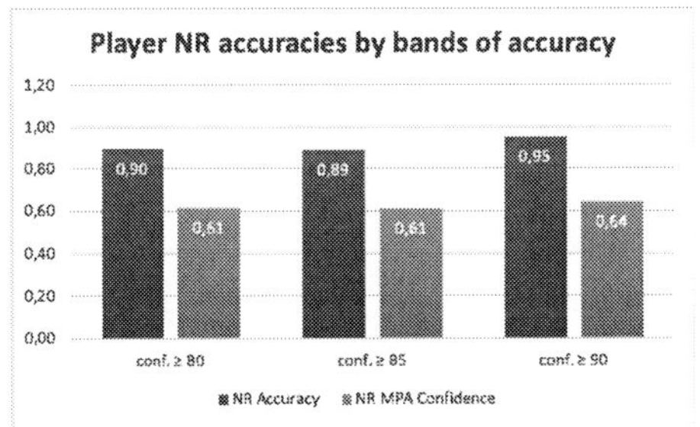

Figure 16: Non-referring accuracy and MPA confidence scores for each band of NR MPA confidence

Figure 15, 16 and 17 groups all players by their DN MPA confidence scores, instead of their observation groups. The bands "conf. $\geq$ 80", "conf. $\geq$ 85" and "conf. $\geq$ 90" are players whose DN confidence scores were higher than 0.8, 0.85 and 0.9 respectively and they are not exclusive of each other. We observe that a majority of players score higher than 0.85 DN MPA confidence in Figure 15. 43% of players score higher than 0.9 while 71% score higher than 0.85.

We do not observe significant difference in terms of non-referring task competence between bands "conf. $\geq$ 80" and "conf. $\geq$ 85" bands (Figure 16). A slight increase is observed in the "conf. $\geq$ 90" band, however we do not have yet sufficient evidence to conclude that the threshold should be set to 0.9. Players in "conf. $\geq$ 90" band do produce more NR annotations per player (Figure 16), however setting the threshold at this level would rule out 57% of players who perform sufficiently well in terms of accuracy at the lower levels (Paun et al., 2018). We hope that future studies with more players, more data, and more levels of complexity can could provide more definitive results.

4. Discussion

In this paper, we have tested 4 different scenarios of skills progression in Wormingo. The fact that the players have voluntarily come to the game rather than for a paid reward, assures more relevance of this data to the general GWAP audience. However, the few number of participants that arrived within the limited time hinders the accuracy of our measurements, leaving room for future research on the area, possibly with more advanced tasks added.

Players who score high on discourse new tasks also achieve high accuracy on non-referring tasks. This fact is encouraging, as it supports the claim that allowing only competent players to do more complicated tasks produces cleaner data. However, this comes with a cost. Setting a threshold too high will hinder the players who have the potential to score adequately on the more complicated tasks. Setting it too low pollutes the produced data. The results show that players can perform higher accuracy on more advanced tasks, if they have were sufficiently trained on the preceding tasks. An optimal threshold that will neither rule out skilled annotators nor pollute the data can be calculated based upon the players' performance on the initial tasks.

5. Acknowledgements

This research was supported in part by the DALI project, ERC Grant 695662, in part by the EPSRC CDT in Intelligent Games and Game Intelligence (IGGI), EP/L015846/1.

6. References

Barrington, L., O'Malley, D., Turnbull, D., and Lanckriet, G. (2009). User-centered design of a social game to tag music. In *Proceedings of the ACM SIGKDD Workshop on Human Computation*, HCOMP '09, pages 7–10, New York, NY, USA. ACM.

Chamberlain, J., Poesio, M., and Kruschwitz, U. (2008). Phrase detectives: A web-based collaborative annotation game. 01.

Chamberlain, J., Kruschwitz, U., and Poesio, M. (2009). Constructing an anaphorically annotated corpus with non-experts: Assessing the quality of collaborative annotations. In *Proceedings of the 2009 Workshop on The People's Web Meets NLP: Collaboratively Constructed Semantic Resources*, People's Web '09, page 57–62, USA. Association for Computational Linguistics.

Chen, L.-J., Wang, B.-C., and Chen, K.-T. (2010). The design of puzzle selection strategies for gwap systems. *Concurrency and Computation: Practice and Experience*, 22(7):890–908.

Csikszentmihalyi, M. (1991). *Flow: The Psychology of Optimal Experience*. Harper Perennial, New York, NY, March.

Fort, K., Guillaume, B., and Chastant, H. (2014). Creating zombilingo, a game with a purpose for dependency syntax annotation. In *Proceedings of the First International Workshop on Gamification for Information Retrieval*, GamifIR '14, page 2–6, New York, NY, USA. Association for Computing Machinery.

Ipeirotis, P. G. and Gabrilovich, E. (2015). Quizz: Targeted crowdsourcing with a billion (potential) users. *CoRR*, abs/1506.01062.

Kicikoglu, D., Bartle, R., Chamberlain, J., and Poesio, M. (2019). Wormingo: a 'true gamification' approach to anaphoric annotation. In *FDG '19*.

Koster, R. and Wright, W. (2004). *A Theory of Fun for Game Design*. Paraglyph Press.

Lafourcade, M., Joubert, A., and Brun, N. L. (2015). *Games with a Purpose (GWAPS) (Focus Series in Cognitive Science and Knowledge Management)*. Wiley-ISTE.

Madge, C., Yu, J., Kruschwitz, U., Paun, S., and Poesio, M. (2019). Progression in a language annotation game with a purpose. In *FDG '19*.

Paun, S., Chamberlain, J., Kruschwitz, U., Yu, J., and Poesio, M. (2018). A probabilistic annotation model for crowdsourcing coreference. In *Proceedings of the 2018 Conference on Empirical Methods in Natural Language Processing*, pages 1926–1937, Brussels, Belgium, October-November. Association for Computational Linguistics.

Poesio, M., Chamberlain, J., Kruschwitz, U., Robaldo, L., and Ducceschi, L. (2013). Phrase detectives: Utilizing collective intelligence for internet-scale language resource creation. *ACM Trans. Interact. Intell. Syst.*, 3(1), April.

von Ahn, L. and Dabbish, L. (2004). Labeling images with a computer game. In *Proceedings of the SIGCHI Conference on Human Factors in Computing Systems*, CHI '04, page 319–326, New York, NY, USA. Association for Computing Machinery.

Zichermann, G. and Cunningham, C. (2011). *Gamification by Design: Implementing Game Mechanics in Web and Mobile Apps*. O'Reilly Media, Inc., 1st edition.

Proceedings of the LREC 2020 Workshop Games and Natural Language Processing, pages 85–93
Language Resources and Evaluation Conference (LREC 2020), Marseille, 11–16 May 2020
© European Language Resources Association (ELRA), licensed under CC-BY-NC

Automatic Annotation of Werewolf Game Corpus with Players Revealing Oneselves as Seer/Medium and Divination/Medium Results

Youchao Lin, Miho Kasamatsu, Tengyang Chen, Takuya Fujita, Huaijin Deng, Takehito Utsuro

Graduate School of Systems and Information Engineering, University of Tsukuba, Tsukuba, 305-8573, Japan

Abstract

While playing the communication game "Are You a Werewolf", a player always guesses other players' roles through discussions, based on his own role and other players' crucial utterances. The underlying goal of this paper is to construct an agent that can analyze the participating players' utterances and play the werewolf game as if it is a human. For a step of this underlying goal, this paper studies how to accumulate werewolf game log data annotated with identification of players revealing oneselves as seer/medium, the acts of the divination and the medium and declaring the results of the divination and the medium. In this paper, we divide the whole task into four sub tasks and apply CNN/SVM classifiers to each sub task and evaluate their performance.

Keywords: werewolf game, annotation, CNN, players revealing oneselves as seer/medium

1. Introduction

Werewolf is a party game created in the USSR in 1986. It models a conflict between an informed minority, the werewolf, and an uninformed majority, the villager. The werewolf game has been popular in many countries including Japan. In Japan, particularly, not only the game itself, but several other activities such as "Werewolf TLPT" (Werewolf: the live playing theater) [1], a improvisation where the actors and actresses play the werewolf game, and a TV variety show[2] where comedians, actors, and actresses play the werewolf game.

In the research community of artificial intelligence, it has been well known that the werewolf game is one of games with imperfect information where certain information are hidden from some players. This situation is quite contrary to games with perfect information such as chess, shogi, and go, where it is known that computer programs won a human champion[3]. In the Japanese research community of artificial intelligence, the werewolf game has been considered to be used as one of standard problems to evaluate the performance of general artificial intelligence since 2014 (Shinoda et al., 2014). Also, research activities aiming at developing a computer agent program which participates in the werewolf game has started and the first competition of the AIWolf (artificial intelligence based werewolf)[4] was held in August 2015 (Toriumi et al., 2014).

However, in those previous studies aiming at developing a computer agent program which participates in the werewolf game, research issues that are closely related to natural language processing and knowledge processing research have not been studied extensively. Those higher level research issues should include, e.g., understanding natural language conversations among the participating players, inferring each player's roles considering the contents of their conversations, and deciding the player to be attacked or executed based on high level inference.

Considering the underlying goal of constructing an agent that can analyze the participating players' utterances and play the werewolf game as if it is a human, as the first step, this paper studies how to accumulate werewolf game log data annotated with identification of players revealing oneselves as seer/medium, the acts of the divination and the medium and declaring the results of the divination and the medium. In this paper, we divide the whole task into four sub tasks and apply CNN/SVM classifiers to each sub task and evaluate their performance.

2. Werewolf Game

In the werewolf game, each player is given a role and all the players are divided into one of the werewolf side and the villager side. Then, players of the both sides aim at winning the game. The werewolf side attacks one player of the villager side per day, while the villager side tries to execute one werewolf per day through arguments and votes. The players on the villager side do not know each player's identity of being a werewolf or a human, while those on the werewolf side know those identifies. The werewolf side tries to make the players on the villager side vote themselves to be executed through misleading arguments by providing false information. Table 1 shows a typical case the list of roles of the both sides of the werewolf game with 15 players. Among those roles, the role of the possessed is on the werewolf side and the possessed wins when the werewolf side wins, although the seer divines the possessed to be a human, the medium declares the possessed to be a human as the result of the act of the medium, and the possessed is counted as a human when one survives.

Table 2 and Table 3 also list the rules and common sense of the werewolf game. The players are usually requested to follow those rules listed in Table 2, while they are just assumed to follow those common sense listed in Table 3. Those common sense are considered to be a kind of conventional strategies that are recommended to adopt so as to

---

[1] `http://7th-castle.com/jinrou/index.php` (in Japanese)

[2] `http://www.fujitv.co.jp/jinroh/index.html` (in Japanese)

[3] `http://www-03.ibm.com/ibm/history/ibm100/us/en/icons/deepblue/`,
    `http://www.shogi.or.jp/kisen/denou/` (in Japanese),
    `https://www.deepmind.com/alpha-go.html`

[4] `http://cedec.cesa.or.jp/2015/session/AC/7649.html` (in Japanese)

side	player type when counting the survivors	role	description	# of players
villager	human	villager	A human who does not have any special skill.	8
		seer	A human who belongs to the villager side. Every night, the seer can choose one player and learn whether the player is "werewolf" or "human". Learning the result, the seer can tell it to other players.	1
		medium	A human who belongs to the villager side. The medium can learn whether the player who was voted to be executed on the previous day is "werewolf" or "human". Learning the result, the medium can tell it to other players.	1
		bodyguard	A human who belongs to the villager side. Every night the bodyguard can choose one player except the bodyguard oneself to defend so that the chosen player can avoid being attacked by the werewolves. However, the bodyguard can not learn whether the player chosen to be defended was actually attacked or not.	1
werewolf		possessed	A human who belongs to the werewolf side. The possessed wins when the the werewolf side wins. However, the possessed and werewolves do not know each others' roles.	1
	werewolf	werewolf	Every night the werewolves choose one player on the villager side to be killed. The werewolves know each others' role and can communicate through a channel that are available only to the werewolves.	3
total			—	15

Table 1: Roles in the Werewolf Game (for 15 players)

1	The number of the players for each of the roles of the seer, the medium, the bodyguard, and the possessed is one.
2	The werewolves know each others role.
3	The werewolves can not attack themselves.
4	When the number of the werewolves is larger than that of humans, the werewolf side wins.
5	When all the werewolves are executed, the villager side wins.

Table 2: Rules of the Werewolf Game

1	The content of the utterances by the villagers, the seer, the medium, and the bodyguard do not conflict with the truth.
2	The seer / the medium reveal themselves as a seer / a medium.
3	The content of the utterances by the werewolves and the possessed may conflict with the truth.

Table 3: Common Sense of the Werewolf Game

task	class		training	evaluation
task 1	revealing oneself as a seer		881	178
	revealing oneself as a medium		259	93
	revealing oneself as neither a seer nor a medium		1,336	778
task 2	X	(X = "utterance declaring	3,206	700
	not X	the results of divination / medium")	3,206	12,324
task 3-1	Dieter		145	41
	Peter		195	33
	Clara		165	35
	Erna		134	40
	Otto		183	35
	Liesa		193	44
	Nicolas		210	49
	Katharina		218	31
	Jacob		161	26
	Walter		120	30
	Fridel		202	38
	Thomas		133	27
	Albin		163	44
	Simon		172	41
	Pamela		185	40
	Simson		176	44
	Joachim		210	44
	Moritz		152	29
	Regina		89	23
task 3-2	human		2,398	500
	werewolf		808	200

Table 5: # of Training and Evaluation Examples for Tasks 1, 2, 3-1 and 3-2

raise the winning rates of both the villagers' and the werewolves' sides.

3. Werewolf Game Log

In this paper, as the werewolf game log data, we use that of werewolf BBS[5], which is a werewolf game site on the Internet, where the participating players communicate with each other with a character-based text input communication channel. This werewolf game site keeps the record of the text data of the previous werewolf game log and makes them publicly available.

---

[5] http://www.wolfg.x0.com/ (in Japanese)

4. Werewolf Game Corpus Annotation Tasks

Table 4 overviews the werewolf game corpus annotation tasks we study in this paper. In this paper, we apply supervised classifier learning techniques to those tasks, and

task	task description
task 1	Identifying Players Revealing Oneselves as Seer/Medium
	input: each player and his/her utterances of the first 3 days
	output: one of the classes of task 1 ($\in$ { (i) revealing oneself as a seer, (ii) revealing oneself as a medium, (iii) revealing oneself as neither a seer nor a medium})
task 2	Identifying Utterances declaring the Results of Divination / Medium
	input: each utterance on the 2nd day or after, of the players who are judged as "revealing oneself as a seer / a medium"
	output: one of the classes of task 2 ($\in \{X, \text{not } X\}$, X = "utterance declaring the results of divination / medium"})
task 3-1	Identifying the Names of the Players whose Roles are Identified by the Act of Divination / Medium
	input: each utterance on the 2nd day or after, of the players who are judged as "revealing oneself as a seer / a medium"
	output: one of the classes of task 3-1 (names of the 19 players listed in Table 5)
task 3-2	Identifying Results of Divination / Medium
	input: each utterance on the 2nd day or after, of the players who are judged as "revealing oneself as a seer / a medium"
	output: one of the classes of task 3-2 ($\in$ { human, werewolf })

Table 4: Overview of the Werewolf Game Corpus Annotation Tasks

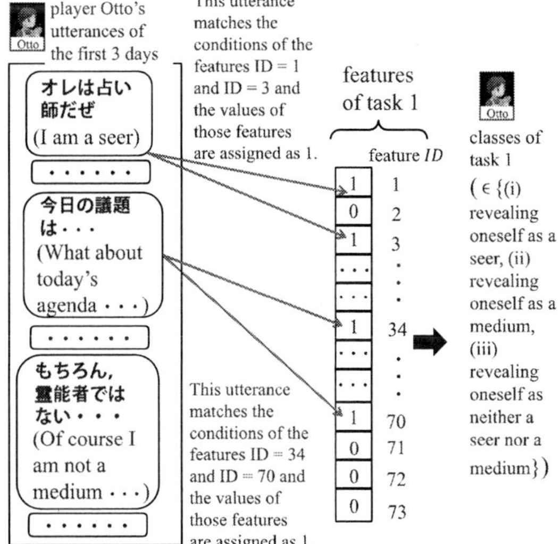

Figure 1: Feature Representation of Task 1 (when manually crafted 73 rules are employed)

Table 5 lists the numbers of training and evaluation examples for each of the four tasks studied in this paper. The following sections introduce each of those four tasks. In the framework of applying classifier learning techniques, where we apply CNN and SVM, we employ manually crafted rules as well as character level text embeddings when designing feature representations of each of those four tasks. Rough idea of the feature representations of those four tasks when manually crafted rules are employed is illustrated in Figure 1 and Figure 2.

4.1. Task 1: Identifying Players Revealing Oneselves as Seer/Medium

The most important information which werewolf game players keep tracking throughout the whole werewolf game, and especially, in the early stage of the game, is that of players who reveal oneselves as a seer / a medium. This is obviously because the players of the roles of the seer / medium provide other players with true information on human / werewolf roles of other players. Thus, among the four tasks, the most important task 1 is that of identifying players who reveal oneselves as a seer / a medium. The input to the task 1 is one of all the 15 players and his/her utterances on the first three days[6], and then as the output of the task 1, the player given to the task 1 is judged as one of the three classes: (i) revealing oneself as a seer, (ii) revealing oneself as a medium, and (iii) revealing oneself as neither a seer nor a medium. Table 6 shows four examples of the task 1, for each of which, the name of the player given as the input, the role of the player, and the date of the utterance in which he/she indicates exactly that he/she is or is not a seer/medium are shown[7].

As illustrated in Figure 1, in the framework of applying classifier learning techniques such as CNN and SVM, we employ manually crafted rules as well as character level text embeddings when designing feature representations of task 1. In the case of task 1, we used 73 manually crafted rules in total, each of which is combined with the quoting notation that is commonly used in the werewolf BBS. Out of the total 73 rules, 14 are for matching Japanese expressions for revealing oneself as a seer, 7 for matching Japanese expressions for revealing oneself as a medium, and 15 for matching Japanese expressions for revealing oneself as not a seer nor a medium, where these in total amount to 36 rules. Another 36 rules are designed to examine the temporal order of the utterances that are matched to

---

[6] The task 1 considers each player's utterances for only first three days, but not for later days. This is because, in werewolf BBS, generally, the seer reveals oneself by the end of the second day and the medium does so by the end of the third day.

[7] In those utterances of werewolf BBS, as shown in the underlined part of each utterance of Table 6, players use notation of quoting the part where he/she exactly indicates that he/she is or is not a seer/medium.

name of the player who utters, the role of the player, the date of the utterance in which he/she indicates exactly that he/she is or is not a seer/medium	Joachim, seer, day 1	Liesa, possessed, day 1	Pamela, werewolf, day 1	Fridel, villager, day 1
utterance	おれおれおれだ よ占い師··· (*Here I AM a seer* ···)	··· あ た し は 占い師でも霊能者 でもない じょー。··· (··· I am *neither a seer nor a medium* ···)	··· 霊能者ＣＯ、霊見 えます··· (··· *medium CO, I can tell the role of the executed* ···)	··· 私は占い師や霊能 者ではありません ··· (··· *I am neither a seer nor a medium* ···)
class of task 1 ($\in$ { (i) revealing oneself as a seer, (ii) revealing oneself as a medium, (iii) revealing oneself as neither a seer nor a medium })	revealing oneself as a seer	revealing oneself as neither a seer nor a medium	revealing oneself as a medium	revealing oneself as neither a seer nor a medium

Table 6: Examples of Reference Dataset of Task 1 (Underlined part of the utterance is quoted by the player who utters, indicating exactly in that part that he/she is or is not a seer/medium) (CO: abbreviation of "coming out")

one of those 36 rules. More specifically, each of another 36 rules judges whether the utterance matching the rule is around the end of the third day compared to remaining other 35 rules. Finally, the last rule is designed for judging whether at least one of the aforementioned 36 rules matches any of the utterances on the first three days, whose value is assigned as 1 when none of the 36 rules matches any of the utterances. The results of matching those 73 rules are represented as feature value assignments as shown in Figure 1.

4.2. Task 2, Task 3-1, Task 3-2: Identifying Utterances declaring the Results of Divination / Medium, the Names of the Players whose Roles are Identified, and Results of Divination / Medium

Once a player is identified as revealing oneself as a seer / a medium as the result of the task 1, then, each of his/her utterances on the 2nd day or after is given to the following task 2, task 3-1, and 3-2 as the input. In those following tasks, task 2 first identifies the utterance U which declares the results of divination / medium, task 3-1 then identifies the name of the player whose role is identified by the act of divination / medium in the utterance U (identified in task 2), and task 3-2 finally identifies the result of the act of divination / medium in the utterance U (identified in task 2). The input to those three tasks task 2, task 3-1, and task 3-2 is each utterance (on the 2nd day or after) of the player who is identified as revealing oneself as a seer / a medium as the result of the task 1. The output of task 2 is one of the two classes: (a) X, and (b) not X (X = "utterance declaring the results of divination / medium"). The output of task 3-1 is one of the 19 player names listed in Table 5[8]. The output of task 3-2 is one of the two classes: (a) human,

(b) and werewolf. Table 7 shows three examples of the task 2, task 3-1, and task 3-2. For those three tasks, the name of the player who utters, the role of the player, and the date of the utterance given to those three tasks as the input are shown.

As illustrated in Figure 2, in the framework of applying classifier learning techniques such as CNN and SVM, we again employ manually crafted rules as well as character level text embeddings when designing feature representations of task 2, task 3-1, and task 3-2.

In task 2, we used 7 manually crafted rules in total. Roughly speaking, those 7 rules judge whether the utterance includes (i) the quoting notation that is commonly used in the werewolf BBS, (ii) player names and the role names such as "human" and "werewolf", (iii) typical Japanese vocabularies representing "acknowledgment" and "identification", (iv) the mixture of (i) and (ii), and (v) the mixture of (i) and (iii). Furthermore, one of those 7 rules judges whether the utterance does not match any of the (i) to (v) above. And, the final one out of those 7 rules represents the order of the utterance among other utterances within the same day. The results of matching those 7 rules are represented as feature value assignments as shown in Figure 2.

Similarly, in task 3-1, we used four rules for each of the 19 player names. Roughly speaking, those four rules judge whether the player is alive or dead, and judge whether the utterance includes the real name or nickname of the player, the quoting notation that is commonly used in the werewolf BBS, and the role names such as "human" and "werewolf". Overall, in task 3-1, we used 77 rules in total (= 19 player names $\times$ 4 rules + one rule for detecting that none of the 19 player names matches the input utterance).

In task 3-2, on the other hand, we used 7 rules, out of which 6 are for matching typical Japanese vocabularies representing the roles of "human" and "werewolf", while the final

---

[8] As shown in Table 1, the werewolf game log data we used in this paper is with 15 players, while the number of the player name candidates is 19 in the werewolf BBS.

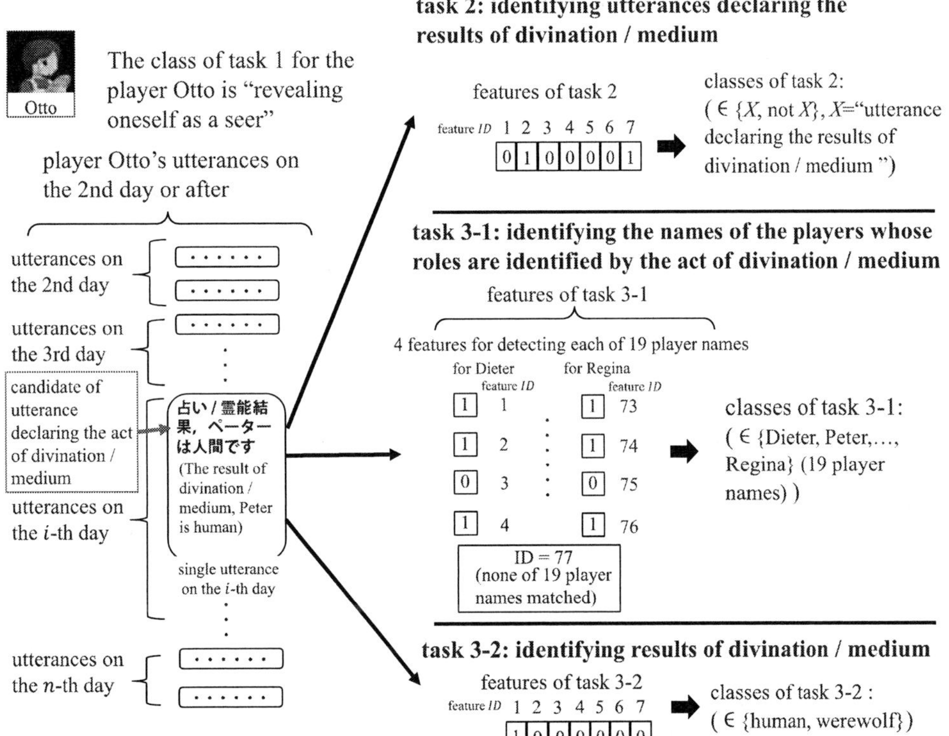

Figure 2: Feature Representations of Task 2, Task 3-1, and Task 3-2 (when manually crafted 7 (task 2) / 77 (task 3-1) / 7 (task 3-2) rules are employed)

name of the player who utters, the role of the player, the date of the utterance given to the tasks 2, 3-1, and 3-2 as the input	Joachim, seer, day 3	Fridel, villager, day 4	Pamela, werewolf, day 4
utterance	⋯ エルナさんは白でした⋯ (⋯ *Erna is white* ⋯)	⋯ ヨアヒムさんが狼だったらどうなるか⋯ (⋯ what will happen if Joachim is a werewolf ⋯)	⋯ 羊狼だと違和感 ⋯ (⋯ it is strange if the role of the player sheep is werewolf ⋯)
class of task 2 (∈ {X, not X}, X = "utterance declaring the results of divination / medium"})	X (X = "utterance declaring the results of divination / medium")	Since the class of task 1 for the player Fridel is "revealing oneself as neither a seer nor a medium", tasks 2, 3-1 and 3-2 are not applied to any of her utterances.	not X (X = "utterance declaring the results of divination / medium")
class of task 3-1 (names of 19 players listed in Table 5)	Erna		Since the class of task 2 for this utterance is "not X", tasks 3-1 and 3-2 are not applied to this utterance.
class of task 3-2 (∈ { human, werewolf })	human		

Table 7: Examples of Reference Dataset of Task 2, Task 3-1 and Task 3-2 (Underlined part of the utterance is quoted by the player who utters, indicating exactly in that part that he/she declares the results of divination / medium, or just his/her guesses.)

one detects that the utterance does not include any of those vocabularies.

5. Classifier

As the classifier, this paper applies CNN and SVM to all of the four tasks: task 1, task 2, task 3-1, and task 3-2.
When applying CNN, the implementation platform within Pytorch[9] is employed, where the following three types of feature representations are evaluated: (i) manually crafted rules are used[10] as shown in Figure 1 and Figure 2, (ii) char-

[9] https://pytorch.org/

[10] We use one convolution layer (40 channels and the filter size as 5), one max-pooling layer (the filter size as 2) and two fully connected layers to build the network. We use ReLU activation function, mini-batch size of 10, learning rate: 0.001, number of epochs: 50 epochs. The cross-entropy loss between training labels and predicted ones is minimized and optimization is performed using SGD.

acter level text embeddings[11] are used, (iii) both (i) and (ii)
are used together. As character level text embeddings[12],
we used the one trained with Wikipedia Japanese text[13] by
FastText (Bojanowski et al., 2017)[14], where the character
level text embeddings are kept static during the procedure
of training the CNN parameters.

When applying SVM[15], the feature representations shown
in Figure 1 and Figure 2 are directly used, where 2nd degree
polynomial is employed and the hyper parameters C and γ
are grid-searched.

6. Evaluation

The CNN and SVM models described in the previous section are evaluated with the training and evaluation examples
whose numbers are as shown in Table 5. As shown in Figure 3 ~ Figure 6, the evaluation results are presented as
the recall-precision curves[16] for the evaluation examples of
each class of the four tasks. For all the tasks, CNN models
with the following three types of feature representations, as
well as the SVM model are evaluated and plotted in the figures: (i) manually crafted rules are used, (ii) character level
text embeddings are used, (iii) both (i) and (ii) are used together. In addition to those three CNN models and the SVM
model, we also dot the recall and precision point when we
evaluate the manually crafted rules as they are originally
designed to judge the class of each task without incorporating into CNN/SVM.

For task 1, as shown in Figure 3, it is obvious that the CNN
model with the feature representation obtained by manually crafted rules performs the best for the two classes: (a)
revealing oneself as a seer, and (b) revealing oneself as a
medium. For the class of (b) revealing oneself as a medium,
7 rules without incorporating into CNN/SVM achieved the
highest recall. One of the reasons why the CNN models
having feature representations with character level text embeddings ((ii) and (iii)) performed much worse than those

---

[11] For both (ii) and (iii), the fundamental formalization of CNN
is based on that of Kim (2014), where one convolution layer (one
channel and the filter size as 3, 4, 5), one max-pooling layer (the
filter size as 2) and one fully connected layer are used to build
the network. We use ReLU activation function, mini-batch size
of 10, learning rate: from 0.001 to 0.0001, number of epochs:
100 epochs. The cross-entropy loss between training labels and
predicted ones is minimized and optimization is performed using
ADAM optimizer (Kingma and Ba, 2015).

[12] We compare word level and character level text embeddings, where the character level embeddings outperformed the
word level embeddings.

[13] We compared text embeddings trained with the Japanese text
data of the 646 werewolf BBS game logs and the one trained with
Wikipedia Japanese text, where the one trained with Wikipedia
Japanese text outperformed the one trained with the werewolf
BBS game logs.

[14] https://fasttext.cc/docs/en/pretrained-
vectors.html

[15] https://www.csie.ntu.edu.tw/~cjlin/lib-
svm/

[16] The evaluation examples are sorted in descending order
of the probability of the softmax function and then the recall-
precision curve is plotted by changing the lower bound of the
probability of the softmax function.

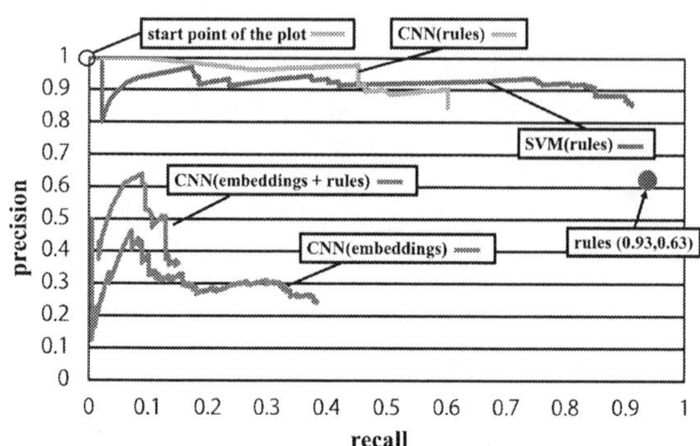

(a) class of "revealing oneself as a seer"

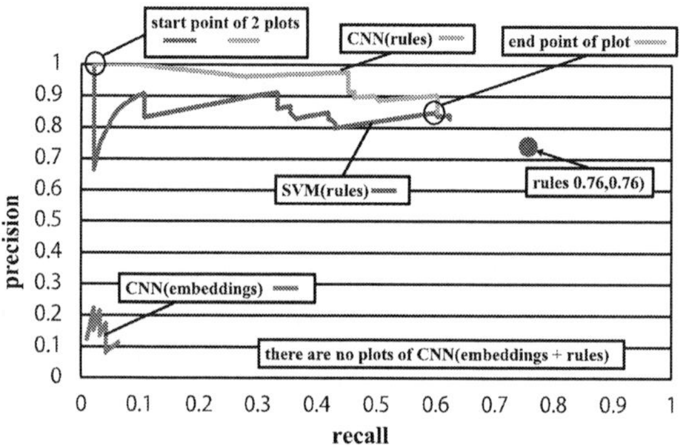

(b) class of "revealing oneself as a medium"

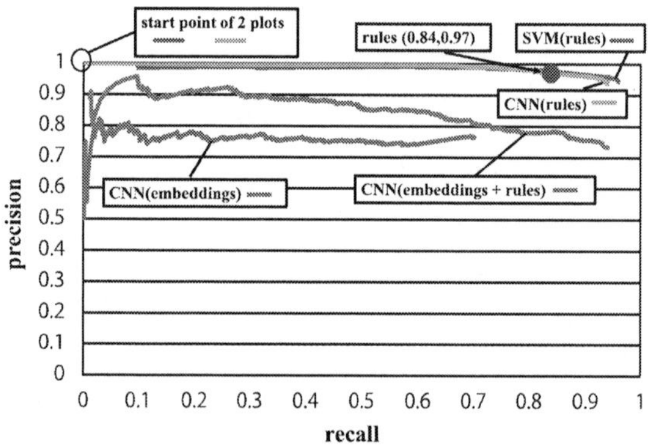

(c) class of "revealing oneself as neither a seer nor a medium"

Figure 3: Evaluation Result of Task 1

by manually crafted rules only is that the number of utterances on the first three days is too large (up to 60 utterances)
when character level text embeddings are incorporated into
the CNN model[17].

For task 2, overall, the CNN model with feature representations by manually crafted rules as well as the SVM model

---

[17] The CNN model with the feature representation (iii) (both (i)
and (ii) are used together) did not predict the class of (b) revealing
oneself as a medium for any of the evaluation examples. This is
mainly because the numbers of both the training and the evaluation examples are much smaller compared to other two classes.

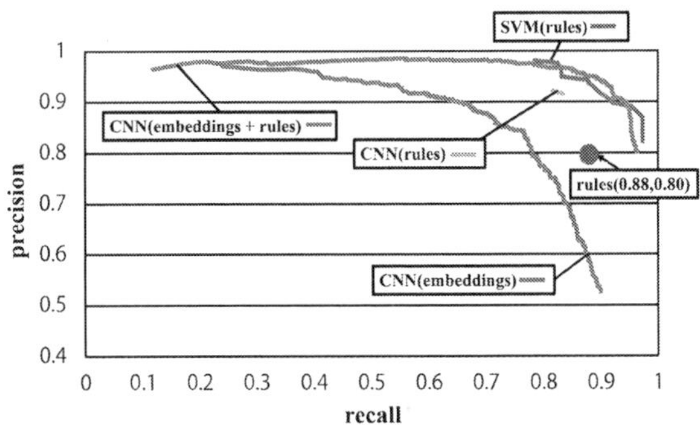

(a) class of X

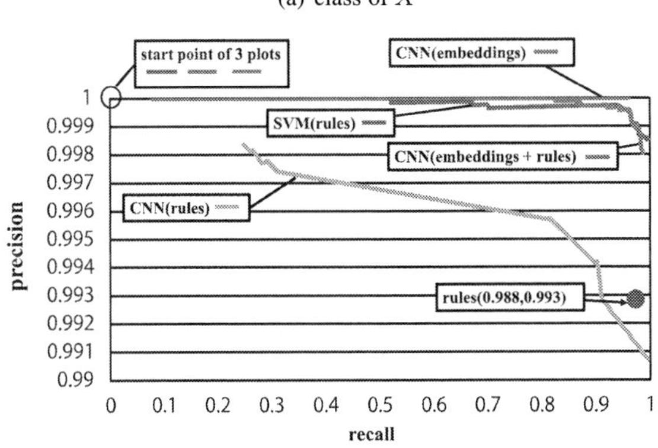

(b) class of not X

Figure 4: Evaluation Result of Task 2 (X = "utterance declaring the results of divination / medium")

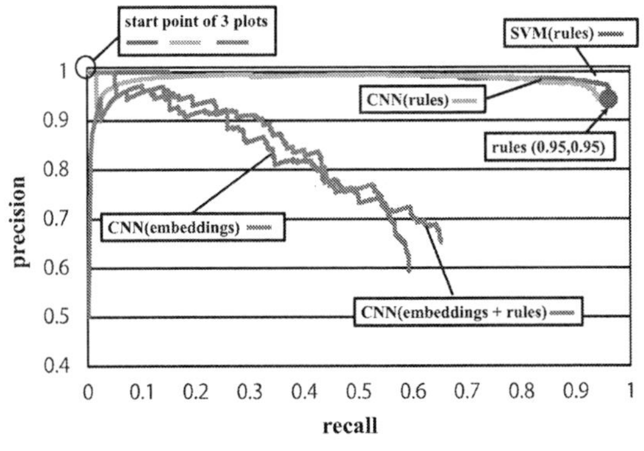

Figure 5: Evaluation Result of Task 3-1

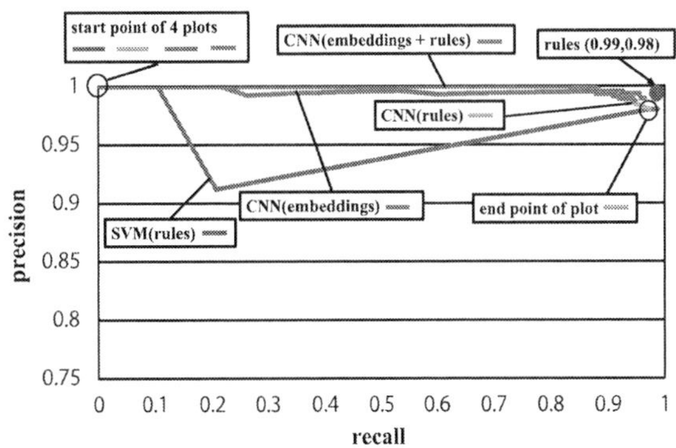

(a) class of "human"

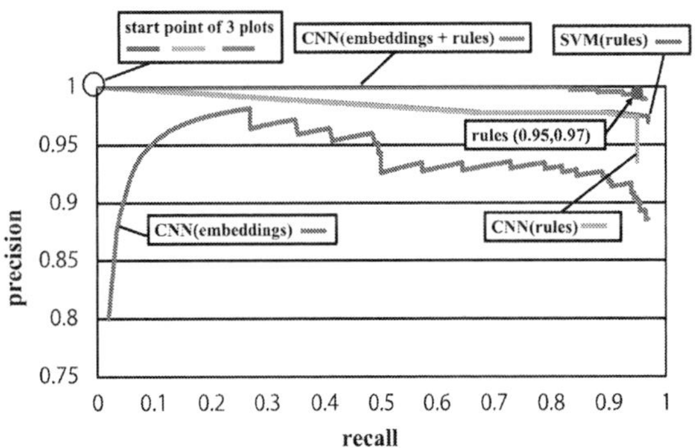

(b) class of "werewolf"

Figure 6: Evaluation Result of Task 3-2

performed the best. Roughly speaking, it can be pointed out that, for the CNN models, the performance improved by incorporating the feature representations (i) manually crafted rules are used, and (ii) character level text embeddings are used, all together into (iii).

For task 3-1, the CNN model with the feature representation obtained by manually crafted rules as well as the SVM model performed the best. Another finding here is that manually crafted rules without incorporating into CNN/SVM achieved almost the highest performance even compared to CNN/SVM. This is mainly because the num-

ber of the classes of task 3-1 is 19, which is quite large, and consequently the number of training examples for each of the 19 classes becomes relatively small, especially for the CNN model with the feature representation obtained by the character level text embeddings.

For task 3-2, overall, the CNN model with the feature representation obtained by manually crafted rules performed the best. Also, in task 3-2, manually crafted rules without incorporating into CNN/SVM achieved almost the highest performance even compared to CNN/SVM. This is mainly because, for this task, 6 rules for matching typical Japanese vocabularies representing the roles of "human" and "werewolf" play almost the most important role in this task. And, once the utterance matches one of the 6 rules, it can be stated that the result of the act of divination / medium can be easily obtained even without incorporating the feature representation into CNN/SVM.

7. Evaluation of Applying the Models of Task 1 to Task 3-2 Sequentially

When we actually annotate a werewolf game log text corpus with information that is closely related to state transitions the werewolf game by applying the models proposed in this paper, it is necessary to apply the models of individual tasks one by one sequentially. This section describes the procedure of such a situation and its evaluation results

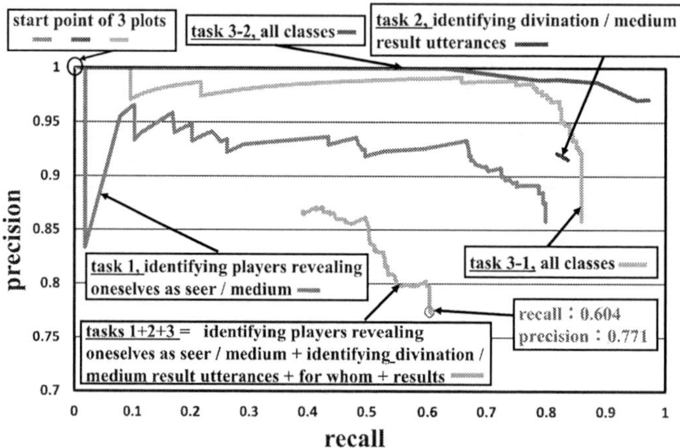

Figure 7: Evaluation Result of Applying the Models of Task 1 to Task 3-2 Sequentially

as in Figure 7[18].

In such a situation, we first apply the model of task 1 to each player (i.e., for each player, to the set of his/her utterances on the first three days), and identify players revealing oneselves as seer/medium (the evaluation result of this individual task is shown as the plot "task 1, identifying players revealing oneselves as seer/medium" in Figure 7), while we ignore players revealing oneselves as neither a seer nor a medium. Next, we apply the model of task 2 to each utterance (on the 2nd day or after) of those identified players, and identify utterances declaring the results of divination/medium (the evaluation result of this individual task is shown as the plot "task 2, identifying divination/medium result utterances" in Figure 7), while we ignore other utterances. Finally, we apply the models of task 3-1 and 3-2 to each utterance U of those identified utterances and obtain the player name whose role is identified by the act of divination / medium in the utterance U and his/her role as the result of the act of divination / medium (the evaluation results of these individual tasks are shown as the plots "task 3-1, all classes" and "task 3-2, all classes" in Figure 7).

When sequentially applying the models of those individual tasks one by one, the recall-precision curve for correctly identifying the outputs of all the four tasks is plotted lower (as shown as the plot "task 1+2+3 = identifying players revealing oneselves as seer/medium + identifying divination/medium result utterances + for whom + result" in Figure 7) compared to those evaluation results of individual tasks. This is obviously because the overall sequential evaluation results are obtained by multiplying each evaluation performance for all the four tasks. However, in this overall evaluation results, we achieved around 60∼70% recall/precision and the highest prevision as over 85% when restricting recall around 40%.

---

[18] In the evaluation results of Figure 7, to all the tasks, the CNN models with the feature representation obtained by manually crafted rules are applied. Evaluation results for the individual tasks are those against the whole evaluation examples whose numbers are as shown in Table 5.

8. Related Work

Most previous work related to the werewolf game (and other similar games) studied issues regarding how to design the werewolf game agent which has the ability of joining natural language conversation of the werewolf games (Gillespie et al., 2016; Hirata et al., 2016; Nishizaki and Ozaki, 2016; Toriumi et al., 2016; Nide and Takata, 2017; Xiong et al., 2017; Kano et al., 2019; Nagayama et al., 2019; Sugawara, 2019; Tellols, 2019; Tsunoda and Kano, 2019). Issues studied in those previous work include tendencies in utterances of the executed or attacked players (Nishizaki and Ozaki, 2016) and analyzing the influence of the features such as the number of each player's utterances, number of the players revealing oneselves as seer/medium, etc., against the winning rate of the werewolf side (Nagayama et al., 2019). Among those previous work, the task studied in Sugawara (2019) is relatively similar to those studied in this paper. Sugawara (2019) applied embedding based technique to the task of classifying speech acts of utterances collected from the natural language text based werewolf game log, where their classification performance is much lower than the results we report in this paper. It is obvious from the results we report in this paper that speech act classification performance should improve by incorporating feature representations obtained by manually crafted rules in addition to those embedding based feature representations. This finding is one of the most important differences between this paper and Sugawara (2019).

9. Conclusion

This paper studied how to accumulate werewolf game log data annotated with identification of players revealing oneselves as seer/medium, the acts of the divination and the medium and declaring the results of the divination and the medium. In this paper, we divided the whole task into four sub tasks and applied CNN/SVM classifiers to each sub task, where we showed the effectiveness of the proposed CNN/SVM models.

10. Bibliographical References

Bojanowski, P., Grave, E., Joulin, A., and Mikolov, T. (2017). Enriching word vectors with subword information. *Transactions of ACL*, 5:135–146.

Gillespie, K., Floyd, M. W., Molineaux, M., Vattam, S. S., and Aha, D. W. (2016). Semantic classification of utterances in a language-driven game. In Tristan Cazenave, et al., editors, *Computer Games. CGW 2016, GIGA 2016*, volume 705 of *CCIS*, pages 116–129. Springer, Cham.

Hirata, Y., Inaba, M., Takahashi, K., Toriumi, F., Osawa, H., Katagami, D., and Shinoda, K. (2016). Werewolf game modeling using action probabilities based on play log analysis. In Aske Plaat, et al., editors, *Computers and Games*, volume 10068 of *LNCS*, pages 103–114. Springer, Cham.

Kano, Y., Aranha, C., Inaba, M., Toriumi, F., Osawa, H., Katagami, D., Otsuki, T., Tsunoda, I., Nagayama, S., Tellols, D., Sugawara, Y., and Nakata, Y. (2019). Overview of AIWolfDial 2019 shared task: Contest of automatic dialog agents to play the werewolf game through conversations. In *Proc. AIWolfDial*, pages 1–6.

Kim, Y. (2014). Convolutional neural networks for sentence classification. In *Proc. EMNLP*, pages 1746–1751.

Kingma, D. P. and Ba, J. (2015). Adam: A method for stochastic optimization. *Proc. ICLR*.

Nagayama, S., Abe, J., Oya, K., Sakamoto, K., Shibuki, H., Mori, T., and Kando, N. (2019). Strategies for an autonomous agent playing the "werewolf game" as a stealth werewolf. In *Proc. AIWolfDial*, pages 20–24.

Nide, N. and Takata, S. (2017). Tracing werewolf game by using extended BDI model. *IEICE Transactions on Information and Systems*, E100-D(12):2888–2896.

Nishizaki, E. and Ozaki, T. (2016). Behavior analysis of executed and attacked players in werewolf game by ILP. In *Proc. 26th ILP*, pages 48–53.

Shinoda, T., Chokai, F., Katagami, D., Osawa, H., and Inaba, T. (2014). "Are you a Werewolf?" becomes a standard problem for general artificial intelligence. In *Proc. 28th Annual Conf. JSAI*. (in Japanese).

Sugawara, Y. (2019). Data augmentation based on distributed expressions in text classification tasks. In *Proc. AIWolfDial*, pages 7–10.

Tellols, D. (2019). Are talkative AI agents more likely to win the werewolf game? In *Proc. AIWolfDial*, pages 11–14.

Toriumi, F., Kajiwara, K., Osawa, H., Inaba, T., Katagami, D., and Shinoda, T. (2014). Development of AI wolf server. *Proc. 19th GPW*, pages 127–132. (in Japanese).

Toriumi, F., Osawa, H., Inaba, M., Katagami, D., Shinoda, K., and Matsubara, H. (2016). AI wolf contest — development of game AI using collective intelligence —. In Tristan Cazenave, et al., editors, *Computer Games. CGW 2016, GIGA 2016*, volume 705 of *CCIS*, pages 101–115. Springer, Cham.

Tsunoda, I. and Kano, Y. (2019). AI werewolf agent with reasoning using role patterns and heuristics. In *Proc. AIWolfDial*, pages 15–19.

Xiong, S., Li, W., Mao, X., and Iida, H. (2017). Mafia game setting research using game refinement measurement. In Adrian David Cheok, et al., editors, *Advances in Computer Entertainment Technology. ACE 2017*, volume 10714 of *LNCS*, pages 830–846. Springer, Cham.

Association for Computational Linguistics
209 N. Eighth Street
Stroudsburg, Pennsylvania 18360

ISBN 978-1-7138-1260-9